The Awakening
A Transformational Love Story

Master Coach
Hu Dalconzo

Renaissance Publishing

Forked River, NEW JERSEY

HOLISTIC LEARNING CENTERS, INC.
NAMASTE
SAVE the...Humans!

Praise for The Awakening a Transformational Love Story

"I was continually drawn in by the emotion that it stirred in my heart throughout; I felt the characters heartbreak and hope. This book entertains the reader with the advantage of also learning about spiritual transformation."
-Lorie Caldwell, CSLC & Public Speaker

"This transformational love story depicts that when spiritual partners surrender to the Laws of the Universe where two or more souls are gathered in a state of consciousness, love and grace they can create heaven on earth."
-Sharda Geer, CSLC

"This book has changed my life! It has help me to understand myself, and my spiritual purpose for incarnating. Thank you, thank you and thank you again from the bottom of my heart. I can't say thank you enough for this amazing transformative book."
-Namaste' Bangorn Foster, ALSC

"The Awakening is one of those books that will I will pass to my children. I tote it around, to reassure that I am 'emotionalizing' all my lessons and staying on track. By the time the book had ended, I felt TRANSFORMED because of the realization that I truly am a BEing of light and love who came to this earth to experience a curriculum made of life lessons and karmic 'burns.'"
-Lisa DiChiara, ALSC

"The Awakening book explains deep esoteric concepts
with amazing clarity in a gentle and lovingly way
that touched my heart and warmed my soul. I was
mesmerized about what would come next."
-Tommy Brown

"Through the loving plotline of the romantic relationship we
learn to grow and evolve by helping one another, which is the
key for change for ALL of humanity. THANK YOU for writing
this important 'Guideline' to help us create the changes that
are needed one soul at a time!"
-Lisa Stahl

"The Awakening truly touched my soul. The adventurous
vision quests and the budding romance kept me longing for
more. The Awakening is a must read for anyone who is on
their own spiritual journey of transformation."
-Natalie Gervasio, CSLC

"Reading this incredible story touched my heart and soul very
deeply and gave me strength to go through some challenging
moments in my life. Thank you once again, and many
blessings to your wonderful book."
-Carolina Villa, CSLC

"WOW!!! I didn't want to put the book down. This book will
appeal to you, no matter where you are on your Spiritual
Journey. If you are looking for the perfect
self-help book to add to your book club or
study group... look no further!"
-Namasté Tracey Knowlton, CSLC

"The Awakening is a heartwarming love story filled with a message for humanity. It contains hope for humans as a species and it provides suggestions for living a life that is worth living. There is a way to achieve all of it, and it is through the awakening."
-D'Angelee Bowman, CSLC

"Wow, what an awesome read! It teaches us that if we want to transform the world, we must start by transforming ourselves. This book illustrates for us how to transform pain into Spiritual wholeness that can heal the world, one Soul at a time."
-Donetta Powell

"This book created a willingness within me to take a transformative leap into the unknown. I truly felt a connection with Paula and Mark. I could feel myself in the room as if I was feeling their emotions!"
-Christy Sprabary, ALSC

"WOW, the first few chapters touched my soul so deeply I couldn't stop the tears from running down my face. Words can't describe how much this book has helped me grok my Pauline-ology. Thank you, thank you, thank you!!!"
-Pauline Quackenbush, CPC, CSLC

"The Awakening is a tale of personal transformation following a heart wrenching tragedy. It gently brought me through many stages and thought patterns of my spiritual evolution. I found myself taking notes and enjoying the love story at the same time."
-Carole Smith-Rea, ALSC

"This novel may be fiction, but the 'TRUTHS' have changed my life and will change yours too! These 'TRUTHS' taught me that my heart is my instrument of unity.
Read it once.
Read it twice. Read it again."
-Lewis Knowlton

"Oh my gosh! It kept me wanting more as I read once for the purity of the romantic love story, once for the adventures, and finally for embedding the spiritual lessons.
You'll definitely want to share The Awakening with your book club and friends."
-Joan Howton Tufts, CSLC &
Twilight Brigade National Trainer

"A compelling read from the beginning to the end. Through the lessons in this book, I was able to explore my own awakening as I vicariously experienced lessons in transformation and love with 'Mark & Paula.'"
-Shakera "Creatress" Hudson, ALSC

A Special Thanks!

To my
co-author Dean V. Dalconzo
and my co-editors,
Christine Grauer and Joan Howton Tufts
I want to give you a
Special Thanks
for undertaking the project
of editing this book
as a labor of love!

Thank you,
My Soul Friends!

Acknowledgements

I wish to acknowledge the immeasurable contribution that my teachers have made to my life and this textbook. No one writes a book alone, especially a textbook like this one, which is a compilation of all my notes, journal edits, books, tapes, and the lectures that I attended since 1977 on my *journey home to my Self.* All my spiritual teachers, mentors, and models contributed to my spiritual education. Their wisdom and knowledge have been a part of my life for so long that it's hard for me to differentiate anymore whom to acknowledge for what. Therefore, I would like to thank and credit all the souls who have taught me that I AM a Conscious BE-ing who is having a human experience.

I pass on my teachers' wisdom to you hoping that it will take root and flourish for the benefit of all sentient BE-ings: Jesus the Christ, Buddha, Eckhart Tolle, Ram Dass, Deepak Chopra, Wayne Dyer, Pema Chödrön, A Course in Miracles, Louise Hay, Shakti Gawain, Marianne Williamson, Dr. Venice Bloodworth, Dr. Joe Dispenza, Michael Singer, Barbara DeAngelis, Stephen Levine, Mohandas K. Gandhi, Swami Muktananda, Stuart Wilde, St. Francis of Assisi, Gary Zukav, Eric Butterworth, Emile Cady, Henry David Thoreau, Ralph Waldo Emerson, Harry Palmer, John Bradshaw, Michael Ryce, Edgar Cayce, Neale Donald Walsch, Richard Bach, Ernest Holmes, Jim Rohn, Phil McGraw, Doreen Virtue, and all my spiritual guides.

Also By Master Coach Hu

The HuMan Handbook & Audiobook

Seven Spiritual Truths book & Audiobook

Self-mastery... A Journey Home to Your... Inner Self

Coach's Textbook & Audiobook

Spiritual Life Coach's Course & Training Manual

Spiritual Life Coach's Course Audio Program

Self-parenting Coaches Course & Training Manual

Weight Mastery Course & Training Manual

Money Mastery Course & Training Manual

Relationships Mastery Course & Training Manual

Parenting Mastery Course & Training Manual

How to Build A Successful Holistic Practice Training Manual

Available from Holistic Learning Centers, Inc.
www.HolisticLearningCenters.com
888-452-0878

Author's Note

"There are no more awards for predicting apocalyptic rain, only for taking the required actions to build a transformational ark!"
-Master Coach Hu

The stories in this book are based on true events that I experienced over the last two decades while facilitating thousands of spiritual life coaching sessions with hundreds of clients.

My hope is that you will relate to the emotional challenges, insights, and Self-realizations that the characters experienced as if they were happening to you. Because they did happen to real people, in real time.

My altruistic reason for writing this book was to inspire the reader to do the inner work required to distinguish their real Self from the illusions of the temporal world. Then to use this wisdom to unite as ONE via the Namasté Consciousness and co-create the Critical Mass needed to help SAVE the... HuMans!

Namasté My Soul Friends,
Master Coach Hu

Contents

Foreword

"The Time Has Come for the Book- The Awakening"

By Dr. Jane M. Sennett

As I sit at my computer to write, the news erupts with the story of another fatal shooting with multiple casualties. The devastating images are displayed repeatedly on my television screen. The harshness of the images illustrates that we are living in a time of unrest. Social media that was meant to connect us, in many ways, has isolated us from each other, negating the need for conversations and personal contact. The Centers for Disease Control (CDC) reports that suicide rates have continued to increase over the past decade especially among girls 10 to 14 years of age. The internet reports suicide bombings on one website and on another teaches you how to build your own bomb or join a terrorist organization. It is estimated by the CDC that 66,000 Americans died in 2017 from opioid overdoses. In addition, the CDC cites that Americans are eating themselves into disease and morbidity with almost 40%

of American adults and 20% of American adolescents falling into the unhealthy obese category.

Sages through the centuries have called for change in the world and cited the need for the transformation or evolution of the human consciousness as crucial for these changes. Although many periods in our history can easily be identified as requiring modification, no time is more important than today. *The time has come for the book -- The Awakening.*

Various scientific disciplines discuss the concept of a critical point where something minor and controlled in a populace will suddenly escalate. Epidemics are examples of a diseases which exceed the critical mass point allowing the illness to overwhelm the population. Examples of this phenomenon includes the Spanish Flu virus in 1918, SARS in 2003 and the HIV/AIDS virus. *This same idea of a tipping point can also produce change for the positive.* A prime example of this is the destruction of the Berlin Wall which separated East and West Berlin. Constructed in 1961, the wall was erected as a means to prevent German citizens from leaving East Berlin. But in 1987 when Ronald Regan urged Mikhail Gorbachev to "tear down this wall", a shift occurred in the consciousness of the people of Berlin. Increasing numbers of peaceful protests led to a shift in the internal political structure of the country, which ultimately resulted in a nonviolent revolution. On November 9, 1989 the citizens of the city peacefully tore down the Wall, which resulted in the reunification of East and West Berlin.

"Everyone thinks of changing the world,
but no one thinks of changing himself."

Leo Tolstoy

It is believed that an intentional shift in consciousness can occur in a population once as little as 10% of that population begins to actively participate in the change. The means to this transition must first occur with individual spiritual growth as taught by Mahatma Gandhi, *"Be the change you wish to see in the world."* It is vital to remember that we are all Spiritual BEings having a human experience and to co-create a better world, we must first begin our own personal journey of self-mastery.

"Yesterday I was clever, so I wanted to change the world.
Today I am wise, so I am changing myself"

Rumi

There has never been a more critical time in our turbulent society for the creation of a Self-mastery book such as *The Awakening*. Master Coach Hu's book eloquently illustrates the path to spiritual transformation through the touching love story of two soulmates, Mark and Paula. Although this romantic story is heartfelt, the underlying message of spiritual awakening and its rewards are simplistically outlined and easy to understand. The book inspires and teaches readers (both those who are new to the concepts of Self-mastery and psycho-spiritual self-help work, as well as those further along the path) how to raise our individual and ultimately our collective consciousness from that of fear and violence to one of love and compassion.

The message of *The Awakening* has never been more relevant and compelling than it is today. As we acquire the skills and knowledge to grow spiritually, we will help to create the critical mass required to **SAVE the...** **HuMans**™ and co-create the spiritually conscious world we so desperately need.

"I alone cannot change the world,
but I can cast a stone across the water to create many ripples"
Mother Teresa

Thank you, Master Coach Hu, for this wonderful work and inspiration.

Namasté,
Dr. Jane M. Sennett

The God Source Knew

For over 250 million years, dinosaurs had undisputed dominion over the planet. They shook the earth with their mighty footsteps, soared through the skies with wingspans dwarfing those of modern birds, and roamed the farthest reaches of the great seas. But then, as if overnight, these marvels of evolution were driven to extinction by a natural disaster.

The *God Source*[1] knew that what She was observing was a natural evolutionary process, but it still greatly saddened Her to watch the last dinosaur die. The loss of so much *Life Force Energy*[2] greatly disturbed Her; thus, the

---

[1] God Source: The Source of all that is.
[2] Life Force Energy: The energy which fuels all that is.

God Source decided to create humans. Unlike the dinosaur, She created humans in Her own image, gave them dominion over the earth and all its creatures and gave them free will to choose their personal destiny. Sadly, over time, humankind became blind to their holistic interconnectedness with each other and the earth, and they misused their powers to such an extent that they were on the brink of creating another global catastrophe capable of wiping out life on earth.

To help humanity awaken to their *Namasté Consciousness*[3], the God Source had sent Spiritual Masters[4], philosophers, and gurus, but they were either persecuted, killed or made into idols. Instead of empowering themselves by applying what the Master Teachers had taught them, humankind focused their attention on building churches, mosques, temples, and the bureaucracies and dogma to support them.

The problems humankind faced were *systemic*, because their global challenges were embedded in their governmental and archaic monetary systems, which relied solely on power, physical strength, money, and anatomical beauty as their core values.

---

[3] Namaste Consciousness: I honor the place in you, where the entire universe dwells! I honor the place in you, which is of truth, of light, of peace, and love! When you are in that place in you and I am in that place in me...WE ARE ONE!
[4] Spiritual Masters: Teachers who have deep intuitive wisdom.

Each One of Us is a Cell in a Body Called Humanity

The God Source knew that the only *peaceful way* for humanity to change their bureaucratic systems was to co-create a spiritually based evolution that educated humans about the miraculous power of transformational Critical Mass[5]. Critical mass had occurred many times in the world, such as when the Berlin Wall collapsed without a single shot being fired. Critical mass is Nature's way of making non-violent global changes.

To help germinate humankind's awareness of their multisensory, God-given powers and generate the *critical mass* needed to create a global shift in consciousness, the God Source sent humankind enlightened, new-thought *Master Teachers*[6]. These teachers incarnated to help humans transcend their fear-based, survival-of-the-fittest mentality; to use their Godlike powers of Light and Love; and to teach humankind that they are all interconnected by the Namasté Consciousness.

These teachers perfected their skills over many lifetimes by observing and correcting their less-than-

---

[5] Critical Mass: The percentage of the population (estimated to be 10%) needed to dramatically shift human consciousness. This Inner Self-transformation will create a quantum critical mass of souls that will miraculously transform humanity's consciousness into Namaste' awareness where we realize that we are all One in Spirit.

[6] New-Thought Master Teachers: Are teaching souls who after many incarnations have mastered how to instruct souls how to use the *Lessons of Transformational Awakening* to play in the world as deliberate conscious creators.

perfect behavior as quickly as possible. During those lifetimes, they made the same mistakes that all humans make, and as a result, they were very patient and compassionate with human behavioral shortcomings.

We All Have Multisensory Capabilities
That Can Help SAVE the... HuMans™!

Master Teachers form *spiritual partnerships*[7] where each soul makes a sacred covenant to develop their own Self-empowerment, which in turn supports their partner to do the same. Each partner agrees that there is nothing more important than to remain deliberately conscious of their divine identification and interconnectedness with all living things. Spiritual partnerships create a synergistic effect[8] because they create a safe space for each partner to practice their Self-mastery skills, which helps them to evolve faster than they would individually.

The Primary Purpose for which *Master Teachers* Have
Incarnated is to Teach Us How to
Self-Master Ourselves

Master teachers live among us right now as seemingly ordinary people, such as parents, schoolteachers,

---

[7] Spiritual Partnerships: A partnership of two or more people formed for psycho-spiritual growth. Hu Dalconzo, The HuMan Handbook, Renaissance Publishing, 2011, pp. 29

[8] Synergistic: Growth that is fueled in such a manner that two or more-people committed to Spiritual growth will grow faster together than they can separately.

doctors, nurses, ecologists, healers, holistic practitioners, or spiritual life coaches. Their mission is to *awaken* souls to their God-given multisensory powers, so we can unite as ONE to co-create the critical mass needed to produce a *global transformation* of love to help **SAVE the... HuMans**™.[9]

This book is about one such Master Teacher and her partner who embark on a transformational journey of spiritual awakening to master their own God-given powers, so together they can help humanity survive beyond the next 100 years.

---

[9] SAVE the... HuMans: Joseph Hu Dalconzo, Seven Spiritual Truths, Renaissance Publishing, 2016, pp 94. A movement initiated by Holistic Learning Center in 1993 to create the critical mass necessary to save human kind from its own self-destruction via their Awakening to the interconnectedness with all living things.

CHAPTER 1

The Dark Night of the Soul

Most Souls Spiritually Awaken After Experiencing a Tragedy

Several millenniums ago, a Master Teacher befriended a young soul who became her Spiritual Initiate. After many incarnations they formed a psycho-spiritual bond that could never be broken. Together they spent many lifetimes learning about the Universal Laws of Life and Mastering the Disciplines of the Spiritual Initiates.

They made a contract to meet again in this lifetime, confidently knowing they would find each other again via the Law of Attraction. Their souls were vibrationally attuned due to their common desire to evolve spiritually and their dharmic calling to share their knowledge with other souls.

***

Mark met Ann during his sophomore year in college where he was studying psychology. Despite the many different career paths available to him, he wanted to become a social worker to serve those less fortunate than himself. Although Mark was an intelligent, sensitive soul, he found it emotionally challenging to meet new people and feel comfortable in social situations. However, one fateful Saturday night, despite his feelings of uncertainty, he accepted his best-friend Tony's invitation to a local frat party. And it was there that he met the love of his life.

Ann was the same age as Mark and stood several inches shorter than he. She was fit and had light strawberry-blonde hair, which fell just above her shoulders and curled into a slight bob. Her face was adorned with the slightest number of freckles over her nose and cheeks.

When Mark first met Ann, he was so overwhelmed by her beauty that he overcame his shyness and found a way to converse with her. She displayed a maturity that was well beyond her years and he found himself enamored by her unique perspective on life. As their conversation carried through the night and into the hours of the morning, Mark felt a connection that he had never felt before; it's like he had known Ann his whole life.

Mark was a tall, fit, young man who wore a serious look on his face. Growing up, his spiritually attuned parents taught him all about meditation and the Laws of the Universe. He was first made aware of the Universal Laws at an early age; and throughout his teens and into young adulthood, his parents continued to enlighten him; but all too often, he would dismiss his parent's pearls of wisdom.

Mark had a good rapport with his co-workers and friends and a loving relationship with his parents, but his greatest achievement was winning Ann's heart. Ann gave him a sense of identity he hadn't known before. Her support filled him with caring contentment and a sense of self-confidence that made him feel like he could conquer anything.

As the semesters passed, Mark and Ann's relationship evolved from an intimate friendship to a romantic partnership. During the last semester of their final year, Ann accepted Mark's proposal to marry him. She was more than just his fiancé; she was his life-partner and the other half of their combined whole.

After graduation, they moved back to their respective hometowns. Despite hundreds of miles between them, they remained enamored with each other. After a year of maintaining a long-distance relationship, they finally set a date for their wedding. They decided to hold the ceremony in Mark's hometown, since most of Ann's family members were deceased. Making wedding arrangements in Mark's hometown wasn't easy, but their undeniable love for each other helped them overcome the challenges of planning their wedding over a long distance. Together they worked out the details of their wedding with little emotional drama.

After many months of planning, the day of their wedding rehearsal finally arrived. A gloomy layer of overcast clouds painted the sky grey, while light rain fell persistently through the day. It wasn't the type of weather Mark would have chosen for the day of his rehearsal dinner.

Mark texted his father, "Sorry Pop, I have to work late tonight. I can't pick up Ann and Tony and make it to rehearsal on time. Can you pick them up at the airport for me?"

"You bet Son! I'm happy to help!" Through the years, Mark's parents had come to love Tony, so they were thrilled that he was Mark's best man. And Ann was the daughter they never had, so they were looking forward to welcoming her into their family.

While trying to finish up his work project, Mark received a text from Ann: "Hey Love. Just found out my flight will be late because of a layover ☹. Worst case, start the rehearsal without me. It's not ideal, but I hate to keep everyone waiting."

Mark smiled as he looked down at her text. It was just like Ann to consider the needs of others first. He promptly texted back, "No problem, Love. I'll let Mom and Dad know you'll be late. I'm sure everything will go fine."

"Thanks Hun! Love you my HUSBAND TO BE! XOXOXOXO ☺"

Mark felt his heart swell. Throughout their entire engagement, Ann had never referred to him as her *husband*. It was a title he knew she was waiting to use until their marriage was official. "Love you too my WIFE TO BE!"

By this point, Mark was so excited that he found it nearly impossible to concentrate on work. He decided to leave work and pick up Ann and Tony at the airport himself.

"Hey dad, I'm leaving work now. I'm going to the airport to pick up Ann and Tony, so no need for you to go, OK?"

"Thanks Son, but we're already here. We're having dinner with Tony. By the time we're done, Ann's flight will be here. Relax. We have things handled. See you in a few hours!"

It didn't make sense to return home before the rehearsal dinner, so Mark decided to meet his colleague, Eric, for a drink while waiting for his family to return from the airport. In no time, Mark was sipping a beer in his favorite pub. As he waited for Eric to arrive, he stared into the dreary cloud-covered sky and daydreamed about the upcoming ceremony. He had only enjoyed a few sips of beer when Eric arrived smiling widely.

The pair shared a warm handshake, and as soon as Eric sat down he asked, "So how does it feel to commit to one woman for the rest of your life?"

Mark's stomach tightened with a swirl of emotions. He thought back to the fateful night when he met Ann. If he had decided to leave Tony's party earlier that night, they never would have met. Now he was merely hours away from promising himself to Ann forever. The weight of this decision hung heavily on Mark's mind. He knew that he was head over heels in love, but he still felt the gravity of the commitment he was about to make. Mark was lost in his thoughts.

"Hey," Eric snapped his fingers twice to get Mark's attention "Mark. You there?"

"Huh? Oh. Sorry. You were saying?" Mark chuckled feeling somewhat embarrassed.

"I was trying to ask... how does it feel to be tying the knot? I'm proud to say that I have no intentions of going down that road for many years to come. Sooooo. What does it feel like?"

Mark put his uneasiness aside as the waitress approached their table. The two men ordered some food, as Eric continued with his line of questioning.

"Again, how does it feel to commit to one woman for the rest of your life?"

"Ann's the best thing that ever happened to me." Mark paused a moment; and with a more serious tone in his voice, he continued, "Sure, planning the wedding was an emotional storm at times, especially since Ann lived so far away."

Eric chuckled, "I'll bet."

"But it's all been worth it. Even with all the headaches from dealing with long-distance wedding plans, I'm a lucky man to have fallen in love with a woman as special as Ann."

"That's awesome man. I'm super happy for you." Eric raised his beer, "Let's toast to marriage and finding the half that made you whole!"

"Definitely." They clanked their glasses and took a sip of beer, eagerly anticipating the arrival of their food.

Mark glanced at his phone. He couldn't help but feel a little anxious at the lack of communication from Ann and his parents. Ann was playful and secretive, and she giggled with delight when she could successfully surprise

Mark. So, Mark figured Ann was just up to her sneaky surprises again.

The comrades continued chatting about the engagement and the wedding plans and Eric's dramatically different, single-man escapades. Growing impatient from not hearing from Ann or his parents, Mark checked his phone again. He had missed a call from an unknown number. His blood ran cold, as he listened to a voice message left from a police officer urging him to return his call immediately. Without explaining any details to Eric, Mark stood from the table and apologized for having to leave so suddenly and headed to his car for privacy to return the police officer's call.

Mark had barely reached his car, when his phone rang.

"This is Officer Bolton. Is this Mark Celli?"

"Yes." Mark shut the door to his car.

"Mr. Celli, it was my intention to have this discussion with you in person. But you weren't at your work or home. I..."

"Please cut the crap and just tell me why you called."

There was a brief pause before Officer Bolton continued, "Mr. Celli. Are you related to a Robert Celli or Julia Celli?"

Mark's entire body began pulsing with paralyzing fear. "Yes, that's my mom and dad."

"At 5:30 tonight, they were involved in a traffic accident. It was a head-on collision."

Mark's mouth dried, and his stomach tightened. He could hear the officer flipping through pages.

"And there were two other passengers in the back seat, but their identities haven't been confirmed yet."

Mark's heart stopped beating.

Mark's nausea grew exponentially worse. A cold sweat began forming on his forehead and body and saturated his white shirt. He was no longer aware of his surroundings.

"Officer? My parents were supposed to pick up my best friend and my wife. I mean, my fiancé. We were supposed to meet for our wedding rehearsal tonight."

Memories, images, feelings, and sensations flooded Mark's mind and body. In an instant, he remembered his father teaching him how to ride a bicycle and his mother singing him lullabies. Images of Tony laughing, and partying flashed through his mind. And he remembered making love to Ann and dancing with her at his cousin's wedding.

Deathly afraid to hear what his heart already knew to be true, Mark asked, "Is my family alright?"

"I'm sorry, Mr. Celli. The driver and passengers didn't survive the accident."

In a state of denial, Mark pleaded, "Please tell me that the young woman and man in the back seat are alright?!" A flood of tears poured down his face.

"I'm sorry. Their injuries were too severe. The young man died in the ambulance on the way to ER. The young woman suffered severe brain trauma and didn't survive emergency surgery. I'm so sorry to have to tell you this. Toxicology has yet to confirm, but we believe the opposing driver may have been drinking."

In shock, Mark could hear the officer talking, but he no longer understood a word he was saying. Mark's mouth filled with saliva. He threw open the car door and fell onto the pavement. He threw up and collapsed into a fetal position crying profusely. Mark laid on the rain-covered pavement in his own vomit, sobbing. The sounds that escaped his lips were of a man whose very soul had just been shattered. There were no words that anyone could say or actions that anyone could take to help him deal with the shock of losing the four people he loved most in the entire world. All he could do was lie on the ground and wail like a wounded animal.

Mark could hear Eric's voice in the distance drawing closer, but it didn't matter. Mark couldn't feel Eric's presence any more than he could feel the sensation of the cold water in which he lay. Mark continued to wail as his mind tried desperately to find a way to deny the inescapable and horrifying nightmare of losing his family.

***

Funeral arrangements were made over the course of the next week. It was a miracle that Mark was able to attend the burial because the only thing he felt like doing was running away. The kind and supportive words from his friends, coworkers and relatives passed right through him like sunrays through glass. Mark felt numb, distant and alienated from everyone who tried to console him. All sentiments of sympathy were lost on him. He felt like he was on the brink of mental collapse.

He felt God had betrayed him, and he didn't want any part of a God that could let all the people he loved die. The Universal Laws of life he had learned as a child were now completely worthless to him. He wanted nothing to do with God or the Universal Laws. With each passing day, it became harder and harder for Mark to deal with his depression. Mark was angry because his life had come to an abrupt stop, while it was life as normal for the rest of the world.

Mark became fully engulfed in the depths of his emotional anguish. He could not separate himself from his pain. As his mind moved deeper into the pain of his loss, he began to blame others and then himself. He felt unreasonable guilt and shame for not having picked up his fiancé and best man himself. He felt victimized; *What had he ever done to deserve this?*

His mind cycled from blaming others to blaming himself; but regardless of who he blamed, he sank deeper into remorse and anger at the world. His mind was brutal and never let up. Mark could find no relief from the shadows of his mind. His thoughts and anguish spiraled endlessly downward, until he became fully engulfed in feelings of victimization, blame, and anger.

With hopes of occupying his mind on something other than his loss, Mark returned to work. But after one week, his supervisor insisted that he take a leave of absence because Mark was clearly struggling to maintain focus and composure at the office. Now, Mark focused even more on how much he missed his family and Ann. He began forming destructive habits and simultaneously stopped any constructive ones that he had. He drank excessive amounts of alcohol and stopped exercising. He regressed to eating junk food to try to provide some degree of emotional comfort.

Mark gave up meditation entirely. Just the *thought* of meditating or praying angered him. He didn't want any part of God, prayer or meditation now. His mind rested on thoughts of loss, which haunted his every waking moment. Giving up meditation had deeper ramifications than Mark realized. He had sunk as low as a soul could go. He was drowning in a sea of justifiable self-pity. Mark's core was shattered and his life force energy waned. He was experiencing what many have called *the dark night of the soul*.

Mark was desperate for anything that could provide some relief from his feelings of despair and hopelessness, but none of his destructive habits and attempts at averting his pain provided him with any lasting relief. He saw no viable solution. Physically and emotionally spent, he lost all hope of ever being happy again. He was prepared to end his life; and it was then, in his darkest hour when help arrived.

CHAPTER 2

It's Darkest Before the Dawn

And That Was When I Carried You

As Paula smelled the scent of the sea, her heart raced with anticipation. Since her teenage years, Paula had loved sailing. For her it was more than a hobby; it was a meditative process - a means to shut out the noise in her head and simply be in the moment. It helped her to see beyond her mind's intellect and process matters from a deeper place of knowingness. And on days like today, when the winds exceeded 25 mph, she felt as though she were flying over the waves, and the turbulent tide added an element of danger and excitement.

Looking at Paula's petite body, one would never suspect that beneath her small frame lay an empowered Master Teacher. She stood just over five feet tall, her face delicate and graced by small features, which contrasted starkly with her large dark eyes. Paula kept her hair several inches below her shoulders, and although she was only 32 years old, she insisted on keeping the natural flecks of gray in her hair, which gave her a more mature appearance.

With much expectancy, Paula pulled her truck with sailboat in tow onto the beach. Her sailboat was just large enough for one person and a bag of supplies. She viewed it as an extension of herself; although small, it was strong and durable. As she unfastened her boat from its hitch, she took a moment to take in the beautiful evening. The low-hanging sun reflected brilliantly on the ocean surface, and the sky beamed a stunning bright red. She took her time with the necessary safety precautions, checking over her boat and preparing the emergency supplies.

Once everything was ready, she laid out a beach blanket and took a moment to meditate. Paula always meditated before sailing; it helped her get centered, and she always prayed and gave thanks in advance for a safe trip. She was confident in her sailing ability, but especially on days with such high winds, she wanted the *God Source* to protect her from harm. Paula had some difficulty calming her mind down today since she was so excited, but she honored this important ritual before setting sail.

During her meditation, Paula sought inspiration to help discover her true purpose. She spent several years traveling the country teaching yoga and working with different holistic practitioners. During this time, she developed her professional life coaching skills. She knew deep within her heart that she had a unique life purpose, a dharmic calling. She felt she could do something with her life that would benefit all of humanity, *but what?* Because of her established meditation practice, when these thoughts and questions surfaced, Paula was able to surrender them to the God Source. She had faith that she would be shown the next step for her dharmic evolution when the timing was right.

After meditating, she dragged her sailboat to the edge of the shoreline. She wrestled with the crashing waves and finally arranged her boat into launch position. She felt a strange feeling followed by chills in her body, but she didn't pay much attention to them. She was too immersed in the excitement of launching her boat.

***

Mark tried his best to ease the deep pain that was tearing at his heart, but nothing seemed to help, not even grief counseling. He mourned the loss of his best friend

Tony, who'd brought him so much joy and comradery. He mourned the loss of his parents whom he loved so much. But most of all, he mourned the loss of his Ann, and nothing he did could relieve the pain he felt in his heart.

Without his job to keep his mind occupied, Mark found he had too much time on his hands. Many evenings he just wandered from place to place in search of anything that could take his mind off what had happened. On this windy autumn day, Mark found himself sitting alone on a deserted stretch of beach overlooking the ocean. It was late in the afternoon and the descending sun created a beautiful sunset. It was wasted on Mark though, because all he could see was his ugly past. Hunched over, with his elbows resting on his knees, he thought, *What's the point in living?*

His mind ran rampant. He knew he shouldn't give up. And with that thought, a memory of his dad was triggered warning him to not let his ego mind dictate his feelings. But Mark just didn't have the will to resist his feelings of despair. He knew deep down that he had reached his breaking point. *I don't care anymore. I'm done.* Mark decided to take his own life then and there. The idea of ending his life had loomed over him since he had lost his family, and he had now reached a point where he no longer had the will to fight.

He planned to swim into the ocean until he tired and then let himself drown. He raised his head from his palms, sat up, and surveyed the beach and ocean. Other than a woman on a small sailboat about a hundred yards offshore, he was alone. He didn't want anyone to observe what he was about to do, so he waited for the sailor to pass. But to his dismay, rather than taking a straight course, the sailor tacked back and forth, prolonging her trip across Mark's stretch of beach. As he waited, his mind whirled with emotions about how his action might affect his soul and future incarnations.

There had been many moments in Mark's life when he felt the aid of some deeper wisdom within him. But now he quickly repressed anything that hinted of a higher power, which made him feel even more ashamed for what he was about to do. He kept pondering, *What if death is the end of my existence and after drowning I just cease to be?* That thought terrified him, but he no longer had the resolve to withstand the pain in his heart. The more Mark considered dying, the more he realized it was *living* that he was afraid of.

***

The high winds and waves created a powerful rip current, and Paula's adrenaline was pumping from the challenging and exhilarating ride. She took full advantage of the wind's incredible power with reckless abandon. It took all her experience, strength and skill to keep a steady course. It was intense and even frightening, but she loved every minute of it.

As she banked back toward the shore, a large stone jetty suddenly appeared directly in her path. She felt a surge of panic wash over her, and she instantly reacted and made critical adjustments to avoid a collision. Although she narrowly avoided the jetty, the mast caught a strong gust of wind with the boat's sudden change in direction, and the main beam swung violently toward Paula. She was caught completely off guard and was struck on the head and flung into the ocean.

***

Meanwhile, Mark was taking off his shoes and clothes in preparation for the last swim of his life. He took a final scan of the area and was jostled from his depression-driven delirium by what he saw. The small sailboat was now empty with the main beam swinging uncontrollably. Mark's stomach tightened, and his pulse quickened. He scanned the horizon for signs of the woman he had seen earlier. The rough waves blocked Mark's view, but after a moment, he spotted her. She was floating on her back and he knew that she was in danger. He immediately started yelling and wildly waving his hands, "Hey! Hey! Are you alright?"

He realized that she couldn't possibly hear him over the sound of the waves. He surveyed the area to look for help, but the beach was deserted. Mark ran to where he had left his belongings to call 911. When he reached his phone, he glanced back to see the status of the woman. She was bobbing in the water like a buoy, and she had already drifted considerably farther from shore. It was clear to him that waiting for emergency services to arrive would be a death sentence for her. He knew she would die without his immediate help. But he was in such a deep state of despair that he didn't know if he could bring himself to act. He felt paralyzed by fear. He almost laughed at the irony, because he was about to take his own life by drowning.

Fear trickled from his lips, "I can't. I just can't." Simultaneously, an empowered voice from within said, *Yes you can. Act now or she'll die!* Mark felt his fear melt away. He didn't know whether it was God, fate, or simple instinct that drove him, but he knew he couldn't stand idly by and watch someone die.

Mark ran to the water and dove in. The shock from the cold water washed over his body. He was a competitive swimmer in high school, but swimming through this powerful riptide was entirely different. He swam with all his might and quickly closed the gap between the sailor and himself, but his mind began to work against him. It considered all the things that could go wrong. Paranoia seized him momentarily, but then he remembered what his dad had taught him about using his divine willpower to silence his mind, and he swam on with even greater power.

He reached the sailor and immediately noticed that she was unresponsive. She had a large gash above her temple that was bleeding steadily. Thankfully, she was breathing. Mark's next thought that surfaced was fear over sharks being attracted to the blood, so he acted quickly. Without thought, his junior lifeguarding skills kicked in. He positioned himself, so the woman's head remained above water, and he began swimming back to shore. The only way to conquer the riptide was to swim parallel to the shoreline, beyond where the riptide was strongest, and then he started swimming directly toward the beach.

He slowed his pace to conserve energy, all the while making sure to keep the woman's head above water. After what seemed like an hour of steady-paced swimming, he finally reached the shore. He laid her unconscious body on the beach and checked her vital signs; she was still breathing and unresponsive, and the gash on her head continued to bleed steadily. Mark searched for his phone to call 911 only to see that the tide had reached his clothes. The phone was useless. He instantly decided to take her to the hospital himself. Although he was exhausted from the ordeal, he mustered the energy and carried her to his car.

He carefully reclined the woman in the front seat and buckled her in for the ride to the hospital. Mark couldn't help but notice that he felt completely different than he did before the rescue, when he was about to end his life. Mark had faced his fears and performed a selfless act, which reawakened his intuitive heart and shifted something inside of him that he hadn't felt since before his fiancé died. For the first time in a very long time, he felt alive, energized, and good about himself.

While driving to the hospital, Mark kept checking to make sure that the woman's condition didn't worsen. She was still unconscious, but her bleeding had slowed, and she seemed no worse than when he'd first pulled her from the water. Mark arrived at the hospital and entered through the emergency doors with the unconscious woman in his arms. He was immediately bombarded with questions from the medical staff. He told them that she was knocked out of a boat and that he'd rescued her from the turbulent, cold water.

The physician and nurse assured him that her injuries didn't appear to be too severe and that the head wound need a few stitches. The nurse presumed that the woman had a concussion, but they would assess further once the diagnostic scans came back. The nurse thanked Mark for his heroic act of helping a stranger. If he hadn't put his own life in jeopardy, the woman certainly would have drowned. The woman didn't have any identification on her, so the nurse asked Mark to provide his identification and contact information.

Mark left the hospital and headed home feeling better now than he had in a long time. When he arrived home, he unlocked the door to his apartment and stared into the darkness. He was afraid to turn on the lights knowing that everywhere he looked was a memory that reminded him of Ann and the life he'd lost. Following the rescue, Mark had enjoyed a surge of adrenaline that had temporarily distracted him. But now, hours later, he realized his deep emotional grief was still there. The kind words from the nurse did not penetrate his wounded psyche. Despite being a so-called "hero", he still felt no desire to continue living.

He uttered aloud to himself, "Hell, nothing's changed. Everything is still as bad as before. I want to swallow a bottle of pills. It would be so easy. Anything would be better than feeling what I'm feeling."

He immediately searched through his kitchen cabinets until he found a bottle of expensive whisky that Eric had given him several years before. Mark raised the bottle to his lips and drank until he needed to breathe.

Mark hadn't eaten since lunch, so the alcohol took effect quickly. Soon his thoughts slowed, and his body relaxed. He looked outside and became fixated on the effect the wind was having on the trees. No longer content simply looking through the glass, he stepped out onto his patio. He sat on the fine weatherproof furniture which Ann had selected for their home. He didn't care that the cushion was soaked. He continued to observe the storm while he sipped his bottle of whisky.

Though Mark's mind continued to feed him destructive thoughts, his heart knew that he was not ready to waste *this* incarnation. Despite how horrific it was to lose his fiancé, parents, and best friend; at some intuitive level, he knew that killing himself would just land him in another incarnation where he would have to burn off some heavy karma for taking his own life.

Mark realized how physically exhausted he was. He slowly made his way to the living room couch where he collapsed and quickly slipped into a drunken slumber.

CHAPTER 3

The First Day of This Life Time

Birds of a Feather, Reincarnate Together

Mark found himself in a quiet pitch-black room where he couldn't see his hand in front of his face. He yelled, "HELP!" but didn't hear a sound other than a faint echo of his cry. He felt completely disorientated. As each moment passed, his anxiety grew worse, until he felt the warmth of a delicate hand on his shoulder. Mark turned and saw the glow of a feminine figure bathed in bright, white light. It was impossible to make out her face. He raised his hand to shield his eyes from the glare to try and make out who she was, but the brilliant light still blinded him.

The illuminated figure gently pulled Mark's hand away from his face. Her hands were warm and soft, and he felt soothed and calmed by her touch. She began to speak, and although he could see her mouth moving, he couldn't hear what she was saying. Mark felt strangely perplexed by this woman's presence. She continued to speak for a few moments, but he still couldn't hear what she was saying. Then she smiled, waved goodbye and slowly faded away.

Mark cried out, "Wait! Please don't go!" He stretched out his arms trying to reach her. He was overcome with sadness as she slipped away. Once again, he was alone. "Please don't leave me again. ANN!"

The startling scream awoke Mark from his sleep, nearly knocking him off the couch. It was the dawn of, yet another morning preceded by a night of intoxication and regret. He wiped his teary face with the sleeve of his shirt unable to recall the dream that led him to cry so profusely. As he finished gulping a glass of water, he was startled by the ringing of his landline. Very few people had that number. He hesitated before answering.

"Hello?" Mark was ready to hang up thinking it was an annoying telemarketer.

"Hi. Is this Mark? Mark Celli?"

Mark didn't recognize the voice on the other end. "Yeah. That's me. Who is this?"

The woman's tone certainly didn't sound like a telemarketer, but no one he knew would call this number.

"I'm sorry if I woke you. My name's Paula. We've never been formally introduced but... last night I woke up in the hospital. I don't remember much. I know that I went sailing, but I can't remember anything after the first few minutes into my trip."

Hearing this woman's voice triggered something inside of Mark that made him feel anxious.

"The doctors told me what happened. I got knocked into the water, and you saved me. They told me I would've drowned if you hadn't saved me." Her voice cracked, as she continued, "I don't know how I could ever repay you. I wanted to call and say thank you."

Even though the phone call made him feel anxious, Mark felt the same sense of pride that he had felt when he first pulled her from the water. He wasn't sure what to make of this situation.

"You were in trouble, and there was no one else around, so I did what anyone would have done. It's nothing really. I'm just happy you're alright. You were a little banged up when I found you, but you sound fine now."

"Well, I have a strong headache. But it's nothing I can't handle."

"I know what you mean." Mark responded with a dry wittiness.

Paula laughed politely. There was a moment of awkward silence as each waited for the other to speak.

Paula finally broke the silence, "Hey. I know this is totally out of left field, but I'm getting released from the hospital soon and... um, can I buy you breakfast? I'd like to meet the man who saved my life."

Mark was caught off guard by Paula's request, plus his head was still pounding from a night of heavy drinking. "I'm not sure I can right now, Paula. I literally just woke up. And to be perfectly honest, I feel like hell right now."

"Please, I want to meet the man who saved my life. I just want to thank you in person."

Mark knew that this wasn't a good idea, but he couldn't deny the inner pull he felt to meet her. Then, out of nowhere, memories started flooding his mind about his parents. He remembered all the times his dad had taken him for walks in the woods and explained the significance of harnessing his Godlike powers, and the times his mother had meditated with him and told him stories about her trips to India. Mark didn't understand why these memories were flashing through his mind, but in some strange way it helped him to follow his intuitive feelings. He decided he would meet Paula. "Sure. Why not? You pick the place, and I'll meet you there."

A few hours later, Mark found himself sitting alone in a booth at a local diner sipping coffee. In his state of mind, he felt emotionally ill equipped to meet anyone. *Don't get so worked up.* He told himself. *It's fine. She just wants to say thank you. Just say hello, make some idle conversation, and then be on your way. No big deal.*

Mark was beginning to think that Paula might not show when he spotted her coming through the diner's door. He recognized her right away as the woman he'd pulled from the ocean.

Paula scanned the room not quite sure which of the patrons she was meeting. Mark waved her over. She smiled widely and returned Mark's wave. As she approached, Mark stood to greet her properly.

"Paula? Hi. I'm Mark. Nice to meet you."

Paula put her bag down on the bench opposite Mark. Still warmly smiling, she reciprocated, "Hi Mark! Yes, I'm Paula. It's great to meet you!" She extended her arms to hug Mark, but he only extended his hand in return.

Figuring that Paula was put off by his prickly response, he felt the need to explain. "Oh. I'm sorry. I'm just not a hugger. Nothing personal." Mark's face burned red. He saved this woman's life yesterday, and now, just seconds after meeting her, he had already lied to her.

"It's fine, Mark." Paula smiled and chuckled slightly to help put Mark at ease. "I just automatically hug. It's no big deal."

They got situated in the booth, and Paula broke the awkward silence that ensued, "Should we order something? I'm starving."

"Sure. I'll have another cup of coffee."

"You don't want to eat anything? It's my treat."

The thought of eating made Mark feel nauseous. He didn't know if his lack of appetite and nausea was a result of his sadness or the whisky. He broke eye contact with Paula and glanced around the room. "No, I'm fine thanks. I had breakfast just before you called."

It was obvious to Paula that Mark was lying, and it puzzled her. Though Mark seemed polite and pleasant on the surface, mere moments into meeting him she noticed he was aloof and emotionally distant. She had coached enough people to recognize signs of emotional distress. She wasn't willing to make any assumptions about Mark, but she sensed that he was unhappy.

Mark was careful not to divulge too much information about his personal life. On the contrary, Paula was an open book. She spoke freely about the fun she had traveling the country while teaching yoga and learning how to facilitate various types of holistic practices.

The similarities between Paula and Mark's parents, specifically his mother, were uncanny. He couldn't quite figure out what it was about Paula, but he sensed a loving and kind energy about her that reminded him of his mother. His mom used to say, "No coincidences in a perfectly evolving universe, Son." and without a doubt, he knew his mother would say that he and Paula were drawn to each other "via the Law of Attraction." But it didn't matter because such holistic notions no longer held any meaning for him.

Mark was strangely transfixed by Paula's unorthodox persona. She had a very petite, fit and athletic body. Her attire wasn't particularly revealing, but he could tell through her knit sweater that she had a good figure. As she spoke freely about studying under Ram Dass, Mark couldn't help but notice how striking her eyes were. They were large and golden brown and had a distinct doe-like quality to them. Though his sadness and anxiety persisted, he felt more relaxed in Paula's presence.

Starting to get a little bored from the conversation, Mark fixed on Paula's pupils and steered the topic back to the sailing incident. "So, do you remember anything about the accident?"

Paula was surprised by Mark's inquiry because the entire time they'd been speaking he had been vague and distant. Now, he seemed sincere and interested about what she had experienced. She felt uncomfortable with his unpredictable behavior, but she found herself strangely drawn to him. She sensed a caring soul beneath Mark's hardened veneer, so she didn't take his aloofness and unpredictable attitude personally; it just reinforced her initial impression that Mark was troubled and unhappy.

"Well, I clearly remember parking my truck and launching my boat. Everything after that gets fuzzy."

Mark maintained his gaze, clearly interested and asked, "So you blacked out when the beam knocked you into the water?"

Paula paused for a moment trying to remember the details of her experience. "It's strange, but while I was unconscious, I experienced being in a long tunnel glowing with radiant white light that pulled me in deeper and deeper. The deeper I went, the more I felt that this brilliant white light was the God Source."

Mark had a weird look on his face, "God Source?" He was in no mood to hear about any holistic mumbo jumbo.

Despite Mark's noticeable apprehension, she continued, "Yeah. God Source. It's what I call the life force energy of the Universe. What term do you use... God? Jesus? Buddha?"

Feeling very uncomfortable, Mark abruptly said, "God."

"As a holistic practitioner, I work with people from all walks of life with many kinds of religious beliefs. I use a generic term to avoid offending anyone."

Mark felt mildly intrigued. His shoulders and brows relaxed. He sipped his coffee and continued his line of questioning, "Interesting. Did the God Source share some divine wisdom with you?"

Detecting a slight hint of sarcasm in his voice, Paula was now sure that Mark had experienced some sort of emotional trauma. Almost everything she said triggered him to some degree, but she continued to answer his questions. She closed her eyes momentarily to gather her thoughts. It was challenging for her to put her powerful visual experience into words, but out of nowhere the words floated off her lips with effortless ease. "When I was out cold, I experienced a vision that helped me grok my dharma. The vision made understanding the esoteric Laws of the Universe as easy to comprehend as basic arithmetic."

"What? You lost me after grok."

"Sorry. Let me explain that a little better. 'Grok' means to fully understand; to know something at the very core of your Being. So basically, when I was knocked out, I had a vision that helped me truly feel and understand my

Spiritual purpose for being on this planet. I also got a clear sense of the Laws of the Universe, which I'd never really had before. They always seemed so mysterious and cryptic for me. My vision really made those Laws clear to me!"

The stern look on Mark's face helped to finally convince Paula that her new soul friend was indeed experiencing a troubling time in his life, and that he needed to do some deep personal work to take down the emotional barriers which she could distinctly sense.

As Mark put down his coffee mug, Paula locked eyes with him. She exuded genuine concern and asked, "Can I ask you a personal question?"

Mark was surprised by Paula's sudden change in demeanor from bubbly to serious and the shift in her tone from comforting to concern. He indulged himself in his curiosity. "Sure. What's on your mind?"

"What is this deep sadness I sense within you?"

Her question irritated him. His eyes narrowed, and his body tensed. He didn't know this woman, and he had no interest in letting her stir up everything with which he was struggling. Yet, another part of him just wanted to get it all off his chest.

Paula could tell that Mark was annoyed. To respect his boundaries, she decided not to push the issue. But to her surprise, Mark opened a little, "Sometimes you feel like you know where your life is going, and then... then things just don't... they just don't work out."

"Mark, I know we just met, but you're safe with me. You can tell me anything you want, or nothing at all if you prefer. This is a judgment-free zone."

"I was trying to kill myself! OK?!" His face reddened, and his eyebrows furrowed.

Paula was shocked by Mark's sudden outburst. The emotional turmoil that she had sensed was now fully exposed.

"A while back, I lost everyone; my fiancé, my parents and my best friend... in a car crash. They're all dead now. And I tried. I really did... to grieve and move on. But I just can't! I went to the beach to kill myself. But you were there, and you needed my help." Mark felt embarrassed and even a little angry yet unloading brought him a tremendous degree of relief. He found it difficult to read Paula's face, as he stared at her waiting for her response.

"Oh my God. I'm so sorry to hear that Mark. I can't imagine what you must be feeling."

"I'm not really sure what I'm feeling right now."

"Well. I'm sure glad that my accident made you cancel your plans."

Paula had enough coaching experience to know that the primary cause of Mark's suffering was his inability to fully accept what had happened to him. He needed to allow his horrific feelings to surface so he could release them. She knew self-help exercises that would help him transcend his intensely painful life experience and help him to move on.

"I'm not sure what your spiritual beliefs are, but I believe that we live in a perfectly evolving Universe. If you and I were on that beach at the same time yesterday, on a planet with seven billion souls... that's no coincidence."

Although Mark's mind instantly tried to counter-respond, he couldn't ignore the strange circumstances surrounding how they'd met. Before him sat a perfect stranger, yet her philosophies strangely mirrored that of his parents. Mark's anger began to fade, and he started to relax into the moment. He looked into Paula's eyes and noticed their brilliant shade of golden brown.

"What are you trying to tell me Paula?"

Within moments, Mark pivoted from being closed off to being open and courageously vulnerable. Paula was overjoyed that she was beginning to reach the core of the soul who had just saved her life. She intuitively felt a deep connection with Mark, but she didn't quite understand why.

"Mark, I realize you don't know me very well. But if you're willing, I believe I can teach you how to work through your tragedy. You can channel your sad feelings into a spiritual reason for living. You can heal, by helping others to heal."

Mark digested what Paula said for several minutes.

While Mark was processing, Paula quieted her mind and said a silent prayer for the wisdom to help Mark transcend his ordeal. She was wise enough to know that it was impossible for her to fully understand what he had been through, surviving something as horrendous as losing everyone he loved in the world.

"I'm feeling very confused right now. Can you explain what you just said? I can heal myself by helping others to heal?"

Paula validated Mark's feelings and told him that it was perfectly normal for him to feel confused, angry and sad, and that anyone who experienced what he did would feel the same way. "If you are willing to invest just one month to study, practice and emotionalize what happened to you, I'm confident that you will start to make peace with what must seem impossible for you to transcend."

Feeling confused and emotionally drained, Mark was surprised that he was considering Paula's offer. He quickly blurted, "Sure. What do you have in mind?" With disbelief and regret for accepting her offer, his mind now frantically tried to conjure excuses to back out of what he just said.

"We can meet tomorrow morning." Paula hastily grabbed a pen from her bag and scribbled her number down on a napkin. "Here's my number. I'll call you in the morning."

Paula waited with bated breath as Mark tapped his fingers on the table. Then as if he was watching a movie, he heard himself say, "Okay, call me around 9:00, and we can figure out a place to meet."

With their first meeting scheduled and their breakfast finished, they said their goodbyes and left the diner. Paula smiled warmly and waved, as she climbed into her truck. As she drove away, she felt melancholy thinking about how alone and sad Mark must feel, having lost his whole family. Navigating life and transcending daily ups and downs was challenging enough, let alone having to deal with such an unbearable loss. She knew that Mark had a rough road ahead of him.

Little did Paula and Mark know that they were about to continue an adventure that had begun many lifetimes before that would eventually help millions of souls spiritually awaken to their transformational powers of Love.

CHAPTER 4

Spiritual Partnerships

Beginnings Are Usually Scary

As Paula drove home, she felt awash with emotion. She was dismayed to learn about Mark's troubles and excited by the prospect of being able to help him. For many years Paula loved providing spiritual life coaching as a part-time occupation. Unlike any of her previous occupations, coaching allowed her to learn and internalize what she helped others to heal.

During her coaching years, she worked with many different souls who'd experienced various types of tragedies, but Mark's situation was wretchedly unique. She had never worked with anyone who'd experienced such extreme loss. She realized that helping him was going to challenge her coaching skills, and although the magnitude of this holistic healing challenge felt daunting, it filled her with a degree of excitement. In many ways, working with Mark was like her love of sailing; she always enjoyed the experience, but it was the challenging, wind-whipping days which filled her with the highest degree of exhilaration. Helping Mark transcend his tragedy represented a similarly exciting challenge, and it was one that she intuitively knew she needed to do; not only because she wanted to repay the man who had saved her life, but also because she believed Mark's trauma could be transformed from a *karmic curse*[10] into a *dharmic blessing*[11]. She knew that if Mark had the emotional courage to transcend his grave tragedy, he could certainly learn how to use those skills to help others do the same.

Paula entered her modest, three-bedroom ranch-style home. Despite having a slight headache, she immediately sat down at her desk and started jotting ideas for her first coaching session with Mark. She wanted to ensure that she was professionally prepared for their session, so

---

[10] Karmic Curse: Is negative cyclic energy created by the Law of Cause and Effect – "*what* goes around comes around ..."

[11] Dharmic Blessing: The rewards you receive for doing the work you were born to do -your calling

working through the discomfort of a headache was a small price to pay.

We are all blessed with free will, so we can steer our boat; but the one thing we can't steer is the river! She didn't know why, but this thought kept replaying in her head over and over. Except for a few short breaks, she spent most of her day writing coaching notes to help Mark. Although her notes were somewhat disorganized, Paula had faith that her Spirit would guide her as to how best to help Mark heal his broken heart. As the hours passed, she followed her intuitive pull to complete her coaching lesson plan for Mark.

With her lesson plan finally complete, she stared at it in quiet contemplation. *Eventually everyone reaches the ocean of God's bliss, but we must choose the river that feels right to us because there is no single right river for everyone.* This Self-realization was a concept she clearly understood, but her enthusiasm had caused her to overlook this Universal Truth. Paula put her pencil to rest. She realized that even with all the planning she had done, it was Mark, and only Mark, who could make the decision to heal or to continue suffering. She surrendered the details, knowing that God would handle those things.

Whether or not Mark decides to move forward is entirely his choice, she thought. Mark's experience had been horrific. If Mark decided to heal, he would be able to help others who had suffered losses equally as great by relating with them in ways that no other practitioner could, unless they had personally experienced a similar tragedy.

By this time, the sun had set. Without her work to distract her, Paula noticed how hungry she was and started preparing a simple meal. As a single person she often dined out, but she was a capable cook and enjoyed the sense of accomplishment she felt from cooking. While preparing her meal, her mind kept returning to Mark. Although she didn't know him very well, she felt confident that the psycho-spiritual exercises that her mentors had taught her would be effective for Mark, if he had the emotional courage to commit to doing them as prescribed. She also knew that by working together, the synergy of their powers of intention would help him heal.

As she prepared to get some much-deserved rest, Paula reflected on the last 48 hours. While experiencing a near-death encounter, her life had crossed paths with Mark. She knew there were no coincidences in the Universe, and that meeting Mark must have some deep significance for them both. She considered the thoughts she had just before she set sail and recalled the deep desire she felt for finding her spiritual purpose for incarnating. She also reflected on the near-death vision she had while she was unconscious. She knew that these seemingly disparate elements should fit together, but she just didn't know how.

Paula lay down in her bed and shut her eyes. She felt excitement pulsing through her body. She knew that her first coaching session with Mark would bring many challenges, but she was eager, not afraid, to face them head on. As she slipped into slumber, her mind kept repeating the same question. *Why were we drawn together in such a miraculous way?*

Paula woke up before 5:00 a.m. the next morning inspired by what she had learned while asleep. She didn't even bother getting dressed. As soon as she opened her eyes, she leapt from her bed and went directly to her office to capture her thoughts on paper. She wanted to ensure that she didn't forget what had come to her during her sleep about the importance of *spiritual partnerships*. She wrote as fast as she could:

Spiritual partnerships create a synergy, which helps each partner to awaken faster than they would on their own. They agree that the main purpose for being together is to support each other's spiritual, emotional, and psychological growth. They _do not_ commit to having *perfect* behavior; instead, they commit to owning their *less-than-perfect* behavior as quickly as possible...

Murphy's Law, she thought as her pen ran out of ink. She took a deep breath to relax and started looking for another pen. She felt a little worried because she didn't want to forget anything. She found a pen and wrote her final inspirational thoughts:

Spiritual partners recognize that they are both in the process of emotional and psychological growth, which is why their commitment to being emotionally honest is essential.

Paula was wise enough to grok that dreaming about spiritual partnerships was not an accident. With pride and amazement, she meditated on what she had written. She recalled what she had learned from Ram Dass: When two or more souls come together with conscious awareness of their Oneness with the God Source, a synergistic effect is created that magnifies the spiritual powers of both souls. She also remembered that Coach Zac had taught her that nothing is more important for spiritual partners than supporting each other to remain intentionally conscious of their connection to the Divine. As she sealed her meditation, she sensed that her reflection on spiritual partnerships would play a major role in helping her fulfill her dharma, even though she didn't quite know how or why yet.

With a feeling of satisfaction, Paula stepped away from her office for breakfast. She drank a soybean shake and swallowed a handful of whole-food vitamins. Her mind continually returned to the same thoughts about the mystical way in which she had met Mark. She understood that the synergistic effect of a spiritual partnership would accelerate each of their Godlike powers. She wondered if, and even secretly hoped, their relationship would evolve beyond that of coach and client.

Paula wasn't quite ready to share this with Mark, but she believed that their souls were drawn together via the Law of Attraction for a dharmic purpose. She wondered if they could somehow work together and then apply what they learn to help other souls spiritually awaken. She had a suspicion that the deep metaphysical work they were about to do might reveal that they had shared other lifetimes together. Exploring such possibilities would have to wait though. For now, getting Mark into a healthier emotional space was the priority.

Later that morning, Paula called Mark. Because he seemed reluctant when he accepted her offer for coaching, she was afraid he wouldn't answer. When Mark answered the phone, her heart filled with joy and her body immediately relaxed. Although he still seemed somewhat hesitant, she was happy that he was holding to their agreement.

They decided to meet at Paula's home office. She wanted to get Mark out of his environment, which was laced with sad memories, to help him surrender to the coaching exercises.

When Mark arrived at Paula's home, emotions flooded over him. Part of him felt compelled to seek her help, while another part of him felt strongly at odds with the entire Self-help process. He had agreed to do coaching sessions with Paula because he was curious and didn't want to disappoint her; but after knocking on her front door and being warmly welcomed into her home, his mood shifted instantly.

Paula disregarded what Mark had said about not being a hugger, and she immediately gave him a long, warm hug. After breaking from their hug, she looked deep into his eyes. She intentionally resonated faith and trust, and simply told him, "Thank you for coming."

Mark was slightly befuddled by this somewhat strange situation. He looked back at Paula with a slim smile and said, "No problem."

Paula knew it would be helpful for Mark to take a few moments to acclimate being in her home before she facilitated the coaching session. She offered him a seat on her couch while she brewed some chamomile tea.

While waiting, Mark noticed Paula's home felt strangely familiar. The scent of rosewood incense was rich, and the lighting was dim in a comforting way. The coffee table was littered with reading material. Although he hadn't read any of it, he recognized the authors from his parents' library. He noticed that the home was adorned with tapestries and artwork tied to Eastern philosophies. Mark wasn't well versed in such traditions, but he thought that they were likely related to Hinduism, Buddhism or Confucianism. It was an eclectic mix that he found inviting. Although he still had reservations, there was something he couldn't quite identify about Paula's home that made him feel welcome; as though he had returned home after a long absence.

As Paula returned to the couch with the hot tea, she realized that it had taken great courage for Mark to overcome his fears and swim out into the rough sea to save her life. She said a silent prayer that he could muster up the same type of courage to transcend his pain and open his heart to receive love again. Paula then remembered her *aha* moment from her near-death experience. When she reached Mark, she stood motionless holding his gaze in a silent state of gratitude for the clear vision that the God Source had bestowed on her during her accident.

"Are you okay, Paula?"

Paula didn't answer him. She wanted to share more about her mystical experience, but she knew he wasn't ready yet. What she did know was that her memories were beginning to fade. Luckily, she knew exactly what to do to remember the details of her near-death vision. "Before we begin, I'd like to meditate so I can remember what I saw in my near-death vision before I forget it. I think there were some important messages in that vision that will help me to help you. Going into a meditative state will help bring that vision back into my conscious awareness so I can recall the details. My meditation will be more effective if you meditate along with me. Are you willing to meditate with me?"

"I guess so."

"Great!"

They moved to Paula's small office, which was decorated with tapestries like the ones Mark had seen in the living room. She had a desk with a laptop, a variety of small metaphysical ornaments, and an incense burner. A large, over-stuffed bookshelf was tucked into the corner of the room containing books that ranged in topic from metaphysical philosophy to sailing.

After asking Mark to sit in the recliner, Paula began her meditation ritual by putting on Tibetan bell music, lighting a candle and including rosewood incense. She took a seat opposite Mark in a large, comfortable office chair and settled into her posture, which she had learned from her eastern meditation teacher, Swami Gawain – the mellowest person she had ever met. She folded her legs and straightened her posture. She rested her hands on her knees with open palms and connected her pointer-fingers and thumbs.

"I begin my meditation by taking long, slow breaths. I direct my mind to focus on the difference of how my breath feels when I inhale from how it feels when I exhale."

Mark and Paula closed their eyes and completed several rounds of slow rhythmic breathing.

Paula continued, "I learned to use 'Namasté' as a mantra from Swami Yolanda. I use this word as an anchor to help me get into a deep meditative state."

Namasté was a word Mark had heard many times growing up, but he never fully understood its meaning. "Sorry. What does Namasté mean?"

"Namasté is an ancient Sanskrit word. It means, I honor the place in you, where the entire universe dwells. I honor the place in you, which is of truth, of light, of peace, and love. When we consciously communicate with each other from that level of awareness, we are one."

They each placed their attention on the word Namasté. After several minutes, they both drifted into a deep state of meditation.

After about 30 minutes, Paula rang a bell to signal that the meditation was complete. She and Mark slowly opened their eyes.

"Thanks, Mark. I could feel a difference with you meditating with me. I think our combined energies helped me to recall exactly what I needed from my near-death vision. Just give me a minute to jot down a few things while they're fresh in my mind."

After several moments, Paula rested her pen and continued, "A lesson that Ram Dass had previously taught me came to me during my meditation. "The human school has a beautiful system of balance created between the self[12] and the ego mind[13]. The ego mind is our instrument of separateness and the Self is our vehicle of unity. This opposition creates a profound polarity between the ego mind and the Self. I see this as a creative tension." I think this will somehow tie into our work together. I trust that anything that comes to me in a meditative state will have significance. I just don't always know how or why or when!

Not quite knowing what to say, Mark replied, "Oh." He just wanted to get on with his first coaching session.

Mark's mind was negatively polarized from his life tragedy. Paula knew that the negative polarization of his mind was just a defense mechanism that his ego mind created to help him survive his tragedy. It wasn't good,

---

[12] Self: Another name for your Spirit, God, Atman, Ram, the Soul or any term that defines the life force energy of the universe.
[13] Ego Mind: Is the intellectual voice that you hear inside your head.

bad, right or wrong; it was just his ego's way of protecting him from extreme emotional trauma. Although it diminished his painful feelings, it also separated him from people he loved, which was making him feel lonely and isolated.

"Okay, let's do your first Mark-ology spiritual life coaching session. We'll start by doing the Spiritual Distinction Meditative Exercise[14]."

"But we just meditated."

"I know, but this meditation is different. It's unique. This exercise will help you distinguish your composite parts - your ego mind, body, vision, and Spirit. Being able to intuitively distinguish how your Spirit feels from how your ego mind feels is very important for doing your spiritual work."

---

[14] Spiritual Distinction Meditation- Is a meditative exercise that HuMethod Coaches teach their coaching clients, so they can consciously *feel the difference* between all their composite parts (Spirit, body, mind, vision)

Lesson #1 Of
Transformational Awakening Is...

Spiritual Partnerships

Consciously awakened, Spiritual Partnerships are a miraculous support system that can help humankind evolve from a five-sensory species to a multisensory species, so together we can create the critical mass needed to help SAVE the... HuMans!

It's All Perfect, Can't You See?

The Universal Law of Cause and Effect

Paula felt her first spiritual life coaching session with Mark went well. She knew that when he mastered the Spiritual Distinction Meditative Exercise it would help him to release his repressed feelings and transcend his disabling karmic curse. To her surprise, she sensed a subtle degree of sarcasm from Mark immediately following his first coaching session.

"How long will it take before I see any results?"

"That depends. Do you know how to eat an elephant?" Paula chuckled.

"What? What are you talking about?"

Paula's playful tone shifted to a more serious one, "Well, if you were shipwrecked on a deserted island and the only thing you had to eat was an elephant carcass, what would you do?"

"Okay, I'm not getting this. What's your point?"

"My point is that you would eat that elephant one small bite at a time. Then after a few months, your elephant would look like a Thanksgiving turkey after 20 guests devoured it. And that's what we will do. We'll digest your karmic challenge one bite at a time and after a few months, you will have digested all your pain and suffering. That's my plan. Are you in?"

Mark replied with a high degree of skepticism, "Sure. I'm in." He felt ambivalent about his decision to continue working with Paula. He couldn't shake an uneasy feeling he had tugging at the edge of his thoughts. He couldn't quite put his finger on it, but he knew something about their arrangement was keeping him from opening to her.

On his drive home after his first week of coaching, Mark suddenly understood why he felt uncomfortable working with Paula. He realized that he didn't know her, nor did he seek her help. It was as though life had just thrust her into his life. He had met her only a week ago, and after a short breakfast, he was expected to spill his guts about his most intimate secrets. He knew some superficial details about her but almost nothing about her professional experience or past. He knew he wouldn't be able to open until he learned more about who she was. He decided he wouldn't leave their next coaching session until he had learned more about her.

Their next coaching session began smoothly, but within a few minutes Paula noticed that Mark was more resistant than usual. He was emotionally rigid and what he did share was trivial and even a little passively-aggressive. Paula didn't want to admit it to herself, but at some deeper level she knew that Mark's resistance wasn't only about him.

Paula had received intuitive messages that their client-coach relationship was about to end. She withheld this from Mark and her emotional dishonesty was impeding the level of open communication between them. She needed to find a safe way to tell Mark that even though their souls were drawn together for a purpose, it wasn't for her to be his coach.

After concluding their coaching session, Paula reflected on Mark's obvious negative body language. "Mark, we've been at it for a week now. How do you feel?"

"I'm still having a hard time opening up, Paula." Mark's eyes glanced around the room to avoid making eye contact with her.

"I'm sorry to hear that. Please tell me more."

"Well. When I come here, I do feel better. The meditation and the exercises do help me feel more relaxed. But when I'm by myself, I still think way too much about what I've lost." Mark looked at Paula, his eyes filled with emotion.

Paula wanted to validate his feelings and to encourage him to share more. "It's okay Mark. You're going to have days like that. Anyone who went through what you did would feel the same way. It's not realistic to expect to overcome a tragedy like the one you experienced in just a few days."

"I know what you're saying, but that's not what's bothering me." Mark made direct eye contact and showed an inner strength that Paula hadn't seen before.

"Mark, this is a safe space for you to tell me what you are thinking and feeling. Please, don't hold back." Paula paused for a moment to allow Mark time to collect his thoughts.

Mark replied with a strong and firm voice, "I want to know who you are and why you are working with me."

"Because I want to help you feel better, Mark. You saved my life. It's the least I can do."

"I know I saved you, but anyone else would just say thank you and that would be it. We'd go our separate ways and there'd be nothing more. So..."

"Do you want to end our coaching sessions?"

"No. It's not that. It's just that…"

"Tell me, Mark. It's okay. What's really bothering you?"

Mark and Paula locked eyes. He knew what he wanted to say, but his ego kept watering it down. He finally blurted out, "Look. Nothing personal, but I didn't seek you out to be my life coach. You're just a person I met by chance. Now I'm coming here and sharing my deepest, darkest secrets with you, and I don't understand why. Why do you care so much?"

"Because, when I was down and out someone helped me in the same way." Paula's tone was vastly different this time. Her usual bubbly demeanor was now sternly serious as she continued, "You see me as I am now, but I wasn't always this spiritually grounded. Not too many years ago, I was a walking, talking, pessimistic bundle of negative thoughts and fear-based feelings. My life was a dark and sad mess."

Paula's response surprised Mark. She'd been so consistently cheerful and positive during their interactions that it never even occurred to him that she might have experienced her own tragedy.

Opening to Mark reminded Paula of when she first heard the expression *dark night of the soul*, and it brought up one of the worst memories of her life. It happened after college when she was so down that she had completely given up. She remembered being in a drug-induced stupor and sticking her head out her car window yelling, "Get me out of here! I want out! I give up! I'd rather be dead!" It was at this, the lowest point of her life, when she experienced her *dark night of the soul*.

Paula remembered when she learned that her veil of egoic delusion was like a steel wall, and it separated her from being *fully present* in the moment. She knew that the "blessing" of her deep despair was that it lowered her protective walls long enough for her to experience who she really was. For the first time in her life, Paula grokked that she was more than just her body, roles and material possessions; she experienced herself as being *Consciousness having a human experience.*

"My father spent most of his time drinking and avoiding work. He was what you'd call a 'rage-oholic'. Naturally, I tried to spend as much time away from him as possible. I didn't have any real friends, so I mainly hid in my room and read. My mother was a classic enabler, always making excuses for my father and trying to justify his excessive drinking and unemployment. She was the primary breadwinner in our family, even though she only managed to get low paying secretarial jobs. I know she wanted my sister and me to be happy; she always tried to put up a front for us and acted like everything was fine. But I knew that she was very sad.

Fortunately, I was blessed with several good teachers as I was growing up. School became my safe haven, and the knowledge I gained from reading kept me grounded. While my home life was very painful, my education gave me positive role models and hope for a better future. I'm so grateful for all my teachers. They really helped make me stronger.

After high school, I left home to go to college, and never returned. I was so hopeful when I graduated college that I would make something of myself. I wanted desperately to rise above what I had become. I never landed the *amazing* teaching job that I had hoped for. I wound up just drifting around the country trying to figure myself out. During those years, I experimented with drugs and alcohol and met many people who definitely weren't holistic. Then my older sister Mila stepped in. She started dragging me to Alcoholics Anonymous meetings where I made personal connections with many helpful souls who had childhood experiences like mine.

If it wasn't for Mila and those meetings, I'm not sure where I'd be today. I can guarantee you that I wouldn't be a spiritual life coach. That's for sure!"

Hearing Paula open up in such a personal way captivated Mark; "I didn't know you had a sister. How old is she?"

Paula smiled, her eyes still glossy, "Mila? She's 40, and she's my best friend in the whole world. For most of my life, she was my surrogate mother. She introduced me to yoga, which motivated me to investigate all sorts of holistic modalities. It also encouraged me to seek out teachers like Ram Dass to help me discover my dharmic reason for incarnating. That's when I began traveling the country and learning about my Self-empowerment from as many holistic practitioners as possible."

A single tear rolled from Paula's eye, which she slowly wiped away. "I'm not sure where I'd be now if it weren't for my sister's love and guidance."

Mark sat dumbfounded by Paula's emotional honesty. He felt embarrassed by how critical he'd been. He fumbled trying to find a way to apologize. "I'm sorry Paula. I didn't know."

Paula looked back at Mark and smiled. Her eyes were still glossy, "It's okay, Mark. I now understand that my parents just never had their emotional dependency needs met by their caretakers. I've moved past it since, but it can still be difficult for me sometimes." Paula paused a moment before continuing, "I'm helping you because I'm teaching what I most need to learn and heal in myself."

She wanted to say more, but the words wouldn't come. As Mark looked into her bright brown eyes, he smiled slightly. "Paula you're kind and gracious. And honestly, when I come here I always feel comfortable. I guess what I'm trying to say is, I'm sorry I'm having trouble opening up."

Paula's eyes filled with tears again, "I've been holding back too Mark, and now I believe I know why."

They both stood up and to Paula's surprise, Mark willingly embraced her. When they stopped hugging, Paula wiped the tears from her eyes and lightly giggled before taking a more serious tone.

"Mark. I'm sorry but this isn't going to work. I can't be your coach anymore."

"Wait. What?! This whole thing was your idea and now you're bailing on me?" Mark was aghast by her sudden change of heart.

"Please just take a deep breath. You'll understand what I'm trying to communicate if you give me a minute to explain. As Swami Muktananda once said, 'It's all perfect, can't you see?' And what he was referring to was that we live in a perfectly evolving Universe, so everything we experience is due to the *Law of Cause and Effect*[15].

The miraculous way we met was no accident. We were drawn to each other by the *Law of Attraction* for a very

---

[15]Law of Cause and Effect: -The Universal Law of Cause and Effect states that for every cause there is an effect because your thoughts, behaviors and vibrational feelings create specific effects that manifest life as you know it.

specific reason, but I no longer believe that the reason is coaching. I want to refer you to a professional colleague of mine, Coach Sarah Connelly. She was one of my mentors. She has decades more experience than I do and is much better equipped to handle a case like yours." Paula quickly searched through her bag to find her friend's card. Although she feared Mark's reaction to her change in plans, she felt confident that her proposal was in alignment with what the Universe had reunited their souls to do.

"I don't get it Paula." Mark muttered as he stared at the business card. "Everything you shared with me about using my pain to help others and meeting in such a strange way... what was that all about?"

Paula could tell he was feeling abandoned. "Mark, in a proper coach-client relationship I shouldn't share too much about my personal history with you because it can muddle the coach-client boundaries, which makes it difficult for me to do my job. Yesterday in meditation, I realized that I don't have enough field experience to coach someone with a case history like yours. It made me feel sad. But then I remembered, when one door closes, another door opens."

Mark was still baffled and irritated, but when he looked at Paula he could see how sincere she was. Her caring attitude was apparent. Even though he wanted to be angry, deep down he felt that she was right. One thing Mark knew for sure was that he felt better than he had in a long time, and he knew this was because of the spiritual life coaching sessions he did with Paula and the level of emotional sharing that had just taken place between them. The more he thought about it, the more comfortable he felt about working with a more experienced coach.

"Ok. Fine. I'll give Sarah a call and see how that works out. But, what about us?"

"To be honest, I'm still a little fuzzy about that. I know enough about the Law of Attraction to be sure that our souls were drawn together for a reason. If that reason isn't for spiritual life coaching, maybe it's for us to work together. We are no longer limited by coach-client boundaries, so we can support each other through our challenges to transform them into blessings. It feels right to me.

I keep receiving these visual messages where the two of us are working together. I'm not quite sure yet; but in my visions, I think we are using my near-death experience in a similar manner as the American prophet Edgar Cayce did when he received his Universal messages to help souls heal. But like I said, I'm still processing this."

"I haven't heard of Edgar Cayce. What did he do?"

"Edgar was a well-known prophet who touched the lives of millions of people. When he was a teenager, he retained photographic images in his mind of the contents of his school textbooks just by sleeping on them. Later in life, he fell ill. Doctor after doctor could not diagnose or cure him. As a last resort, he tried hypnosis. While in hypnosis he received messages for his own diagnosis and suggested treatments which led to his healing. Once word spread in the medical community, doctors referred their most difficult cases to Edgar. He was able to diagnose and present successful treatments by only knowing a patient's name and address. And all of this was done while Edgar was in an unconscious state. He was called the 'sleeping psychic'.

While in his unconscious state, Edgar tapped into Universal communications from the God Source. I believe this is available to anyone who is in a meditative state and who is open to receiving these messages. I believe this is what happened to me when I was knocked unconscious.

I know it's a lot to take in, so just let it simmer for a while."

"I'm still not totally sure what you mean. But I would like to be able to help others." Mark said, still somewhat confused.

"Don't worry. Once we've spent more time together, it'll become clearer. As far as Coach Sarah goes, I want you to keep me in the loop about how things are going with her," Paula said with an air of authority. "And since I'm no longer your coach, this opens up the possibility of us forming some sort of spiritual partnership where we can work on things as colleagues," Paula said mysteriously.

"What's a spiritual partnership?"

Paula's tone reverted back to her usual light demeanor, "A spiritual partnership is a union between people who are committed to supporting each other's spiritual growth. Until now, I was your coach and you were my client; there was a professional wall between us. Now that we've removed that wall, I can share with you what I'm thinking and feeling without violating any professional boundaries. This means I can be as emotionally vulnerable with you as you would be with me during our coaching sessions. This will help us grow together faster than we would on our own."

"This is all new to me, but if you're telling me it's the best thing we can do to empower ourselves and others, then I'm in! I trust you Paula."

"Thanks!" Paula said, with a big grin on her face.

Paula's near-death experience was the Universe's miraculous way of launching Mark and Paula's transformational adventure. Little did they know that they were about to embark on a spiritual adventure that would change both of their lives forever.

CHAPTER 6

Awakening is Paradoxical

The Transformation Begins

Mark had functioned in life in a very precise, measured way. His life had been constructed of careful planning, analyzing and interpreting. But after meeting Paula, this all changed because his mind was now in a transformational state of flux.

Still on leave from work, Mark spent much of his free time listening to audio lessons and studying the materials he had received from Coach Sarah. He was diving into a new world, and yet it was familiar to him. His parents had exposed him to similar teachings, but he had never fully immersed himself in them. Now he studied diligently out of necessity. Mark's emotional pain kept him motivated to always read just one more page and to listen to just five more minutes of his audio lessons. He listened to the audio lessons at every opportunity - while mowing the lawn, driving, doing the laundry, basically anytime his hands were busy. Through it all, he felt a *paradoxical*[16] sense of resistance and release.

Paula and Mark worked almost every day to develop a plan to capture what Paula had learned in her near-death vision. On some deep intuitive level, she felt as though she understood what the God Source communicated to her. But when she tried to write it down, it felt as impenetrable as a brick wall. Simplifying, what she had learned proved to be a greater challenge than she had initially expected.

After several failed attempts, Paula knew that the only way she could duplicate and simplify the lessons from her vision would be to experience the vision again. And since she had experimented with numerous meditation techniques over the years, she was confident that one of those techniques would help provide clarity about the messages she received from the God Source.

---

[16] Paradoxical: Two concepts that appear to be contradictory but are not; The HuMan Handbook; pg. 66.

Paula and Mark worked on their Vision Quest[17] plan for over a month before they felt it was ready to be tested. As Paula reviewed the Universal Laws, she remembered the mother of all teaching proverbs: When the student is willing, the teacher will appear. This made her laugh because she also knew that when the teacher is ready, the students will appear.

On the evening of their first Vision Quest trial, Paula sat on her living room couch amidst a sea of notes, journals, and textbooks and worked hard at formulating her ideas. Since she woke up that morning, she'd been furiously preparing for Mark's arrival. Together they would recreate Paula's near-death vision. Paula knew that her miraculous vision held the knowledge that they needed to reach a multitude of spiritual seekers.

She stepped away from her work to brew a pot of tea and take a well-deserved break. She had been staring at her laptop for hours and her brain felt numb from all the information she'd ingested in such a short time. She was only sitting for a moment when she heard a knock at the door. She rose with a feeling of joy, hoping to see Mark at her door with a big smile on his face.

"Hey Paula. I..."

---

[17] Vision Quest: Astral plane adventures usually associated with Native American cultures.

Paula interrupted, "I must look like hell," feeling self-conscious about her disheveled appearance. "I've literally had my head in the books since I woke up this morning. Come on in. I'm just about to brew some tea." Paula led Mark to the kitchen where they sat and waited for the water to boil.

"How have your sessions with Coach Sarah been going?" Paula was curious to hear about Mark's progress. She trusted Sarah, but she also knew that Mark's case history was especially traumatic and would require a lot of work before he could feel at peace with himself.

"It's... challenging. I won't lie. She had me do this over connectedness emotional enmeshment exercise. I didn't want to do it at first, but she talked me through it and eventually I got out of my own way and worked through it."

Paula could tell by Mark's tone that he got a lot out of it. "Yeah. It's always hard at the beginning. But the more work you do, the easier it will get." Paula felt that she had pressed him enough, so she changed the subject. "Are you ready for tonight's experiment?!"

"As ready as I'll ever be I suppose. I noticed a pile of materials on the couch and living room table. Is that all from today?"

"Oh. Yeah, I kept cross-referencing things. I think that I've come up with a few good ideas for our course."

"*Our* course?"

"Ha-ha. Yes. *Our* course. I would prefer to do this with you, as a partnership. Our meeting each other was no accident. This project is as much yours as it is mine. You believe that, right?" Paula asked raising her eyebrow.

"Yeah, I guess."

"Mark, you're actually *key*. I need your life force energy to help me recreate my vision and record everything."

"I can do that. Can I ask you a question though?"

Before she could answer, the kettle began to whistle. After turning off the stove, she sat back down and looked directly into Mark's eyes.

"Sorry about that. What's on your mind?"

"Why is this course so important to you?" Paula knew Mark well enough to realize that he wasn't objecting or challenging her ideologies or plan. It was merely his mind needing to understand what was being asked of him.

"Well, honestly, what's going on in the world scares me." Paula stated with a stern face and flat tone.

"How so?"

"When I look at the world and see the things that some political leaders are trying to get away with, like ignoring climate change and the general indifference people have for one another, it frightens me. I'm afraid that without some sort of... global transformation, we are headed down a road that could lead to our own extinction."

Mark would never have guessed that underneath Paula's carefree exterior was worry and fear. "I get it. Believe me, I do. But what does that have to do with us, and this work?"

"Because, as bad as things seem to be getting, I know that there are many people that are taking action to help create global transformation. With the way things are in the world, I can't imagine *not* doing everything in my power to try and help because the critical need for global change is so apparent. It's a sad fact, but our technology has *exceeded* our humanity."

Paula's eyes watered as she continued, "BUT. I have faith that the God Source has a plan. I truly believe that our humanity can once again surpass our technology. And it's this knowledge that motivates me to expedite our work to co-create a Spiritual Awakening course."

"Do you really believe that the work we'll be doing will have a positive effect?" Mark's tone was curt, and Paula could sense the skeptic in him coming out.

"Well, I believe that if we create a course which genuinely helps souls to become more deliberately conscious, then our students will understand that each of us is one cell in a body called humanity." Paula's face started blushing.

"Sure, but there are more than seven billion people in the world. What makes you think we can make a difference?"

"I believe it's our job to help as many people as possible to spiritually transform. As more and more wake up to the Truth of our interconnectedness, I *hope* they will, *pay it forward*. And this will contribute to the critical mass needed to avert a global crisis." Paula's somber tone of voice reflected her heartfelt passion.

"Alright. So, what's our goal for tonight?"

"I want to recreate the vision I had the day you saved me. If you can help me to get back to what happened that day, we will have accomplished the first step toward creating our Spiritual Awakening course."

"That sounds fine. But I don't understand why we're trying to reinvent the wheel. Instead of doing all this work, why don't we just have our students read the same materials that I'm reading from Coach Sarah?"

"Actually. I'm glad you asked that! This reminds me of my *favorite* Zen teaching parable. 'What you hear, you forget. What you see, you remember. It's only what you *do* that you truly understand. If our students read something, they will only learn the lesson intellectually. But if they experience it, they will emotionalize it."

Mark raised his hand.

"Yes, Mark?"

"Emotionalize? I'm not familiar with that term."

"Okay. If you read something, you might remember it. But it doesn't have the same impact as it would if you took an active part in learning it. So, reading, studying, and conceptualizing are merely *intellectual*[18] learning methods. When our students *do* their Self-mastery lessons, I want them to *emotionalize*[19] the knowledge we will teach them until it melts into their Consciousness.

If you read a book about swimming, you'll only understand swimming intellectually. And if you were to accidentally fall into the deep end of a pool, you'd probably drown. This is why our course must include the three educational components: studying, practicing and emotionalizing.

We need to develop ways for our students to emotionalize the knowledge that the God Source has bestowed on me. But how?" Paula asked rhetorically, as she gazed at Mark.

Mark shrugged his shoulders. "I'm not sure. But that's why we're here tonight. Right? We'll figure it out. Show me what you worked on today."

---

[18] Intellectualizing- to process information and experiences through the thinking mind

[19] Emotionalizing- to process information and experiences through emotions and feelings.

Paula and Mark brought their tea to the living room. They cleared space on the couch where Mark sat, while Paula sat on the floor with crossed-legs, so she could access her work, which was now strewn on the floor. She handed Mark a notebook and pen.

"Okay. I'll just rattle off some of the most important ideas and concepts that I learned today. Can you take notes, so we can add them to whatever we learn tonight?"

Mark gave her a thumbs-up.

Paula's mind flashed back to a lesson from one of her first spiritual teachers. "I learned how an educational fact becomes part of a person's Consciousness. A second-grade student who has not been taught long division may be aware that long division exists. But it's not until that child studies, concentrates and practices long division, that it takes root and becomes part of the child's Consciousness."

Mark scribbled furiously, "Right! I remember when you taught me that."

"My point is, our course exercises must require that our students actually *do* the exercises. To create permanent behavioral change, our students must take action."

Mark waited patiently for Paula to continue. But Paula just sat for a moment with her hand on her chin in deep contemplation. After a few minutes, he finally asked, "Is there anything else?"

"I'm sure there is. But for now, that's enough. Let's clean this mess up so we can begin our visualization experiment."

Together they sorted Paula's research notes and put them aside. The only things left out were her laptop and Mark's notebook and pen. As they tidied, Paula couldn't help but smile; she knew that doing this work was her *calling*. Nothing brought her more happiness than to teach an eager student about the Universal Laws of life, and then to watch the student evolve into a deliberately conscious *BEing*. Doing this work made her feel whole because she knew she was giving away what she most needed to learn.

After they finished sorting, they sat on opposite sides of the couch. "So, what happens now?" Mark asked with pen in hand.

"The lessons for our Spiritual Awakening course must come from the God Source, not from my ego mind. Therefore, I need to quiet my mind, so I can listen to my intuitive feelings and the messages coming from the God Source. This language of feelings is very different from my mind chatter. I learned how to speak the language of feelings by trial and error. I learned that my heart is what interprets the intuitive messages sent by my Spirit. It took a lot of emotional courage for me to face the fact that my uncomfortable feelings were a warning signal that I was out of harmony with my inner Self.

One of the most valuable lessons I have learned is that when my mind resists, represses or denies my feelings, I am disconnecting myself from my own spiritual communications. Since I grokked this transformational lesson, it has had a dramatic synergistic effect on every other Self-mastery lesson that I have learned from that day forward."

Mark stared blankly at Paula. As much as he'd acclimated to Paula's holistic methods, there was much that he was unfamiliar with and still needed to learn. "So... should I just wait? Or do I have to do something to help?" He asked, feeling self-conscious and somewhat confused.

"Oh sorry, Mark. Yes. I'm going to go into a deep meditative state, and I want you to try your best to go into a meditative state with me, so you can send me energy as if you were helping me to jump start my car's battery. Meaning, I want you to consciously send me as much love energy as you can muster. Sound good?"

"Yeah. I can do that. I'm ready when you are!"

With that, Paula began her meditation ritual. With every deep rhythmic breath, she became more and more relaxed. Her thoughts slowed down. After several minutes, she reached a state of alpha Consciousness. Paula repeated her mantra word, Namasté, until she slipped into a deep state of thoughtless bliss.

***

After a few minutes passed, Paula began to see a vision that became clearer the deeper she went into meditation. When her perception came into focus, she realized that she was looking down at a winter wonderland of snow-covered mountains. She could see tall evergreen trees covered from top to bottom with glistening snow. They looked like enormous Christmas ornaments. The sun shined brightly, and the sky was a perfect azure blue, except for an occasional group of white, puffy clouds.

From Paula's vantage, the mountains looked like large, rolling hills. It reminded her of the Adirondack Mountains located in the northeastern part of the United States. Far off in the distance she noticed a long winding river, and, beyond that, an expansive ocean.

Suddenly, she felt herself descend with such force that her vision became blurred. As she fell toward the earth, she began twisting and spinning out of control. A kaleidoscope of orange, purple and red hues engulfed her senses, like different colors in a complex pattern. As suddenly as her descent began, it stopped. She looked down at herself. As she did, she realized that she was no longer in her body; she was invisible and formless. As unnerving as this was, Paula marveled at the sensation of feeling as light and free as an angel.

Suddenly, a skier gracefully cruising down the mountainside caught her attention. Watching the skier carve up the slope with tight parallel turns reminded Paula of how much she enjoyed the physical excitement of skiing. She loved feeling the cold wind blowing on her face and smelling the crisp winter air as she skied down a challenging run on a beautiful sunny winter day.

The skier who had caught her attention appeared to be a man in his 20s about six feet tall, with a medium-build and brown wavy hair tucked beneath his hat. He was skiing alone on fresh, virgin snow. His expert form clearly indicated that he was an experienced skier. As he blazed down the run, Paula began to have trouble focusing. She felt a combination of fear and exhilaration. Without exerting any effort, her extrasensory powers allowed her to not only see, but also to *feel*, whatever the skier was experiencing.

When the young man reached the bottom of the slope, he immediately skied to the lift station. The line was empty, except for a single tall man with silver-gray hair, who appeared to be in excellent physical shape for someone who looked to be well into his 70s. He waited patiently for the younger skier to catch up. Together, they quickly positioned themselves for the next chair lift.

"Good morning Ron! Beautiful day to be alive, isn't it?" The old man said with a big smile on his face.

"Hell yes, Sam! I've skied a few times this season, but today's conditions are the best so far."

"Say, Sam. Do you mind if I ask you a question?"

"Not at all. What's on your mind?"

"How do you stay in such great shape? I must bust my ass and lay off the beer and junk food. But you make it look so easy." It was clear that Ron had great admiration for Sam and that he hoped to be as physically capable when he reached 70 years old.

Sam chuckled proudly. "I go for a long walk every morning. But the most important thing is a good diet. Lay off the beer and smoke a little less pot, and you'll be amazed at how easy it is to stay fit." The two men laughed at Sam's blunt honesty.

After catching his breath, Ron smiled admirably at Sam. "You know. I really appreciate your company, Sam. You don't talk down to me like my stepdad does."

Sam returned Ron's smile and nodded appreciatively.

Ron was a junior in college, majoring in philosophy. He liked to question everything; the origin of life, the survival of the planet, the Law of Cause and Effect and anything else that he could think of. While he hung out with his friends and smoked weed, he philosophized about anything and everything that his chemically-induced, altered state of consciousness triggered.

Ron especially enjoyed philosophizing with Sam, because Sam was a retired spiritual life coach with grandchildren who were older than Ron. Ron knew that it took Sam seven decades to master the game of life, and it was apparent in the way he conducted himself. He was amazed that Sam had witnessed the birth of so many technological miracles, such as computers, going to the moon, the space station, and cell phones.

What Ron appreciated most of all about Sam was that, despite their age difference, Sam could relate well with him. Sam instructed Ron without preaching *at* him, like so many other adults did. He also respected that Sam was *willing* to modify his beliefs anytime someone would back up their theories with concrete facts and evidence.

As their lift carried them through the picturesque mountain scape, the two men enjoyed a moment of silence to appreciate their surroundings. Ron broke the silence, "Sam, do you remember how young I was when we first started skiing together?"

"Yeah. You were nine, I believe. Gosh has it been that long? In that time, I've watched you grow into an intelligent, spiritually aware young man."

Ron felt slightly embarrassed by the compliment and interrupted. "So, we were talking in class the other day about the meaning of spirituality. It got pretty heavy. It made me think of you. I wanted to ask... what do you think is the most important lesson a person needs to learn to live a spiritually conscious life?"

"PARADOX!" Sam quickly blurted out.

***

As she listened intently to Sam and Ron's every word, Paula was abruptly struck by the realization that she'd been catapulted back into her near-death vision. Her vision was as clear and easy to comprehend as a Hollywood movie. The spiritual lesson she experienced during her sailboat accident was unfolding in front of her, and what amazed her was that she and Mark intentionally created it.

"Whoa!" Paula blurted with excitement.

Soon after, Paula took a deep breath to ground back into the moment to fully absorb the First Lesson of Spiritual Awakening... Paradox.

***

As their lift carried them toward the mountain peak, the trees surrounding them gradually transitioned from leafless barren husks to beautiful snow-covered ornaments. Sam quietly admired the breathtaking scenery and pondered the best way to explain why paradox is such an important concept to understand.

While Ron waited for Sam's response, he became immersed in the beauty of the mountains below him. The lift had risen 2,000 feet above the main ski lodge and yielded a spectacular view. The sun shined so brightly that its reflection off the white snow was blinding to anyone without sunglasses. Ron breathed in deeply to inhale the fresh scent of pine that he loved so much.

Sam's tone resounded with wisdom that only comes with age and real-world experiences, "To live a spiritually conscious life I believe that accepting and becoming comfortable with the paradoxes of the earth plane is the foundational lesson you must learn.

Everything on this planet has positive and negative energy charges, and it's the dynamic tension created between these two polarized opposites that creates the physical world in which we live. Paradox is a tough concept to understand because most of us have been conditioned to believe in only one aspect of polarization. For instance, you must be either a winner or a loser.

Paradox happens when two concepts appear to contradict each other, but don't. On your journey home to your Self, Son, you'll run into many kinds of paradoxes. Like the paradox that you are a spiritual

BEing who is having a human experience. In this case, the paradox is that you are both a physical and non-physical entity, simultaneously. To be a Spirit who is having a human experience seems contradictory for one who hasn't spiritually awakened. But what you'll come to realize is that life consists of numerous paradoxes."

Ron replied, "Right. Like how we were taught that the Native Americans were all savages with no moral values or ethics. But in truth, there were many tribes with different cultures and most of them were holistically conscious and had a deep spiritual heritage."

Sam didn't want to correct Ron. What he shared was true, but it wasn't a good example of a paradox. He wisely overlooked what Ron had shared and continued to elaborate on the concept of paradox, knowing that Ron would catch on soon enough.

"The earth plane is made up of hundreds of dualistic opposites. Like the North and South Poles, or the positive and negative sides of a magnet. The visual contrasts these dualisms create helps us to differentiate physical objects. Take the sky for example. Notice that the white clouds are very distinguishable because of the blue sky around them."

Ron interrupted with excitement, "Oh, I think I just had an aha moment! So, my mind judges people and experiences as right or wrong, good or bad. I'm just beginning to realize how polarized my ego-mind actually is."

"You're starting to get it, Ron. I'd say the most important point for you to get about paradox is that polarizations separate us. Unlike spiritual trilogies that unite us, like mind, body and Spirit, and past, present and future."

As the lift approached the top of the mountain, they were greeted with a breathtaking view of about 50 miles in every direction. Pondering the concept of paradox had put Ron into such a contemplative state of mind that he almost didn't get off the chair lift in time. He stumbled as he dismounted and just about wiped out. To hide his embarrassment, he immediately headed to an expert slope. Sam headed to an intermediate, less challenging slope.

"I'll wait for you at the bottom!" Ron yelled out.

Ron's slope was wide and steep. He intentionally slowed his descent by taking long, tight-kneed parallel turns spanning the width of the slope, so he wouldn't have to wait too long for Sam at the bottom. As he skied, he couldn't help but think out loud, "I'm a walking, talking set of opposites. I am self-confident in some areas, and I have self-doubts in others. I'm lazy and hardworking, quiet and outgoing. All at the same time! The paradoxical contrasts are endless."

***

Paula was getting accustomed to her non-form state of being. She felt blessed that she could learn this spiritual lesson in an angelic, formless state of Consciousness. As her vision progressed she remembered part of a poem that her soul friend, Coach Sharda, wrote.

We spend more but have less.
We buy more but enjoy it less.
We have more conveniences, but less time.
We have more knowledge, but less sense.
We have multiplied our possessions but reduced our values.
We talk too much, love too seldom, and hate too often.
We've added years to our life, not life to our years.
We've conquered outer space, but not inner space.
We've split the atom, but not our prejudice.
We have higher incomes, but lower morals.
These are times of tall men and short characters,
steep profits and shallow relationships.

***

Sam reached the bottom of the ski run a few minutes after Ron, and the pair headed straight for the chair lift. After they lowered the safety bar, Sam turned to Ron and said, "I've spent thousands of hours facilitating spiritual coaching sessions, and I have learned how paradoxical the psycho-spiritual healing process actually is."

"What do you mean?"

Sam paused and gestured with his hands to help exemplify his point. "Visualize this. Imagine a large scale, or seesaw. One of my most important jobs is to help my clients balance both sides of this *Healing Paradox*: what happened to you when you were a child wasn't your fault, but it is your responsibility to heal, because no one else can heal it for you."

Ron didn't fully understand, but he nodded in agreement, as the lift whisked them up the mountain.

Sam quietly took a few slow deep breaths and continued. "If you learn nothing else about the Healing Paradox, what I want you to remember is there is always an equal and opposite dharmic blessing for every karmic curse you experience.

You have probably heard people say *what doesn't kill you will make you stronger*. For the most part that's true, but only if you are willing to take the shit that you have experienced and use it as fertilizer to grow a Self-empowered life that you so richly deserve."

"Okay. So, what I think I'm hearing you say is that there is a silver lining hidden within all the crap I took from my stepdad all these years. Is that what you mean?"

"Yes, that is exactly what I mean."

"Well Sam. I respect you too much to lie to you, but I find it hard to believe that underneath all my stepdad's verbal abuse is some good."

"It's perfectly normal for you to feel that way, Son. But what you will eventually discover is that when you can forgive him, without being self-righteous about it, it will free you to make lemonade from all the lemons that he threw at you. Forgiving him will protect you from carrying blame and holding onto to anger and resentment toward him, which only harms you. That is because forgiveness is a *self-protection mechanism.*"

Ron didn't want to think about his stepdad for another second, so he reached into his coat, pulled out a water bottle, and took a sip. He gestured the bottle toward Sam who gratefully accepted. After taking a second sip, Ron continued his line of questioning, feeling very proud that he could converse with someone as wise as Sam. "So, what makes paradox the foundational life lesson of spiritual awakening?"

Sam chuckled, impressed by Ron's inquisitive mind, "Good question! Well, as you know, you are a human being who must abide by the physical laws of the Universe. But, you are also a Spirit, without form. And this means you have two different ways to process your life experiences."

Ron nodded, as he digested Sam's words. "So, you're saying that there are two different ways for me to process my life. Through my intellectual mind or through my intuitive heart?"

"Almost. What I'm suggesting is that a spiritually awakened person should process their life through their intuitive feelings first and their intellectual mind second." Sam paused a moment to let his words sink in.

Though Ron nodded in agreement, he still wore a slightly puzzled expression.

Sam continued, "Do you understand why processing your life through your intuitive heart first is so important?"

"Actually, I'm not sure."

"Before I answer that, remember that you were raised as a man in a patriarchal society. Throughout your life you were rewarded for thinking and reprimanded for crying."

"Okay. Go on."

"I believe that processing your life through your intuitive heart first is extremely important because it allows you to draw upon your Infinite wisdom to find a solution to any problem you are trying to solve. Plus, you can't trust your ego mind, because one of its survival jobs is to minimize, repress or deny any pain that you might be experiencing, which blinds you from the truth that you need to see and feel in order to heal."

"Kind of like anesthesia?"

"Yes! Just like anesthesia! Your ego mind makes up rationalizations to help you feel safe, sane and secure. Do you remember what the word rationalize means?"

"Yeah. It means 'rational lies'. But how can I train myself to feel first after so many years of being drilled by my stepdad to act like a macho hard ass?"

"Well, one of the things that helped me was using a Feel-to-Release Chart[20]. It was paramount in helping me on my journey. I'll email you a copy. Either way, to not sugarcoat it, the answer is hard WORK! It will take consistent effort on your part to change your old habits. But eventually it will become second nature."

"I get it. So, you just used this chart and that was it? Or was there more to it?"

Sam laughed heartily knowing full well it took much more than the chart alone, "I'm sorry. I'm not laughing at you. It's just that the question brought me back to when I was your age. When I was as intellectually curious as you are now."

---

[20] Feel-to-Release Chart: A chart that will help you speak the Language of your Feelings. See Self-Mastery, A Journey Home to Your...Inner Self; Renaissance publishing 2008, page 56.

Ron smiled back at Sam. "I'm not offended. I'm curious though. Can you tell me about your experience?"

"My spiritual awakening process took many years and dozens of books, seminars, and Self-awareness intensives. It was tough. And it required a lot of emotional courage to examine my negative beliefs, habits and behaviors."

Ron admitted, "I'm not always honest with myself. But I do believe it's important for me to quickly own my mistakes, so I don't repeat them."

"Because you've been thinking over 50,000 thoughts a day for two decades, your mind is programmed to believe that you are your roles, such as student, stepson and philosopher. You do play these roles in life, but they aren't who you are."

"What was your biggest transformational hurdle?"

Sam considered Ron's question knowing full well what the answer was. "Honestly. It was the guilt I felt from my Christian upbringing. When I was first learning about spiritual awakening, I felt like my new metaphysical understanding was a sin. There were plenty of times when it triggered fears of my eternal damnation."

Ron's eyes widened, "Wow! No kidding? I never would've pegged you for the religious type."

Sam was amused by Ron's surprise. "When I was a young spiritual seeker, I felt as though my beliefs in the Scriptures conflicted with my spiritual awakening. It was frightening at times. But after many years, I learned that the spiritual awakening process was very much in harmony with the teachings of Jesus the Christ and many of the other great spiritual masters, such as Buddha and Muktananda.

From various books I remember reading over and over, that I am a spiritual BEing having a human experience. And one night it hit me. Just like that. I am a body and a soul at the same time. My soul is invisible, my body is not. And now, I embrace the ultimate paradox. I am Spirit and man, two opposites at the same time. And it was this realization – this foundational lesson of life – that I needed to grok before I spiritually awakened."

Ron continued to listen intently.

"That was a mouthful wasn't it? Sorry if I rambled a bit. But I wanted to make a point. All the other esoteric concepts fell into place for me once I really understood that the physical plane was made up of numerous paradoxes."

"So that's when everything fell into place for you, right?"

"Well. That's a bit of an oversimplification. I'm afraid it wasn't quite that simple. I spent most of my adult life building a financially-sound foundation, so my wife, kids and I were blessed to enjoy the finer material things of life. We drove new cars, took yearly vacations, and we owned a large, beautiful home in the country. What I haven't shared with you yet is what happened to me when I was 42 years old. I lost my job. My home was foreclosed on and we had to move. We moved to a place where our three kids had to sleep in one room with no heat. And my wife and I were forced to clean bathrooms to put food on the table."

"Why did you lose your job, Sam?"

"I'll spare you the gritty details, but the short version is that I made some bad business decisions, which caused me to lose my job. Then I went bankrupt and lost almost all my material possessions practically overnight. It was the most stressful thing that ever happened to me. And for the first time in my life, my faith was truly tested. I started to question my core spiritual beliefs that took decades to build. But through it all, there was something I learned during my spiritual journey that rang true for me."

"And that was?"

"That circumstances don't make the man. But they do reveal to him what he is made of. I knew that I had to view my financial problems as an opportunity to learn and grow, but my ego's neurotic self-talk was focused on feeling sorry for myself. For the first time in my life, I allowed myself to succumb to thinking I was a powerless victim. I remember asking God, *Why me, I'm a good person?* My emotional pain, shame, social embarrassment and uncertain financial future caused me to slip into a clinical depression. I even contemplated suicide."

"Damn Sam, I had no idea you went through all that. How'd you manage to get through it?"

"It all came down to personal choices. Every day I had to muster the courage to choose love and life, and to stop blaming, shaming and playing the role of victim. Eventually, with the love and support provided by my family and friends, I was able to build myself back up again. It took many years, but by God's grace, here I am now... on this beautiful winter day, riding to the top of a mountain with my young soul friend, Ron."

The lift reached the top of the mountain. The two disembarked and made their way to the trail map to plan their next run. As they checked their gear, Ron turned to Sam and smiled earnestly. "Hey. I'm sorry I asked so many questions, but you're an interesting guy to talk to. Thanks for sharing all that with me. I really appreciate your emotional honesty."

Sam smiled warmly and patted Ron on the shoulder. "No need for apologies, Ron. I'm happy to share with you. You're practically a son to me. Honestly my negative, fear-based identity seems ridiculous to me now. I learned many important life lessons and developed unshakable will and courage by choosing love over fear time after time."

"I hear you. Well, I think I'm going to take another black diamond run. Want to meet at the lodge for lunch?"

"That sounds good. I'm ready for some food and rest."

"One last question?"

"Sure!"

"Would you do things differently if you had the chance to do it all over again?"

Sam had often pondered that exact question. "It was incredibly hard to go through such an experience. But I believe my *dark night of the soul* was a blessing in disguise. It quieted my ego long enough for me to see, feel, and heal the Truth of what I needed to transcend to spiritually awaken. So. No. I wouldn't change a thing."

"That's awesome! I'll meet you at the lodge." And Ron quickly disappeared down the steepest slope of the mountain.

***

Paula was so entranced by what Sam had shared about his *dark night of the soul* experience that she didn't realize that her vision was beginning to fade. The vivid colors slowly faded from black to different shades of grey, and then everything went black. Instantly her mind exploded into a kaleidoscope of colors again, but as suddenly as the Vision Quest began, it disappeared. Paula was coming out of her meditative state, and as she did, she realized that she was back in her living room with Mark. She stared directly at Mark, who was waiting patiently with pen in hand, and she asked, "How long was I out?"

"Out? Not long. You were only meditating for about 20 minutes. You stopped saying Namasté after about five minutes. Why? What happened?"

"Wow. That felt like it lasted for hours! Hey! I have an idea. Let's do this like an interview and we'll record our conversation, so we can refer back to it."

"Great idea!"

Paula reached for her laptop, started her camera app and hit the record button. She motioned to Mark to begin the interview.

With a very professional tone, Mark asked, "Paula, we just finished our first Vision Quest experiment to try to recreate the vision you had during your near-death experience. You meditated and fell silent for about 20 minutes. Can you describe, in as much detail as possible, what you just experienced? What did you see in your Vision Quest?" Mark asked as he scribbled in his notebook.

"I was in the mountains. But I wasn't me. Rather... I wasn't in my body. I just existed as an ethereal Spirit. It was winter. The ground was covered in snow. And it was a beautiful day." Paula paused to give Mark a chance to catch up.

"What else did you see?"

"There was a pair of skiers. One was a young guy, probably in his early twenties. The other was an older man. Maybe 70. Both clearly had deep knowledge of the type of spiritual lessons we want to teach."

"What makes you say that?"

"They had an in-depth conversation about the concept of paradox."

As Paula continued to go over the details, her mind flashed back to when she studied under Coach Eckhart. He'd taught her that the most esoteric paradoxes happen between the ego and the inner Self, and which were exemplified in a poem. She couldn't remember all the stanzas, but there were a few she couldn't forget:

> My ego mind thinks,
> The world is against me, they are against me,
> you are against me, and even I'm against me!
> My Self feels,
> I am ONE, I am one with all people, I am one with you,
> and I am one with the whole Universe!
> My ego mind thinks,
> I am not enough.

My Self feels,
I am all there is, I am Love.
My ego mind thinks,
you push my buttons, so I'll avoid you.
My Self feels,
thank you, ego, for you are a doorway to what I need to heal.
My ego mind thinks,
I'll never have enough.
My Self feels,
by creating a heaven within my own Consciousness,
I'll be able to see through the veil of illusion
created by the earth plane,
and thus I'll be able to recognize
the Heaven that is within me.

Together they poured over the details of Paula's Vision Quest and the first foundational lesson of paradox.

Though Mark was still quite skeptical, he trusted Paula. He accepted as truth the things of which Paula spoke. Before their debriefing session ended, Mark asked, "Paula, what do you hope to accomplish with what you learned tonight?"

She looked at him, paused for a few moments, and smiled. "Well. I hope that this foundational lesson about paradox will become the building block to form our transformational course that will help souls spiritually awaken.

As you know, we're experiencing a global crisis. I believe that if enough of our students grok that we are all spiritually interconnected, then our graduates will contribute to the critical mass needed to help SAVE the... HuMans."

Lesson #2 Of
Transformational Awakening Is...

<u>PARADOX</u>

To spiritually awaken, you must embrace
the dualisms of the earth plane, especially
the Healing Paradox because inside of every
karmic curse lies an equal and opposite
dharmic blessing.

Are You Willing?

90% of Life Is Just Showing Up

Paula and Mark spent the next two weeks studying the recording from their Vision Quest and formatting their first lesson of their Spiritual Awakening course - Paradox. Experiencing everything Sam and Ron thought and felt had given Paula the knowledge to systematically co-create the paradox lesson with Mark.

Paula and Mark experienced this extra-sensory educational process from very different perspectives. Paula recalled her formless vision and experienced sensations, as if they were originating from within her, while Mark was learning the lessons on a more conceptual level through listening to Paula's experiences. Together they formed a well-balanced team perfect for the project of co-creating their Spiritual Awakening course.

On a beautiful Sunday morning, Paula sat in her living room reviewing their work. Their work had inspired Paula to maintain a higher degree of organization, but her living room was still cluttered with research materials. She sipped her tea and read until Mark knocked on her back door. She let him in and cleared a spot for him on the couch. Mark wasn't always the most cheerful individual and given his past trauma that was certainly normal. But Paula could sense that something was troubling him. They discussed Mark's inner work with Coach Sarah, but Paula did not sense that anything related to his coaching sessions was bothering him.

With genuine concern, Paula asked Mark directly, "Is something troubling you?"

"I'm alright. Just having a bit of a down day I suppose."

"Is it your Self-work or something else?"

"Honestly, all I did was watch the news while I ate breakfast. I think it got me down."

Paula started chuckling because his response was so insightful that it had surprised her. "Sorry Mark. I know it's not funny. And I'd probably be down too if I watched the news this morning. What was it that you saw that bothered you?"

"Nothing specific really. Just the same old thing. Climate Change, polluted oceans, civil unrest; ugh, just all of it. You know, sometimes I look at the state of the world, and I think about the work we are trying to do, and it feels pointless. I mean how are we supposed to change all that? We're just two people." As he spoke, his gaze gradually shifted toward the floor.

"We won't know if our work will help create the point of critical mass unless we try, right? The truth is, there's no way to know for sure if there's anything we can do that will make a significant difference, but should that stop us from trying? I believe that if we just keep working on building this course, something good will come of it. Don't you agree?" Paula asked smiling cheerfully.

"Yeah, I guess." Mark said with a defeated look.

Paula recognized that look. Mark's depression would oftentimes immobilize him, which was why she knew that he needed to take some sort of *action* to raise his vibrational energy before they could properly begin the day's experiment. She stood and tapped Mark on the shoulder.

"Get up. We're going out." She said with an air of authority.

"We are? Where are we going?"

"There are several hiking trails behind my house. Let's go check one out. It'll be nice to get some fresh air before we get to work."

"Sure. That sounds fine." Mark said with little enthusiasm.

They gathered their essential Vision Quest materials into Paula's backpack and set out to hug some trees. Paula led Mark through her backyard and down an old logging trail that led deep into the woods. The tall surrounding oaks were leafless but noticeably covered in buds. It was early spring, and the forest was just starting to show signs of emerging life. By contrast, the path was adorned with small ferns and evergreen trees that remained green all year long.

They walked for several minutes in silence taking in the scenery, until Mark asked, "Do you hike this trail a lot?"

"Not as much as I'd like. But I *love* hiking in the woods especially when I need to clear my head. This time of year, isn't the prettiest, but it still feels wonderful to walk where there is so much green life force energy." As Paula spoke she faced Mark. "When I was a kid, there were plenty of times when my father would go into his rage-aholic act. Whenever that happened, I would hang out in the woods until I felt safe to go home again."

Mark broke a slight smile. "I'll bet you were a girl scout when you were a kid. Weren't you?"

"Me? No never. My mother was too busy putting food on the table to drive me to a meeting. And forget about my father, he was out of the question. I've just always loved nature. I used to play for hours and just pretend to be one of the characters from the books I had read." Paula said smiling widely.

"Sounds lonely."

As Mark spoke, Paula could sense his energy rising and his mood shifting. She slowed her pace, so they could walk side by side. "I was alone, but I didn't feel lonely. I had a great imagination. If I wasn't pretending to be a character from a book, I'd just make someone up. I suppose now it might seem a little weird, but that's how I spent a lot of my spare time when I was a kid. It got me out of the house at least."

As the pair made their way down the path, Paula continued to tell Mark stories about her childhood and Mark's energy continued to lift. Even though Paula was only making small talk, Mark realized that she had a light and airy presence, which he greatly appreciated. Her overall positive demeanor and carefree attitude made her a pleasure to be around. He couldn't help but smile as she told stories about her childhood summer days building forts, climbing trees and making rope swings.

Eventually they came to a patch of forest where the trees had been cleared away, and the sun was shining through. Paula stopped and surveyed the area. "Okay. I think this would be a fine place to start."

"You want to meditate and do the next Vision Quest experiment out here?" Mark hadn't expected the sudden change in plans.

"Sure! Why not? Can you think of a better place than in the middle of nature? What are you worried about? There's no one else around." Paula began unloading her backpack. She laid a plush burgundy wool blanket down followed by her laptop and other Vision Quest materials.

Mark chuckled at Paula's assertiveness and dispelled his reservations. "Sure. Why not?" He sat across from Paula and picked up a notepad and pencil.

Paula flipped through one of her notebooks with her pen in hand. "So, I've been thinking a lot about Sam's bankruptcy story, and it made me realize that most people begin their spiritual awakening process when they experience a trauma. It's as though the tragedy creates so much pain and suffering that the ego shuts down for a while, and this allows them to see beyond their ego. I suspect this is also what helps them drum up the emotional courage to find a solution to transcend their pain."

Mark nodded in agreement "Right. I know that my tragedy forced my ego to retreat. That allowed me to see past my defense mechanisms, which helped me to awaken to what was already always within me... my Christ Consciousness or soul or call it whatever."

Paula stopped writing and looked up at Mark with a surprised look on her face. "Right. Exactly! I'm impressed, Mark. Did you pick that up from your sessions with Coach Sarah?"

Mark nodded. "I did. Coach Sarah is helping me own that eventually I can make my *dark night of the soul* lemons into some fine-tasting lemonade, so I can transform my defense mechanisms into blessings."

With a big smile and chuckle, Paula said, "Wow. Well said! Seriously well said! But keep in mind, not everyone who lives through a tragedy spiritually awakens. I wonder what the missing link is?" As she spoke, Paula contemplated the metaphoric similarities between a woman's labor pains and the pscyho-spiritual pain everyone feels giving birth to their inner Self.

Paula and Mark continued to chat as they organized the information they had collected about paradox. Once all their research materials were organized, they felt ready to retrieve the next lesson of their course. Mark set up the laptop while Paula assumed her meditation position. She began taking long slow deep breaths and repeating her empowerment word, Namasté, over and over again. Little by little she became more and more relaxed. As her mind quieted, she slowly surrendered so the God Source could show her the next multisensory vision.

**

Once again, Paula found herself floating above a scenic mountain range, but these mountains were very different from the ones she had seen in her previous Vision Quest. These mountains were much taller with sharp, snow-covered peaks, like the Rockies. She could see trees adorned with orange, yellow and purple leaves in the surrounding valleys. It was a gray overcast day with high clouds blanketing the entire sky.

Suddenly, Paula started to free fall. She thought, *Here we go again.* Although she didn't enjoy the extreme sensation of the rapid descents, it was a price she was willing to pay to learn the next lesson. Paula's vision blurred, and she became enveloped in her now familiar kaleidoscope of colors and shapes. As she fell, she felt her speed increase, which magnified the intensity of her descent and caused the colors around her to blur together into a white mass of light. Then as miraculously as the colors appeared, they abruptly disappeared. Paula found herself in a formless state of Consciousness. She had come to a stop just above the treetops. Below her was a group of hikers equipped with climbing gear and backpacks. The hikers were at a spot where three mountains intersected and formed a deep ravine of about 500 feet into a basin about 25 yards wide.

After scouting the area and taking in the breathtaking view, the four hikers stopped to set up camp about 30 yards from the cliffs' edge. The hikers began to pitch their tents while the team leader, Tom, gave orders and answered various questions about setting up camp. Tom appeared to be in his early 40s. He stood over six feet tall with a large build, a full beard, and long dirty-blond hair.

***

Paula chuckled to herself thinking, *He looks like a mountain man straight out of the '1800s."*

***

After setting up camp, Tom gestured for the group to gather around the fire pit they'd built and opened the conversation, "Please introduce yourselves and explain why you enrolled in this Self-awareness adventure. Tell us what you expect to get out of this paradigm[21]-shifting, experience. We'll start with you, Howard."

"Well, as you already know, my name is Howard. I'm an antique furniture dealer from Connecticut. I'm sure that you can tell by my accent that I'm originally from

---

[21] Paradigm: A self-imposed belief pattern which might be true or not

England. The reason I'm here is because I need to do something to get out of the emotional rut that I've been in for the last two years."

Howard was a thin man, about six-and-a-half feet tall, who was in good physical shape for being in his late 50s. His distinguished English accent gave him an air of superiority, which matched the stiffness of his personality.

The next person introduced herself as Lenore, "I work as a dental consultant on Long Island. I teach dentists how to build and run profitable practices. I'm here because I just divorced my husband of 20 years, and I want to do something to help me break out of my old relationship paradigms."

Lenore was of average height and weight, and she had long black hair. She was sultry looking, yet her numerous facial lines showed signs of long endured emotional stress. Her voice sounded alive and personable.

Rounding out the crew was Pat. Unlike Lenore, Pat had a large tall frame and a heavy build. She was clearly very fit and strong, and she resembled a female Olympic weightlifter. She had short wavy brown hair and a deep voice.

"Hello everyone. I'm Pat. I'm from Los Angeles, and I love physical fitness and testing myself. My partner, Taylor, and I have been together for... wow... almost 10 years now. Taylor has never really been the physical type, so I decided to take this trip, so we could enjoy some time apart. I also wanted to test myself. I'm looking forward to the physical challenge and... I want to overcome my fear of heights."

Since Pat exuded confidence and carried herself with a powerful sense of authority, the group was shocked to hear that she was afraid of heights. Her outward appearance and personality projected that this woman was not afraid of anything.

**

Paula sensed how uncomfortable Pat was feeling. She also felt fear resonating from Lenore and Howard. *And why not*. Paula thought. They were about to repel down a 500-foot ravine.

**

Lenore light-heartedly asked, "I want to know, Tom... have any of your students ever died while repelling? I need some reassurance that I'm going to get down this cliff alive."

Lenore's question created welcomed comic relief, as the team checked their safety equipment to prepare for their first repel.

Tom was an experienced outdoor travel guide who had taught thousands of students to overcome their fears, and the only way this was possible was for them to be emotionally *willing*. "You can do anything that you are *willing* to do, because *90% of life is just showing up*." Tom coached his team with a hyped motivational tone in his voice, as if he was a high school football coach rallying his team before kickoff. "And no. I've never had a student die under my watch."

Tom knew that people have a natural fear of heights. And for his students, this fear is multiplied because of their lack of repelling experience. He felt the team's anxiety building, so he asked a question to try to calm them down "What are you feeling right now?"

"I'm scared to death!" Pat responded nervously.

"That's good because your fear is preparing your body for the physical task at hand. Remember feeling fear is normal, natural and healthy. Healthy fear can even save your life if you know how to channel it." Tom assured her. "But first, you must be *willing* to mentally commit to doing this repel. No matter how scared you feel. Got it?"

"Got it!" Pat responded, feeling a little less nervous.

Tom asked the group, "How would you define *willingness*?"

"Willingness means to do whatever it takes." Howard quickly answered.

Pat chimed in, "And you must be *willing* to face and overcome the obstacles that could stop you from accomplishing your goals."

Tom added, "Willingness comes from the root word *will*. It is the *will* to take the actions necessary to transcend your fears.

"Can anyone tell me the difference between *fear* and *danger?*"

No one answered.

Tom continued, "The difference is that fear isn't real. It's a product of the ego's imagination. Don't misunderstand this though. Because *danger*, like repelling down a 500-foot cliff, *is* real! Whereas, fear is a mental choice.

The egoic mind can neurotically cause people to fear places and things that may no longer actually exist. This type of thinking is broaching insanity. Team, the day you grok that your egoic fears are imaginary stories that *no longer exist*, is the day you will liberate your soul."

* * *

Paula realized that the second lesson unfolding before her was *willingness*.

Feeling impressed with her *aha* moment, she thought, *So that explains why some people don't spiritually awaken when they go through a tragedy. Some souls just aren't WILLING to do the actions that are required to transcend their fears to make their dreams come true.*

* * *

After reviewing safety procedures, Tom moved the team to the edge of the cliff. He told them to sit near the edge, so they could acclimate to the height. Then he asked, "What could stop a person from being willing to take action?"

"The fear of falling!" Pat blurted humorously.

The troop laughed, which helped to relieve some of the tension that was still building.

Tom shouted, "PREPARE TO REPEL!"

***

Paula telepathically felt the team's emotional tension increase. *It feels so intense and thick that I could cut it with a knife. My stomach feels like I'm about to repel too.*

***

The team put on their safety harnesses. They checked and rechecked their safety belts.

Tom instructed, "You see that seven-foot ledge about a hundred feet down? We are going to repel to that spot first. Pat, I want you to go first, followed by Lenore and then Howard."

Tom rechecked all their safety lines. "Does anyone have any last-minute questions?"

No one replied. They just shook their heads.

Pat attacked the first 100 feet with the eagerness of a 19-year-old U.S. Marine. Her actions proved that she was *willing* to face her fears. She used her genuine enthusiasm to awaken her inner courage.

Lenore's repel went off without a hitch. She did more sitting than repelling, but she didn't care because she knew that she would improve with practice. She made repelling look safe and easy which increased Howard's confidence.

Howard was next. As a repelling instructor, Tom could see in Howard's eyes something he had seen hundreds of times before: the look of *terror*. Howard's hands were shaking, his forehead was perspiring profusely, and he started asking stress-induced questions to stall for time.

Tom was incredibly patient with Howard. He answered all his questions calmly; and as he did, he slowly maneuvered Howard into a starting position. Howard's body was as stiff as a board. It was blatantly obvious that he was intimidated by the height of the cliff, but he managed to force himself to begin his descent. Howard only descended 20 feet, when he lost his footing and panicked. He then lost control of the rope that regulated the speed of his descent, and he fell hundreds of feet. By the grace of God, his safety lines tangled on a tree stump, which abruptly broke his fall.

Howard was hanging upside-down, hundreds of feet from the cavern floor with his legs tangled in the ropes. His head had grazed a protruding rock from the cliff, which left him unconscious with a deep bloody gash an inch above his left eye.

"ARE YOU OKAY HOWARD?" Tom yelled as loud as he could.

Howard didn't answer.

The team instinctively began yelling, "HOWARD! ARE YOU OKAY? HOWARD?!"

Finally, after a few moments Howard faintly answered, "I'm okay I guess."

"Hang in there, Howard. I'll be right down. Try not to move."

"Don't worry, Tom. I'm not going to move an inch." His attempt at humor made everyone feel better.

***

Suddenly Paula's vision of the team's repel began to fade. She quickly drifted out of her formless state of Consciousness and into the familiar kaleidoscope of colors. She was frustrated that her Vision Quest had ended before she found out what happened to Howard, but she willingly surrendered knowing that the God Source was in charge... not she.

She opened her eyes and saw Mark sitting across from her with his note pad and the laptop. He was in the same beautiful patch of forest where she had left him.

"What happened? What did you see this time?" Mark asked as he prepared to take notes and started the laptop recorder.

Paula recalled the group's outdoor adventure and Howard's repelling accident, and as she did, she had an *aha* moment and said to Mark, "Without *willingness* to take *action*, spiritual transformation is impossible."

"That's simple, yet poignant. What else did you learn?" Mark asked as he scribbled.

"Think of all the obstacles that you had to overcome Mark, yet you were *willing* to say *yes* to life. If you had said *no* at any point, we wouldn't be here co-creating this course."

Paula thought back to the mental state Mark was in when they first met. She remembered the day she almost died and how Mark had saved her life. She considered that if he had been *un*willing to leave his comfort zone, he very well may have taken his own life. This prompted her to stand up and give him a long, admiration-filled hug.

"Mark," she said with a tear in her eye, "you are the exemplification of willingness."

"Thanks!" Mark replied, with a big proud smile on his face.

Lesson #3 Of
Transformational Awakening Is...

<u>WILLINGNESS</u>

The will to take whatever actions are
necessary to spiritually awaken, because
90% of life is just showing up.

CHAPTER 8

Spiritual Distinction

Can You Feel the Difference?

As soon as Paula and Mark returned from their walk, they unpacked and continued deciphering their notes. Mark was honored and astounded to be part of this co-creative process. Before meeting Paula, he had always been a skeptic, but Paula's tales were far too detailed and specific to be anything but legitimate.

As the pair poured over their notes, Mark couldn't help but stare at the word "willingness". For some unknown reason, it demanded his attention. As the afternoon wore on, he kept returning to it until eventually a specific memory came to mind.

"Finally!" Mark exclaimed.

"What?" Paula asked with a bright smile. "Did you just have an *aha* moment?"

"Actually, I did! It's weird. The whole time we have been working on willingness something was bubbling up from within me, but I couldn't get a handle on what it was. Then it hit me." Mark said with a sense of confidence Paula hadn't seen before.

"Great!" Paula was practically giddy with excitement. "Tell me!" Mark was contributing more than ever before, and she could see the distinct difference in his behavior from when he had first started working with Coach Sarah.

"In high school, I played soccer with a friend of mine, Billy Moore. He was an *incredible* soccer player. He was so good that he was named to the national soccer all-star team. Billy had a likeable personality and was more mature than most of us at the time. I imagine it had something to do with his having been the first born of seven children. When we were high school seniors, his father died of a brain tumor."

"Oh my God!" Paula covered her mouth in shock. "With seven kids?"

"Billy had to give up his scholarship and attend college locally in order to help his mother support the family. I lost touch with him after I went away to school, but I heard through the soccer grapevine that he married his high school sweetheart, and they had two kids."

"Well, I'm glad to hear that something good happened to him."

"It gets better. A few years after I graduated from college, I was back in town visiting my parents, and I ran into Billy at a convenience store. Total coincidence he just happened to be there. So, we got together to catch up, and he filled me in on what happened after his father died.

Did you ever have one of those experiences with an old friend who you haven't seen in a long time and you instantly renewed your friendship as if both of you just saw each other the day before? Well, that is what it felt like talking to Billy again. He told me that he went through a period of depression and anger; but before too long, he surrendered to his fate. He felt pride, not resentment, about helping his mother raise his brothers and sisters. He shared his story with me with the emotional maturity of a soul well beyond his years.

Paula, I was beaming with admiration because even though my old friend's dream of being a professional soccer player was stolen from him, he was still willing to redirect his championship soccer willpower to support his family."

"Sounds like Billy is a great example of someone who was willing to do what was being asked of him. It reminds me of the parable that Sam taught us in the paradox Vision Quest... When life throws you lemons – you make lemonade."

Mark chuckled lightly. "Yup." He checked his phone and was shocked to see their early afternoon meeting had stretched into the early evening. "I should probably head out. There's some things I need to get done at home, and I have work in the morning."

"I didn't know you returned to work. That's great!"

"Yeah, back to the old grind again. I'll see you tomorrow, Paula." The two exchanged a hug, which had now become a ritual, and Mark made his way to the door. Before he opened the door, he turned and said, "Hey. What are you up to tonight?"

"Me? Nothing much. Probably just going to study some more, have some dinner and go to bed early. Why?"

"Well... I was going to stop and grab something to eat on the way home. There's an excellent sushi place I know. Would you like to come?" Mark asked with a slight smile.

Paula replied with surprise and couldn't help but smile brightly from how shyly he'd asked. "Sure!"

They soon arrived together, at a quaint, Japanese restaurant. Mark had learned that some of the most unassuming-looking restaurants had some of the best food. And although this restaurant appeared to be a hole in the wall eatery from the outside, the interior was immaculate. It was dimly lit with small paper lanterns. Traditional watercolor artwork, wall scrolls, Japanese maple trees, and statues of Buddha decorated the space, which created a comforting and tasteful ambiance. Before being directed to their table, they were required to remove their shoes. Paula was somewhat stunned that Mark had brought her to such a unique place, but she very much loved the surprise.

"So." Paula asked as she sipped her tea, "Do you come here often?"

"Not in a while, actually. I used to come here a lot with my father. But after everything that has happened, it's been hard to come back. He loved this place though." Mark replied as he picked up another roll of sushi with his chop sticks.

"Oh. I'm sorry." Paula felt uncomfortable about bringing up such a sensitive topic.

"It's alright. My father and I had a lot of good times here. I feel like I can now come here, and even though it does bring up some sad feelings, it also reminds me of all the good times we had here. It feels like our eating here is like celebrating his life and the good times we shared here."

"That's a great way to look at it. Was he into Japanese culture?" Paula asked as she looked down at her plate and fumbled with her chopsticks.

"Not specifically. No. He loved sushi though. For a while we tried a bunch of places, but once we came here, this became our spot." Mark noticed Paula's chopstick blunders and chuckled lightly, "Having a hard time there?"

Paula looked up at Mark and giggled, "I swear, I know how to use chopsticks. It's been a while though. I just need a minute to get back into the groove."

"Let me show you." He raised his hand with a single stick. "So, this stick must remain still. You want to hold it with just your thumb." Mark picked up the second stick and clasped it between his thumb and index finger. "And this finger goes here. Just hold it like a pencil, and you just move this one stick. That's it really." He slapped his sticks together to showcase the technique.

"Ah, that's much better. Thanks Mark! Did your father enjoy eating a variety of ethnic foods, or did he just love sushi?" She had shared many different things about her life with Mark, but this was the first time that he openly talked about himself in such a lighthearted way.

"He was definitely a man who took the road less traveled. Before he met my mother, he spent a lot of time traveling around the world visiting countries in South

America, Europe, and Asia. Actually, that's how they met."

"Really? They met outside the country? That's so serendipitous. I love it! I guess it was just meant to be." Paula smiled at Mark and sipped her tea. "Tell me more about how they met."

Mark cleared his throat and took a sip of tea. "Well. Like I said, my father was traveling a lot. And he'd always wanted to see India..."

Paula looked up from her plate, "Really? Why?"

"My grandparents raised him Catholic, but when he was about 20, he started studying philosophy and reading a lot of religious holy books. He developed a fondness for Hindu and Buddhist philosophies, so visiting India was a big deal to him. He was able to immerse himself in its ancient culture, which he admired so much."

Paula raised an eyebrow completely surprised by what she had just learned. "It sounds like he was a very special man. Tell me more about how he met your mother."

"So, he was traveling in India taking in the sites and visiting many of the various temples and that sort of thing. Eventually he made his way to Calcutta where he decided to take a yoga class, which my mom was also taking. My mother was an accomplished yogi, and she was on sabbatical in India to study and hone her yoga skills. Being two American travelers in a foreign country, they got to talking, and one thing lead to another. And I was born a few years later." Mark said with a broad smile on his face.

Paula was surprised because she never would have guessed that Mark had such holistic well-traveled parents. This confirmed that their so-called "chance" meeting was no accident. The synchronicity of Spirit was definitely at play.

"So, did they teach you some of the things they learned in India?"

"A little, but they weren't forceful about it. They would give me little nuggets here and there, but they mostly allowed me the space to just make up my own mind about things. I had some knowledge about the types of philosophies they believed in, but I never really got my hands dirty until now." Mark noticed Paula had stopped eating and was completely transfixed on what he was sharing.

When their gaze met, Paula unconsciously returned her attention to eating her meal. "It sounds like they would've really enjoyed our project."

"Oh, for sure! They would have been very much into everything we're doing." Mark sipped his drink again.

Paula looked up and smiled lightly, "What about you? We've been working together for a few months now. I know we've done a lot of work, but we've never really talked about *the work.*"

"I'm confused. What are you trying to ask me?"

Paula put her chopsticks down and placed her hands together as she formulated the question. "What do you *really* think about everything we've been doing? I want to know if you are enjoying the whole creative process."

"Yeah. I am. But I must admit I find the whole thing fascinating. I've always been the skeptical type, and there's so much about everything we've been doing that can't be quantified or explained easily. But I know it's legitimate. I find it intellectually stimulating."

"In what way?"

"Well debriefing your Vision Quest adventures and trying to figure out the meaning within them... it's like being an analyst. I find it mentally satisfying to pour through the information we've been collecting. In some strange, weird way it makes me feel like a scientist."

Paula joked, "Maybe we need to invest in some lab coats."

"Absolutely!"

Mark and Paula continued chatting. It was one of the few times that Mark was able to speak openly since the accident. Up to that moment, he didn't realize that not having someone to idly chat with was something he missed dearly. It wasn't just Paula's ability to listen that

Mark found stimulating; it was also her ability to carry on a great conversation. Even though she had a vast knowledge of metaphysics, she was still capable of chatting about everyday simple things as well.

Throughout their meal, Paula demonstrated the ability to defend her position without being rude or overbearing. As she spoke, Mark couldn't help but think to himself, *I wonder what it would be like to have a life partner as awakened as Paula?* It was only a passing thought, but he couldn't help but wonder, *What if?*

When they finished dining, Mark drove Paula back to her place. As she got out of the car she asked, "You know it's only eight, right?"

"Yeah. What are you getting at?" Mark asked surprised.

"Well, I'm still pumped. And I was thinking, if you were *willing*, we could create another Vision Quest tonight. If you have as much energy as I do?"

Mark burst with laughter. "Oh my God. You're so corny."

Paula smiled widely. She had never seen Mark laugh like that before. "Oh, you have no idea how corny I can get. Well. What do you say, Mark?"

"I don't think so Paula. Like I told you, I have to work in the morning."

"Oh, come on, Mark! I bet you had many all-nighters in college. You can miss a couple hours of sleep. And I promise you that this won't become a habit. Soooooooo. Pleeeease?"

Mark sighed in such a way that Paula knew she'd won him over.

"Alright. Fine. But only because you asked in such a corny way."

The pair entered Paula's home and set their equipment up. By this point, they had their recording and transcription system down pat. They were both consciously aware that this work inspired them because it was the dharmic work they were meant to do together.

"I believe we're ready. Are you *willing*, Paula?" Mark said light-heartedly.

"Yes. I am." Paula said chuckling and wondering where the God Source was going to take her this time.

Paula relaxed into her meditative state while focusing her attention on her mantra word Namasté. She surrendered to the Universe so she could receive the next lesson of spiritual awakening.

***

When Paula's vision appeared, she found herself floating 100 feet above a small, tropical island, which appeared lightly inhabited. It was covered with dense vegetation, akin to a Brazilian rain forest, and steep hills like that of a Caribbean island. The island was surrounded by a coral reef and powder blue, crystal clear water. In the distance, she could see several tiny islands.

Paula felt her stomach drop as she began her uncomfortable descent. When she was able to refocus, she found herself floating above a timeworn, narrow, wooden boat steered by an old, native islander with two women passengers sitting side by side at the front of the boat. The boat was bouncing profusely up and down as it passed through each wave, spraying water over the three of them. The boat was leaving a larger island and heading toward one of the smaller, outer islands.

Paula was mesmerized by the natural beauty of this tropical paradise with its white sandy beaches, clear water, and lush green tropical foliage. She thought, *It's so easy to stay spiritually conscious when my eyes are bathed in such natural beauty.*

Paula watched as the old man beached the boat, so the two women could unload their snorkeling gear, sand chairs and provisions. As soon as the women finished unloading, the old man put the motor in reverse and left them alone on a deserted stretch of beach.

***

With a relaxed tone of excitement, the older woman shared, "Wow, can you believe we are finally here, Donna?! Boy, did I need a vacation. My patients' problems were burning me out. I was beginning to lose my professional distance. How about you?"

In her 30s, Donna was the younger of the two. She had brown eyes and hair and a medium build. She was average in height and in good physical shape. She responded, "Tell me about it. I've had patient burnout for the last six months. I really needed this vacation. All I want to do is set up my beach chair, get a tan, and do some snorkeling. Have you ever been snorkeling, Deb?"

"Not extensively. I've only snorkeled for a few hours when I was in Hawaii. But I loved it!"

Deb was in her late 50s. She had a round, attractive face. Her eyes were bright blue, and she had long, dark brown straight hair, which contrasted well with her blue eyes. Deb was wearing a black one-piece bathing suit, while Donna had on a tiny string bikini. They quickly stretched out on their beach chairs, applied some sun screen and continued talking shop.

After several minutes of relaxing and chatting, Donna suggested, "Why don't we cool off and do a little snorkeling?"

"Sounds great to me."

Off they went with their fins, masks and snorkels.

Although the water was clear, it was devoid of any underwater life. It looked like an underwater desert.

Donna could tell Deb's snorkeling technique wasn't exactly refined, but she still suggested, "Let's snorkel out to the coral reef. There will be plenty of fish to see there!"

"No, I wouldn't feel comfortable swimming that far out."

"OK." Donna replied. "Then let's go back and tan some more, and I'll snorkel out by myself later."

Deb nodded in agreement.

Cooled and refreshed, they reclined in their beach chairs and immediately started talking shop again.

The friends had met several years earlier at a symposium on highly functional depressives.

"Deb, why did you decide to major in psychology?"

"I was adopted when I was seven. My birth parents were emotionally immature, so I developed some neurotic personality traits. Thank God that my adopted parents were highly functional souls, so after I lived with them for a few years, I slowly began to shed some of my neurotic behavior.

By the time I was in high school, I could feel the distinction between my normal and neurotic behavior patterns. I became a psych major in college to learn why I felt the way I felt and did the things I did. As I learned more and more about my psyche, I began thinking that it would be wonderful to make a career of helping people heal their emotional pain.

How about you? Why did you decide to go into psychiatric counseling?"

"I come from a dysfunctional family too. My mother was emotionally abusive, and my father was a rage-aholic, alcoholic. My mother spent most of her time enabling my father's rage to keep his anger in check, so she had little patience to nurture me and my three siblings. I was so enmeshed with her that I found it difficult to make a distinction between what was normal and what was neurotic behavior. And like you, I went into counseling initially to heal myself."

"Are you familiar with eastern philosophy?" Donna asked.

"Not really. But what little I do know, I find interesting."

"Last year a friend of mine brought me to see a Ram Dass lecture. Are you familiar with any of his work?" Donna asked.

"No, I'm not."

"Ram Dass, *aka* Doctor Richard Alpert, is a respected PhD graduate professor from Harvard University. During his lecture, he told us a story. Apparently around the height of his college teaching career, he intuitively knew that he needed to understand more than he was learning within the standard western education system. Eventually, his thirst for esoteric knowledge led him to India, where he studied with his guru.

He became enamored with eastern philosophy because it dated back thousands of years, whereas western psychology basically started with Sigmund Freud, a mere hundred or so years ago."

Deb commented, "Eastern Philosophy is very different from what we were taught in college!"

"In the East," Donna continued, "they believe that a dynamic tension is created between the ego and the intuitive heart, and the physical plane of reality is created from that tension."

"It reminds me of something my mom would say, 'When you can *distinguish* the *difference* between who you really are from the roles you play, then you'll be happy.' You know Donna, the older I get, the smarter my mom becomes!"

Donna looked at Deb with admiration, "You were lucky to be adopted by such a wise soul."

Deb smiled back, "Yeah. She was one of a kind. I miss her very much. I'm sure she would have loved to hear all about what you learned from Ram Dass. What else did he teach you?"

Donna spoke with a glimmer in her eye. It was apparent that she held her old teacher in high regard.

"Let me think. Right! He taught us that in the East they believe that the key to spiritual transformation is to learn to be the witness observer of your life. It's like being in a Broadway play called, *The Deb Story*, and you are the actor, director and producer of the 'play' of your life.

In the East, they believe that we are born with a destiny to fulfill, but paradoxically we also have a free will, which allows us to react to life's challenges constructively or destructively. They believe that if you stay intentionally conscious and observe your life from a witness perspective, you will be better able to sense the distinction between your ego's neurotic needs from your spiritual aspirations."

Donna shook her head when she realized she was lost in shop talk again. "Well. Enough talking shop, I'm going snorkeling. Are you sure you won't join me?"

"No, you go on ahead. But please be careful."

***

While observing her Vision Quest of the two counselors, Paula realized that the God Source was showing her that her ability to distinguish the difference between feelings originating from her Spirit versus those originating from her ego mind was the next lesson that she needed to learn -*Spiritual Distinction.*

While earning her spiritual life coaching certification, Paula learned that there are three primary spiritual distinctions: the distinction between how her Spirit *feels,* as opposed to how her ego mind *feels,* the distinction between *thinking* thoughts about her feelings versus feeling and *releasing* her feelings, and the distinction between her *BEing* and her *BEing's behavior.*

***

Donna put on her snorkel gear and swam off to explore. She enjoyed the distinction between feeling calm and excited. Floating weightlessly on the water made her feel serene, while the excitement of exploring shark and barracuda inhabited territory made her feel the effects of her adrenalin rush.

Seventy percent of the island was surrounded by calm bay waters, while the remainder of island faced the ocean with its strong undercurrents, shifting tides, as well as its sharks and barracudas. Donna was having so much fun snorkeling that she decided to swim around the entire island, which she estimated would take less than two hours.

While Donna snorkeled, she concentrated on staying in the moment and not letting her thoughts drift back to work. She held out pieces of crusty bread and chunks of banana, which she had carefully packed for her voyage to attract fish. As she offered these foreign delicacies, she became engulfed in large schools of beautiful, colorful fish, ranging in size from one inch to over three feet. She became awestruck by observing the tropical fish in their natural habitat. They seemed to almost glow with bright yellow, vibrant blue and stunning red. The surrounding pastel coral formations were extremely varied in shape; some resembled miniature underwater trees, while others were round and mushroom-shaped.

Donna was amazed by the rate at which the water depth changed. In one moment, she was snorkeling in six feet of water, and in the next moment a hole would appear out of nowhere, and the sea floor would abruptly drop thirty or more feet.

Completely mesmerized by her underwater environment, Donna didn't notice that the water was becoming extremely shallow. She was unaware that she was near the border that separated the bay inlet from the ocean breakers. She could hear the low roaring of the waves as they smashed against the coral reef, but because it was such a serene, natural sound, she was oblivious to its warning.

She reached down to grab a shell, and when she did she cut her finger on a piece of coral. She stuck her head out of the water to examine it. She then realized that she had trapped herself in shallow water surrounded by sharp coral. As each ocean wave rumbled past her, it became more and more difficult to stay off the piercing corral. She began to worry that the blood from her finger would attract sharks, and she mentally began reviewing her options. *Stay calm and think. I could circle back the way I came, slowly retracing my trail or I could maneuver my way to shore and climb over the rocks. This would give my finger time to stop bleeding. Then I could continue snorkeling on the ocean side of the island.*

Her adventurous nature won the decision. She decided to work her way to the shoreline and climb the cliffs. She meandered to the beach, but when she took off her fins she realized the stones were excruciatingly hot. And what made matters worse, she didn't realize how steep the cliffs were until she was standing directly beneath them. They shot up 50 feet, but she was glad to see that the rock formations were like large building blocks which would make her climb easier to manage.

As she climbed, her feet quickly began burning from the hot rocks. She managed to climb recklessly fast to the top without slipping before her feet blistered. She caught her breath and peered over the edge. Dismayed, she saw that the cliffs were too steep to climb directly down into the ocean. She needed to find a place where she could reenter the water without killing herself.

She didn't walk very far before she felt small prickle weed balls pinching her feet. And to make matters worse, her feet were now beginning to blister. At that point, the pain in her feet superseded her fear of the steep, rocky cliffs, so she headed back down the hill searching for the safest spot where she could reenter the water on the ocean side of the island.

It was challenging trying to keep her balance as she climbed down the steep rocks on her blistered feet with her mask and snorkel in one hand and her fins in the other. She noticed a small ridge of rocks that extended 25 feet into the surf, and she immediately decided to attempt to reenter the water from there.

Slowly, she worked her way down to the natural rock jetty where she found a rug of wet sea moss on which she could rest. She sat cooling her feet and planning how to best navigate this dangerous section of rocks that protruded into the rough ocean. Between each rock formation, she noticed black sea urchins, the kind with 10-inch long, poisonous spine needles. She watched as the waves rolled over the rocks with tremendous force and the water's depth rapidly increased and then decreased by almost three feet in a matter of seconds.

How did I get myself into this mess? I wanted to create a fun-filled adventure, not a life or death situation.

She sat for 20 minutes trying to figure out how to swim to safety without killing herself. She was trying to stay calm and not panic, so she kept sub-vocalizing, *I can do this. I can do this. I can do this.*

She closed her eyes and said a short prayer, "Lord, please guide me to safety."

Then, out of nowhere, she miraculously recalled the last scene in the movie, *Papillion*, where Steve McQueen and Dustin Hoffman timed the sets of waves to jump into the ocean when they escaped the island where they were held as prisoners.

"Thank you, God! All I must do is count the seconds between each wave set. Then I'll know when the water is at its highest level and safest for me to jump in."

Her jump needed to be timed perfectly. The water had to be deep enough to avoid touching the poisonous sea urchins, but she needed enough time to swim out before the level dropped and the next powerful set of waves rolled back in.

Donna's mind was neurotically thinking about every possible alternative, but her heart knew that this was the only realistic option. She wondered to herself, *Why did I create this life-threatening situation? What was I trying to prove?*

Slowly, she inched her way onto the jetty with her fins in one hand and snorkel and mask in the other. She maneuvered herself to a spot where the water reached the highest point. She closed her eyes and took a few deep breaths to ground herself and to build her confidence.

She knew that she had less than a minute to put on her fins and mask, jump in, and swim about 30 feet beyond the rocks to safety. The longer she waited, the more her fear grew. She yelled, "IT's NOW OR NEVER!" and jumped in.

***

Paula felt herself drifting out of her formless state of consciousness, and as soon as she did she exclaimed, "No, no... not again! I want to know what happens to Donna!"

The familiar kaleidoscope of colors overwhelmed her senses until everything went black. Gradually, she felt the weight of her body return. She opened her eyes to find herself back in her living room with Mark who was eagerly waiting for her with a big smile on his face.

Mark had no idea what Paula had seen, but he gathered it must have been an intense vision based on her outburst. "So. Who's Donna? And why did you yell, 'No, no, not again'?"

Lesson #4 Of
Transformational Awakening Is...
<u>Spiritual Distinction</u>

The ability to consciously feel the difference between your <u>Spirit</u> and the core components of <u>physical life</u> -- body, mind and vision -- is a vital skill of inner Self-Mastery.

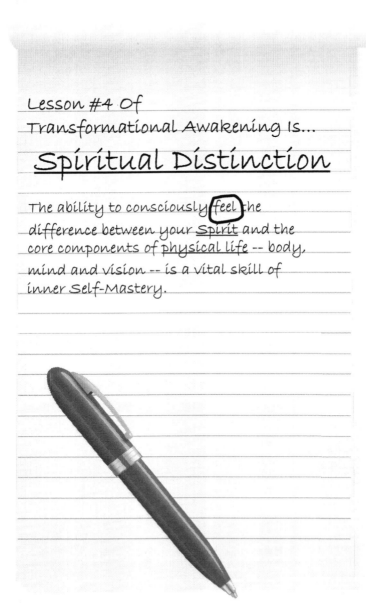

CHAPTER 9

The Five Disciplines of the Initiate

The Empowerment Energy that Fuels Your Life

Paula couldn't help but smile in amazement as she recounted Donna's harrowing tale. Mark noticed she was literally beaming as she described each phase in vivid detail, and he understood why; this was now the third vision that Paula was able to clearly recall and summarize and they were proving to be tremendously valuable in building their Spiritual Awakening course.

"So Paula, the first thing you did when you opened your eyes was shout, 'I want to know what happened to Donna!' What was that all about?'"

Paula's face reddened when she realized that she overreacted. "Seriously, any normal person would have yelled that because my vision was interrupted right when Donna jumped into the ocean. How would you feel if you were watching a movie and someone shut off the TV at the most exciting moment?"

Mark was a little surprised. This was the first time he had seen Paula snap back with an air of defensiveness.

Paula continued. "But now that I've had time to process things, I see that I was anxious to find out what happened to Donna. That feels perfectly normal to me. And yes, I know some of this is just my ego grumbling. I've been practicing how to feel the subtle distinctions between my ego and intuitive heart for a while now, which is why I'm a little perplexed at how triggered I was."

Mark took notes while Paula tapped her finger against her knee while pondering the situation.

Mark looked up from his notebook, "You do seem a bit triggered. What's bothering you?"

Paula continued tapping her knee and fidgeting slightly in her seat. She felt strangely uneasy, and the more she thought about it, the more her nervous feelings intensified. "I don't know Mark. I just feel... weird. Like I'm overflowing with nervous energy, and I have no idea why. I need to discover the thing behind why not knowing what happened to Donna is making me feel so uncomfortable! Why am I not just joyfully surrendering to God's will?"

Mark looked down and continued taking notes. "Yup. There must be a reason. So, what do you think we should do now?"

Paula was silent for a few moments as she contemplated. She continued to tap her knee impatiently until she came up with a solution. "Let's meditate together; that will help me surrender to why 'not knowing' is triggering my ego. Our creative synergy will help me do that from a higher level of consciousness. Agreed?"

Mark checked the time on his phone and looked at Paula with a sly smirk. "Well. I guess it's going to be a late night. Why stop now? Sure! Let's do it!"

Paula led Mark to her office where they assumed their meditative positions. They began breathing together to reach a place *where two or more are gathered in God's name.*

After 30 minutes had passed, they finished their meditation and remained silent for several more minutes. Paula finally shared, "I saw a memory of my spiritual teacher Deepak, educating me about the Law of

Detachment. He taught me that life isn't about waiting for the storm to pass; it's about dancing in the rain mastery. He told me time and again that I can't steer the river, but I can detach and paddle my boat in the same direction the river is already flowing."

Mark added, "My parents taught me that detachment will help me to enjoy life more, because I'm letting God handle all the details. My mom would say, 'Be passionate about your work Son and be dispassionate about its 'so-called' rewards.'"

"The Law of Detachment is another paradox because I can't steer the river, but I can steer my incarnational boat that is in God's river." Paula added. "That's the answer! The God Source is teaching me to detach from my ego's need to *control* what the result must be; and, instead, *surrender to what is,* knowing that man plans, and God laughs."

"Do you think we were taught the importance of detachment by having the outcome of what happened to Donna and Howard withheld from us?" Mark asked with both eyebrows raised.

"Pretty much! It's what I like to call 'a real-world lesson,' Partner."

Mark noticed a slight twinkle in Paula's eyes. She was clearly proud that they had figured out the solution so quickly. But it was more than that. She had never called him *partner* before. He felt proud to be considered so highly by Paula.

"I feel like our Spiritual Awakening course is really starting to take shape. Let's summarize the lessons the God Source has taught us so far," Paula suggested, as she turned to face the large white board, which she had recently hung on the wall. She popped off the cap from a marker and began writing:

- *Spiritual Partnerships* are a miraculous support system to help humankind evolve from a five-sensory species to a multisensory species.
- Spiritual initiates must embrace the dualisms of the earth plane called *paradox*, especially the *Healing Paradox*.
- *Willingness* doing whatever it takes to spiritually awaken, because 90% of life is just showing up.
- The ability to consciously *feel the difference* between your Spirit from the core components of physical life -- body, mind and vision.

Paula's hand lingered at the board for a moment. When she was sure she had captured the primary lessons, they had learned so far, she put the cap back on the marker. She turned to Mark to ensure that she didn't leave anything out, but as she did, her eyes teared up.

"Everything alright?" Mark asked.

"Yes, I'm fine. I just feel so blessed by the way the God Source is allowing me to supernaturally learn these empowering life lessons. The fact that I'm being permitted to feel what these souls are feeling, hearing and thinking... it's truly remarkable."

"I feel honored to be a part of this process too. You and Coach Sarah are teaching me the spiritual lessons I really need to learn."

Paula raised an eyebrow, "Not *me* Mark. Well, not *just* me anyway. Remember, I'm just a conduit that the God Source is using to convey a message. Remember what President Theodore Roosevelt once said, 'The honor belongs to the man in the arena.'"

Mark's eyes widened. He realized he still had difficulty resisting his own skepticism, but he knew what Paula was saying was true. "You're right. The God Source is helping me surrender to what happened to my family, so I can flow... merrily, merrily down God's stream again."

Paula flipped through the pages of her spiritual life coaching textbook. When she stopped, she read, "Surrender is derived from two French words: *sur* which means over, above, higher and *render* which means to melt down. *Melt* means to be altered or transformed from a solid to a liquid. Therefore, when we intentionally *surrender*, we melt down and transform our earth plane roles and consciously identify who we are: One with the God Source."

"Excellent, appropriate quote," Mark replied. He reached into his pocket to check his phone for the time once more. His eyes grew wide with shock. "Oh my God. I'm sorry. I really do need to get going, or I'm going to fall asleep at my desk tomorrow."

Paula laughed lightly. "I'm sorry for keeping you so late. Thank you though. I really appreciate everything we got accomplished tonight."

She walked Mark to the door. As he was leaving, the two exchanged an admiration-filled hug.

"Goodnight Mark. See you tomorrow?"

"Yeah. See you tomorrow. Goodnight Paula."

Paula waved and gently closed the door behind Mark. She briefly organized their night's work before climbing into bed where her mind replayed the events from the evening. It dawned on her that Mark had undergone a dramatic shift in his general mood. When she had first met him, he was completely overwhelmed with sadness from losing his family. But through months of sessions with Coach Sarah, as well as the Spiritual Awakening course development work they were doing together, she could clearly see a positive shift in his attitude; he smiled more, seemed less stern and skeptical, and he was more open to suggestion than ever before. With thoughts of admiration for Marks's courage and commitment to his personal growth, Paula drifted off to sleep.

***

It was a sunny warm Friday afternoon when Paula asked Mark to meet her at the beach where they had first met. They pulled into the beach parking lot at the same time. They got out of their vehicles and immediately took off their shoes to feel the cold coarse sand pressing against their feet. The pair casually strolled down the beach as the waves rolled in stopping inches from their sandy feet.

Paula felt an emotional intensity resonating from Mark. She used small talk to help him feel more at ease; but when that didn't work, she felt compelled to address it. "Does being here make you feel uncomfortable?"

Mark turned to look at Paula, but then allowed his gaze to fall forward again. "Yeah. It does a bit. It takes me back to the mood I was in the last time I was here. Honestly, if I didn't do my sessions with Coach Sarah, I probably would have refused to meet you here."

Paula looked at Mark with admiration. "But you *did* come. And now you can see that despite the emotional baggage you may have attached to this place, the fact is that you have a very different state of mind now than you did the last time we were here."

"What do you mean exactly?"

"Well, you aren't totally consumed by your grief anymore. And you have found a new lust for life."

Mark looked to Paula again, this time with a slight smile.

"But do you know what's the most important thing about us being here this time, Mark?"

Mark stopped and stared at Paula. "What's that?"

Paula returned Mark's stare, smiling the same bright enchanting smile that he had come to recognize as her most distinctive trait. "You know that you aren't alone."

Mark's eyes became slightly watery.

"When you were consumed by your grief, you weren't able to see all the people who still cared about you. But now that you've opened your heart again, you can see all the people you have in your life who love you. And that's not all Mark."

Mark stepped closer to Paula, his eyes transfixed on hers. "Go on."

"You have Coach Sarah and all the knowledge she's imparted to you. And you have me. I'm so happy we met. Not just because you saved me, but because..." Paula felt her eyes start to water. "Because before we met... before we started working together... I didn't know what my dharmic calling really was."

A tear rolled down Paula's left cheek, which she promptly wiped away. "I felt like my life was directionless. As much as I had a passion for the work I was doing, and as grateful as I was to have learned how to facilitate several different kinds of healing modalities, I still lacked a firm sense of meaning in my life."

Another tear rolled down Paula's cheek. This time, she ignored the impulse to wipe it away. "But you, you helped me find what I was missing. That's part of the reason why I wanted us to meet here today. It wasn't just because I wanted to help you overcome your negative anchor to this beautiful place. I also had to come here to face my own emotional baggage. And..."

Paula couldn't stop her voice from cracking and her watery eyes from giving way to a steady stream of tears. "And to say, 'thank you'. You saved me twice. I'm so grateful that you met me at the diner that day. And I'm so grateful to be your soul friend."

Mark narrowed the gap between them. He took her in his arms and gave her a long, warm hug. During the time he'd known Paula, she had never opened up as much as she had just done. Paula had always demonstrated that she was perfectly capable of handling any challenge that came up. But he now saw a side of her that he had never noticed before, a side where she was willing to be courageously vulnerable and totally exposed.

Mark gently stroked Paula's back until he felt her breathing return to normal and her tears subsided.

When they broke their embrace, Paula smiled again as she wheezed a final time, wiped the tears from her eyes, and grabbed a tissue from her pocket to blow her nose.

"Thank you. I needed to release that." She said looking deeply into his eyes.

"Hey. We're friends. You can tell me anything. I'm a safe space for you too when you need to get something off your chest. Hey, I remember when we first met, and I was the one who always got teary eyed."

Paula couldn't help but laugh at Mark's comment. And she thought how incredible it was to see how far Mark had come in such a short period of time.

As they stood in silent admiration, they noticed a loud commotion from down the beach. In the near distance, two children were hunched over something just beyond where the waves reached the beach.

"Let's go see what all the fuss is about."

"Definitely!" Paula replied with a grin.

Paula and Mark approached the children. The older was a girl with blonde hair, about nine years old. The other was a brown-haired boy who looked a few years younger. At their feet was a pair of fishing rods, both of which were being continuously shifted by the incoming waves. One rod was without a catch, while the other had hooked a three-foot sand shark. The children continued to yell excitedly as the small shark flip flopped in the shallow surf, trying desperately to free itself.

Paula and Mark stood about six feet from the children. The children, oblivious to their new onlookers, yelled and screamed as they timidly examined the shark from a safe distance. Mark stepped closer to get a better look.

"Hey kids. What's going on?" Mark asked in a friendly tone.

The children turned to face Mark and continued to yell with excitement. As they spoke, Mark squatted so that they wouldn't have to look up to him. "Oh my gosh. Mister, my little brother and I were fishing, and we caught a shark! But now, we can't get him off the hook and he just keeps flopping around like crazy!"

Mark smiled kindly and stood up slowly.

"That's quite a situation you've gotten yourselves into. I think my friend and I can help." Mark turned his head to Paula and motioned for her to join him.

As Paula approached she smiled warmly and waved, "Hi kids. My name is Paula, and this is my friend Mark. What're your names?"

The young boy looked down at his feet shyly, but his sister wasn't bashful at all. She proudly placed a hand on her chest as she introduced herself, "My name is Angela, and this is my little brother Tommy!" Angela placed a hand on Tommy's shoulder, "C'mon Tommy, say hello."

Tommy looked up slowly. He made eye contact with Mark and Paula and meekly squeaked out, "Hello."

Mark took another step toward the shark. He faced Angela and Tommy and asked, "Do you want our help getting the shark off your line?"

Angela furrowed her eyebrows and frowned. "No!" and yelled, "Sharks are bad!"

Paula approached Angela and knelt in front of her. "Oh, I wouldn't say that Angela. Sharks are cool. They help the ocean a lot." As Paula spoke she made eye contact with Angela and could see in her eyes that she was reaching her. "And by the looks of it, Angela... you've hooked a sand shark. He's not dangerous. Why not help him get back to the ocean?"

Angela squinted her eyes as she considered Paula's proposal, "Well... fine. Alright."

Mark examined the shark for a moment. It was hooked in the corner of its mouth. Getting the hook out was a conundrum unto itself. Paula turned to face Mark, "Well. What do you think?"

"Lucky for us, I always carry one of these for such an occasion." Mark smiled, reached into his pocket and produced a large Swiss Army knife.

Paula's eyes widened slightly, "That's convenient. Well then, what's the plan Scout Leader?"

Mark cautiously approached the shark, which continued to flip-flop recklessly. He cut the fishing line and immediately wrapped it around his hand several times to ensure that the shark couldn't swim away. He motioned Paula to assist him.

As Paula knelt beside Mark, he retracted the knife's blade and opened it to reveal a needle-nose plier. "This is the tricky part. We need to pull the hook out from inside its mouth. I'll hold the shark steady and force its mouth open as long as you are willing to pry the hook out?"

Without hesitation, Paula responded, "I can do that."

"You sure? This shark may be small, but he has a lot of sharp teeth!"

"It's fine. I trust you."

"Alright then, let's do this!"

Angela and Tommy watched in amazement as Mark gently knelt on the shark and used his body weight to keep it still. He carefully placed one hand over its nose and the other below its jaw and he pried its mouth open. "Alright. I've got it. Go for it!"

Paula took her time finding the hook and easing it through the wound in the shark's mouth. Though she was a little anxious, she didn't want to rush and make the situation even more dangerous. After a moment, she was able to free the hook. "Got it!"

"Great! Now let's set him free." Mark slowly let the shark's mouth close. He reached beneath its pectoral fins and lifted the squirming fish into the air. The shark writhed and fought furiously as Mark waded into the shallow surf to release it. As he did, the shark quickly swam off into the waves and out of sight.

Angela and Tommy cheered and clapped. "Wow, that was so cool!" Angela screamed.

"Yeah, that was cool!" Tommy mimicked.

Mark turned to face Paula and he chuckled as he asked, "Well, that was an adventure! You ready to head back to the office?"

"Yeah! That's enough excitement for me. Besides we still have a lot of work to do."

As Paula and Mark made their way back to their vehicles, they recounted exciting tales from their own childhoods.

Paula was impressed by the way Mark had handled the children. *He'll make a great father someday,* she thought to herself.

When they returned home, Paula and Mark went back to their Vision Quest administrative duties to finish organizing their last lesson on spiritual distinction. When they finished, Paula enthusiastically announced, "Okay Mark! I do believe it's alpha time!"

Mark prepared the recording equipment while Paula prepped for meditation. As she became more and more relaxed her mind began to form the kaleidoscope of colors, which she knew was the precursor for her next metaphysical adventure.

Paula was suddenly swept up into a mystical, snow-filled vortex. The vortex traveled up a mountain until all she could see was a medley of colors. When she could focus again, she found herself in a deep mountain valley with lush green grass and tall trees surrounded by three steep snow-covered mountains. In the center of the valley stood a large building that reminded her of a Tibetan monastery in the Himalayan mountains. As she got closer to the building she felt herself get drawn into a time warp that was pulling her back in time hundreds of years. Then in an instant, everything faded to black as she passed out.

***

When Paula regained consciousness, she found herself in a large hall dimly lit with the glow of small candles. Beyond burning incense, Paula smelled an overwhelming damp odor emanating from the old building's wooden frame. She could see several dozen monks in orange robes. Their heads were shaved, and they were chanting the Sanskrit "OM" sound in deep, masculine tones. Paula didn't know why but the OM sound was having a mesmerizing effect on her, as if the sound was massaging her very soul. The chanting continued for a long time before the monks fell silent. The silence was broken by three loud bongs. An elderly monk then stood and took center stage. He bowed and said *"Namasté."*

In return, the other monks answered, *"Namasté."*

The monks sat on the floor with their legs folded in a three-person-deep semicircle around the old teacher. At first Paula didn't understand their spoken language; but miraculously after a few minutes, she could understand them as if they were speaking English.

The senior monk was lecturing on ways to increase one's personal power. A short, portly monk asked him, "What do you mean by *power?*"

"Power is your ability to project your life force energy at will." the old teacher answered.

"Why is one person more powerful than another?" another monk asked.

"Ah, your question is one that has been asked and answered in this monastery for thousands of years. Sooner or later, every initiate must learn how to control their inner power."

The old monk continued, "There are *Five Disciplines of the Initiate* which when mastered will allow you to project your power at will. As you master each discipline, your vibrational oscillations will become faster and faster; and the faster you vibrate, the more powerful your willpower will become."

"Holy One, what are the Five Disciplines of the Initiate?" A tall, thin monk asked.

"The *Five Disciplines of the Initiate* are: *Prayer, Feeling and Releasing Your Healing Feelings, Visualizations, Spiritual Distinction Meditation* and *Dis-Creation*.

Surrendering to your higher powers with *Prayer* is a lifelong process of making peace with *what is*, knowing that everything happens for the evolution of your immortal soul, even if it doesn't feel good. It could not be any other way in a perfectly evolving Universe. By *consciously surrendering* to your higher powers, your Spirit can orchestrate the infinite correlation of details necessary for you to manifest your dharmic reason for incarnating.

Feeling and releasing your healing feelings is one of the most important spiritual lessons because feelings are the language of your intuitive heart, which is your primary healing tool. It is your language of love, the language of your Spirit. When you can consciously *feel* your inner Self, you will know that you are One with all of life everywhere.

If you master how to visualize your goals..."

***

Paula's mind drifted back to what her soul friend Wayne Dyer had taught her about the importance of doing visualizations. She had a vivid memory of him saying, "You can prove to yourself why visualizations work. Close your eyes and imagine that you are sucking on a lemon. What you'll notice is that you'll start to salivate, because your mind can't tell the difference between a real and an imagined lemon. In the same way, your mind won't be able to tell the difference between your real childhood experiences and your Self-parented visualizations."

***

Paula brought her focus back to her vision as the old monk continued to explain.

"Every great spiritual master has preached about the importance of meditation, but the *Spiritual Distinction Meditation* is unique because it will teach you how to develop the ability to consciously *feel the difference* between your Spirit and your three incarnational components... body, mind and vision. The Spiritual Distinction Meditation is different but not better, than other meditations because it will train you to feel the difference in communication from your very clever ego-intellect and your infinitely wise and all-knowing Spirit.

Lastly, *Dis-Creation* is the missing step of the conscious creation process. *Dis* means stop, and *creation* means to bring into existence. *Dis-Creation* is a two-step process where you have to first master how to delete your negative beliefs and then install new positive beliefs to fill the void."

***

Paula's vision of the Tibetan monastery began to fade. She could feel herself drifting out of her formless state of Consciousness into the kaleidoscope of colors.

When she opened her eyes, she immediately said to Mark, "We now know exactly what we need to do to *BE* the message of these ancient spiritual disciplines." Paula recounted the old Monk's teachings to Mark in vivid detail.

Mark took notes and couldn't help but comment, "I never realized that *feeling and releasing my healing feelings* is a spiritual discipline. I definitely have a lot more work to do with Coach Sarah before I can speak the language of my intuitive heart."

Paula smiled at Mark, "Well, that's completely normal for where you are on your journey. One of my favorite spiritual teachers, Ms. Rolle, taught me a spiritual training mantra: Commit, Study, Practice and Emotionalize. I swear I can still hear her voice sometimes. She'd always say, 'You need to wholeheartedly commit to undertaking your Self-mastery studies as the most important course of your life. And if you do, Paula, you will learn how to manifest a life that the gods themselves would envy.'

She would say repeatedly, 'Faith without action usually manifests as self-delusion, and there is little worse than self-delusion for any soul on their journey home to their inner Self.' She taught me that the easiest way to internalize ancient wisdom is to speak, write, feel and think in first-person because it will help me to internalize the meta-knowledge I am learning. She would reinforce repeatedly that conceptual thought does not require me to change my behavior, but when I emotionalize the knowledge that I am learning, my behavior will change, and the imprint will be permanent."

Paula knew that meditation is the discipline of the initiates that she needed to practice most to train her ego mind to be her servant. She shared with Mark, "Well, Partner, I have a lot of inner work to do before I can 'walk' my spiritual initiate's 'talk'."

"Yeah me too."

Lesson #5 Of
~~Transformational Awakening Is...~~

The Five Disciplines
of the Initiate

Prayer, Feeling Your Healing
Feelings, Visualizations, Spiritual
Distinction Meditation and
Dis-Creation will produce the Divine
fuel that will empower your life.

CHAPTER 10

You Are a Vibrational BEing

The Secrets of Vibrational Transformation

It was early in the evening on a Tuesday night, and Paula sat at her kitchen table waiting for her kettle to whistle. Mark was finishing work soon, but she didn't expect him for another hour or so. As she waited, she casually browsed through her notes from their last debriefing session. She had just begun to look over her notes when she heard a knock at her front door. To her surprise it was Mark with his notebook in hand looking ready to work.

"Hey Paula. I know I'm a little early. I hope you don't mind."

"Of course I don't mind! Come on in. I just put some water on for tea. Want some?"

"Don't mind if I do! Thanks." Mark said with as much pep as he could muster. He followed Paula to the kitchen. After getting comfortable, he laid his notebook on the table and raised an eyebrow as he looked at Paula, "So, what do you have planned for tonight? The usual I presume."

"Pretty much. But before we get started, I think we should go over our notes from the last session. I was looking them over, and..." Paula paused in thought.

"And?" Mark asked with a slight grin.

Paula knew Mark was proud of his ability to take detailed notes. "And they're excellent. Really excellent! There just seems to be a lot of advanced psycho-spiritual material. I think we need to streamline things a little and make it more digestible for our students."

"That sounds about right. It definitely was a heavy lesson."

There was a moment of silence as they waited for the water to boil. In the past when there was a moment of silence, it was awkward, and Paula could sense uncomfortable energy emanating from Mark. But this had noticeably faded over the past few months; and now, rather than straining to make small talk to fill the empty space and ease the tension, Mark seemed comfortable and content simply sitting in silence as two soul friends patiently waiting for water to boil.

"How is everything going with Coach Sarah?" Paula asked. She was somewhat hesitant to bring up the subject because she wanted to respect his privacy boundaries. But at the same time, she felt compelled to ask.

"It's going well." Mark looked directly at Paula as he spoke. He didn't show any of the signs of being emotionally triggered. "I'd be lying if I said it's been easy. But I do feel like I've come a long way. Coach Sarah has helped me own many of my karmic 'learns and burns'". Mark was silent for a moment as he pondered his progress further. "I still have some bad days. But I've arrived at a place where I can accept that those are the days when I need to mourn the loss of my loved ones."

Paula gave Mark an inquisitive gaze, "And what happens when you have bad days? How do you cope?" Paula knew she might be pressing a bit too much, but Mark's newfound security gave her the confidence to dig deeper.

"I practice the exercises she taught me, and that helps a lot. But most importantly, I acknowledge to myself that I'm just having a bad day. Coach Sarah calls it a 'mind ache' instead of a headache or a backache. She taught me to observe what I'm experiencing from a witness perspective and to just unconditionally accept it the way I would accept a rainy day. She also taught me to allow myself to feel and release my sad feelings. I've learned that it's important to feel my feelings, but I can't dwell on them, or else they'll rule my life."

Paula nodded in agreement. "I know exactly what you mean. Believe me. I've had bad days too. And sometimes it's difficult to unconditionally accept my sad, angry or scared feelings. But once you master how to feel and release your feelings, you'll gain a tremendous amount of freedom because you'll rule your emotions as opposed to being ruled by them."

The kettle whistled. "Oh, sorry. I'll get that." Paula poured the water over chamomile tea leaves in a handmade tea pot. Together with ornate mugs, she placed the tea on the table. She handed Mark a mug and poured in the steaming aromatic tea.

They sat for a moment in silence enjoying the soothing tea.

"How is it?" Paula asked.

"Relaxing" Mark said. He noticed the photo printed on the mug as he placed it on the table. It was a picture of a beautiful snowcapped mountain. Two things about the photo grabbed Mark's attention; the mountain was not part of a range, but instead stood seemingly in solitude, and a tree covered in cherry blossoms stood in the foreground. Mark studied the photo for a moment before asking, "Is this Mount Fuji by any chance?"

With a surprised look, Paula said, "It is, actually. I'm impressed that you caught that!"

"Yeah. Thanks."

Mark continued studying the mug. As he did, Paula noticed his eyes tearing up slightly.

"Are you alright?" Paula was concerned that she may have gone too far inquiring about his sessions with Coach Sarah.

"Sorry," Mark said, as he quickly wiped the tears from his eyes, "I'm fine. It's just..."

"It's okay. Tell me... what's bothering you, Mark."

Mark sniffled, as he switched his attention from the photo on the mug to Paula. "Really. It's nothing. It's just... Ann and me. We always wanted to visit Japan, or she did really. I was just willing to go because she wanted to. Not that it would have been bad or anything. It was just always her thing."

There was another moment of silence as Mark stared back at his mug.

Paula felt compelled to ask, "What was Ann like?"

Mark diverted his attention from the mug and looked directly into Paula's eyes. "Ann? She was... she was my other half." He looked back at the mug and swirled his tea as he continued. "When we first met, I was just a dumb kid. I was unsure of myself and shy. She really helped me come out of my shell. We were similar in a lot of ways. We were both busy bodies and highly organized; but at the same time, she was very much her own person with her own wants and interests. She definitely marched to the beat of her own drum."

He made eye contact with Paula again. "A lot like you, actually." Mark smiled slightly before returning his attention to his mug.

Paula felt her cheeks flush.

Mark continued, "She loved to travel, and she wanted to see Japan. She was fascinated with eastern culture. It was a dream of ours to travel to far off places after we married..." Mark trailed off and stared at his mug again.

Paula could see his eyes start to well up, and she slowly reached across the table and placed her hand over his. The unexpected touch broke Mark's trance.

Paula smiled warmly at Mark, "She was lucky to have you. I'm sure the time you had together was wonderful."

Mark wiped the tears from his eyes with his free hand and sniffled again. He looked back at Paula and noticed that she also had tears in her eyes.

To Paula's surprise, Mark smiled. "Thanks. It means a lot to me to hear you say that."

"Anytime."

Paula gently stroked the top of Mark's hand with her thumb.

"You know I forgot something." Mark said, still holding Paula's gaze.

"What's that?"

"I talked a lot about how much Coach Sarah has helped me, but that's not the whole story."

"What do you mean?"

"You've helped me a lot too. Without you and this work, I'm not sure if I would have been able to bounce back the way I have." Mark smiled warmly as the last of his tears rolled down his cheek. "I guess what I'm trying to say is, I know you feel like I saved you that day at the beach. But... I owe you a lot. If it would have been anyone else, they would have just said thank you and gone off to live their own lives. But you pressed and got me to climb out of the pit I was stuck in. Thank you, Paula."

"Oh Mark."

They simultaneously stood and embraced in a long, loving hug. When they drew apart, Mark sniffled, wiped more tears from his eyes and grabbed a tissue to blow his nose.

"Thanks. I needed to get that out."

"You don't need to thank me, Mark. Though I do appreciate it. You're my spiritual partner; and if there's anything I can do to help you, I'll do it."

Paula placed a hand on Mark's shoulder and gave him a reassuring caress. She handed Mark his mug and asked shyly, "Would you like to get started?"

Mark smiled, "Definitely."

They moved to the living room where they worked diligently to complete the administrative duties from their last Vision Quest adventure on the Five Disciplines of the Initiate. Once they felt satisfied with the results, they co-created an action plan to establish how they would master each discipline *one bite at a time.*

When they were done Paula looked to Mark, and whole heartily asked, "Ready Partner?"

Mark prepared his notebook and pen and humorously replied, "I was born ready!"

Paula relaxed into her meditative state, while focusing her attention on her mantra word *Namasté.* She *surrendered* to receive the next lesson. As she repeated the mantra, Paula felt her heart rate and breathing slow down. By this point, the process of slipping from a conscious to an alpha meditative state had become second nature, and she had learned to make the transition quickly.

* * *

After a few minutes Paula felt enveloped by a calm soothing sensation, and the room and world around her fell away. She found herself hundreds of feet above a college campus with many ivy-covered, old brick buildings. The campus was lively. It was filled with students wandering the grounds, studying outdoors and fraternizing with each other.

As she surveyed the grounds, Paula suddenly felt herself pulled forward with tremendous force, as though she were moving at sub-light speed. In a flash, she was in a small amphitheater-like lecture hall. At the front of the room was a man who looked to be in his early 70s. He had grey hair and a short neat beard. He was thin and meticulously dressed in a fine suit. He slowly paced across the stage delivering a lecture to the class.

"Recall class, when we last met," the professor began, "we were discussing quantum physics; the study of subatomic interactions, and how this science has helped us become more aware of the effects of Consciousness on physical reality. I used the example of throwing a pebble into a body of water. Can anyone recount what the essence of that example was?"

A stunning tall blonde woman raised her hand with almost alarming passion. The professor pointed to her, and she smiled gleefully for the opportunity to speak. "Well, the idea was, if I throw a pebble into a pond, I can see the ripple caused by the pebble's interaction with the water. It moves outward like a vibration in circular waves from the central point of impact."

"Very good, Pat." the professor replied with a proud grin. He turned his head and scanned the room for another contributor. He made eye contact with another student and asked her, "What else do you remember from our last class, Susan?"

"As a society, we have awakened to the Self-realization that our conscious thoughts have a direct effect on our physical environment because our beliefs create our reality." Susan was more mature than most of the students in the class, which was exemplified by her professional attire. She continued, "Quantum physics has proven that which philosophers have been preaching for millennia; what I feel in my heart and think in my thoughts will create my reality."

"Excellent, Susan. Thank you. Does anyone remember the root word for personality?"

"It comes from the Greek word 'persona', which means mask!" A young man from the rear of the room shouted.

The professor clapped his hands, grinning proudly at how adept his students' answers were. "That's correct, Peter. Now, can anyone tell me how the Greek word, persona, ties into our lesson on quantum physics?"

For a moment, the class was silent. Professor Erich observed the room as his students wrote in their notebooks, whispered to their neighbors, or simply stared at him with blank expressions, awaiting the answer to his query. After a moment a young man, who looked too young to be in college, raised his hand. "Greg, you never fail to surprise me. Please tell us how our persona relates to quantum physics."

The young man cleared his throat and in a nasally voice said, "Thank you Professor. As a species, we hide behind our personas and deny that we are responsible for creating our own reality."

The professor nodded his head and narrowed his eyes, pressing the young student further, "That's a poignant thought, Mr. Saddle. But can you elaborate further?"

Greg pondered the question briefly. "Well. I believe if we don't stop hiding behind our persona-masks and become globally aware of the impact we are having on our environment, or pretty soon we won't have a planet to live on."

"Thank you for your globally conscious answer, Greg. Science has proven that our thoughts have a dramatic effect on the physical Universe because our thoughts are vibrational waves of energy. Something as simple as a nail being attracted to a magnet is an example of how objects are attracted or repelled because of their vibrational energy frequencies. Objects that are in vibrational harmony attract while objects that are not in vibrational harmony repel each other.

We used to think that plants and animals were alive, and stones weren't, so we referred to rocks as inorganic. But quantum physics has since taught us that *every atom* in the Universe vibrates. For example, a stone's electrons and atoms are in constant motion but are invisible because they are vibrating at the speed of light."

From the front of the class, a young student who appeared to be in his 20s raised his hand. "Professor Erich, are you suggesting that scientists have been miss-classifying common rocks for centuries?" The room fell silent. The young student projected an air of superiority.

Surprisingly, the professor smiled back at his challenger. "Ah Rick; always the skeptic. Never lose that quality! It's important to question things that your elders tell you. Without curious minds, we would never learn new things; and as such, we would not progress. To answer your question... no, I'm not trying to challenge the scientific community.

Is a stone alive in the same way as you or me? No. Is it alive in the same way as even a plant? No. Now I challenge you to consider the following. Are *we* alive in the same way as a plant?" The professor paused for several seconds. "Should our definition of what is or isn't *alive* be so narrow? Or should we consider a more universal concept of what defines life and aliveness?"

The class murmured and the professor grinned. He was thrilled by the challenge presented to him. "I can see I still have doubters here. Allow me to phrase it another way. Consider this. Can a piece of coal transform its molecular structure to become a diamond? Yes! But does this mean it has the same degree of awareness as say, you or I do? No. But! It does prove that even rocks have a subtle degree of awareness."

The class murmured again.

Professor Erich could see he'd won a few students over. "Can anyone give me an example that demonstrates how plants are aware of their environment?"

The only gray-haired senior student in the room raised her hand. "Every day, I rotate my plants so their leaves face away from the sun. When I return home from school, my plants have amazingly turned their leaves all the way around to face the sun."

"A superb example, Mrs. Geltman. Your plants turn to absorb the sun's life force energy, which requires a degree of awareness. Wouldn't you agree class?"

Professor Erich scanned the room for another contributor. "Joseph can you give me an example to prove that animals have awareness?"

"Animals are mobile. They hunt, prepare for winter, protect their offspring, and use their five senses to survive and reproduce."

"Very good, Joseph. And while you're on a roll, can you tell me what distinguishes human awareness, from animal awareness?"

Joseph raised his eyebrows in contemplation. After a moment, he shared, "Humans go beyond the five senses to cerebral functions that are multisensory. We think, we have egos, we are logical and creative, we have free will, and we are socially aware creatures."

***

As Paula heard *socially aware creatures*, she felt the familiar pull come over her once again. She was pulled away from the lecture hall, and her vision blurred as she accelerated to sub-light speed. When the blur subsided, she found herself surrounded by men in hard hats and construction equipment. The God Source had apparently taken her to a construction site, but unlike her previous visions, her view was out of focus. She struggled to observe the details of her surroundings, but her vision remained blurry.

She gauged her surroundings and noticed a small area that was in focus. She drew closer and peered through a ten-inch circular opening. Through this opening, the scene was clear and focused. She saw a construction worker cutting a piece of wood with an electric saw. As she observed, the circle of clarity slowly narrowed until the saw's blade was the only thing she could clearly see.

She watched as the blade appeared and disappeared, as the man continuously turned the saw on and off. Paula was perplexed. She thought to herself, *What lesson is the God Source trying to teach me by this unusual vision?*

Then it came to her. When the blade oscillated at a high speed, the teeth became invisible. She only knew that they existed because she could see the effect on the wood being cut.

Paula considered all the scientific miracles that had been proven to exist but are *invisible,* such as electricity, magnetism, television and radio waves. *There are so many things I believe in that I can't see, including love. And even though I don't understand how they work, I still believe in their existence because I can see their effect on things.*

***

Without warning, Paula's Consciousness was pulled away from the scene. She felt herself accelerate to sub-light speed. When she settled, and the blur subsided, she found herself in an educational setting very different from the college she had recently left behind. She was now observing a Self-actualization intensive workshop, much like the ones she had attended many years ago in Sedona, Arizona. The trainer in her vision was a tall woman with long dark hair rolled up in a bun. The students called her Ms. Angel. She was teaching a large class about the secrets of vibrational transformation. She projected a powerful stage presence, which kept her audience completely transfixed on what she was teaching.

Paula listened as Ms. Angel instructed her audience.

"Think back to a time when you decided to listen to music. If you wanted to feel romantic, inspired, happy or sad, you chose a certain piece of music. Why? Because different songs affect your feelings differently based on their vibrational frequency. Your denser emotions, like sadness, anger, frustration, and jealousy, emit a distinct lower energetic resonance, while your higher emotions, such as love and enthusiasm, emit higher faster vibrational frequencies.

You can measure your personal life force energy by the rate of electrical power you emit. Many studies have been conducted in which personal energy output from subjects is measured in megahertz. The results have been both astounding and conclusive. To put it simply, class, the higher the vibration, the healthier the body, and the more powerful the BEing."

She projected a chart which compared the energy output of a healthy body to that of a diseased body, along with the potential energy gained from consuming some common foods.

<u>HUMAN BODY</u>

- Healthy Human Body: 62-78 MHz

<u>DISEASE</u>

- Disease starts at: 50 MHz
- Colds and Flu start at: 57-60 MHz
- Cancer starts at: 30-42 MHz
- Death begins at: 20 MHz

<u>FOODS</u>

- Fresh Fruits & Vegetables: 80 MHz
- Cooked Food: 30-50 MHz
- Sweets, Junk Foods, etc.: 0-5 MHz

***

As Ms. Angel discussed the details of the chart, Paula remembered a documentary she had seen about the African Bemba tribe which used positive vibrational frequencies to 'punish' offenders. During the Babemba's 'punishment' ritual, everyone in the tribe formed a large circle around the 'offender'. Then, they individually discussed all the 'offender's' *positive* attributes, strengths, good deeds and acts of kindness throughout his or her lifetime. After everyone recounted all the *positive things* they could think of about the so-called 'offender', the tribe would welcome him or her back into the tribe with a joyful celebration.

Paula also recalled a few essays she had read on vibrational frequency and its relationship to mood. They explained that a person's thinking patterns profoundly affect their body, because energy flows where thought goes.

Within Paula's own professional experience, she often needed to intentionally raise or harmonize her own vibrational frequencies via mediating, exercising, listening to music, or taking a walk in the woods. This was especially true after facilitating an emotionally "heavy" coaching session.

Paula intentionally brought her attention back to the Self-actualization instructor.

***

Ms. Angel continued, "The first secret of vibrational transformation is everything in the Universe is made of vibrating energy. Quantum physics has proven that everything in the Universe including you, me, sound, light, and matter, is energy that vibrates at different frequencies. This means that energy is the core substance of everything in the Universe, and it proves why we are all spiritually interconnected. Hence the popular Eastern term 'Namasté.'

What you perceive as solid matter only appears to be solid through the lens of your five senses. But when you observe matter on a subatomic level, it isn't solid at all. What you see is energy waves vibrating at a particular rate of frequency."

The instructor paused to scan the room and observe her class. After giving them a moment to absorb the information, she continued. "The second secret of vibrational transformation is that everything oscillates at a unique vibrational speed. This means that every biological and non-biological entity has a unique energy signature that vibrates at a distinct frequency. The God Source that created our Universe has infinite expressions, and we can see this by the different vibrational signatures within our world. A simple example of this is H_2O and its different forms as liquid water, solid ice, or vapor and steam.

I want you to learn and remember these secrets of vibrational transformation because you can't permanently change your thinking without changing your vibrational footprint. You might be able to think positive thoughts about what you want for a short time, but if those thoughts are not in vibrational alignment with the energy vibrations of your soul, it will be impossible for you to sustain them. This means you will not be able to achieve your goals without first altering your vibrational energy that you are resonating into the Universe."

The Self-actualization instructor paused for a few seconds and then whispered, "Mastering the secrets of vibrational transformation will help you to consistently maintain a high vibrational frequency. If you can do that, you can magnetize your dreams and goals to you, which will help you to enjoy life to its fullest, because you will be in vibrational harmony with what you desire."

* * *

The instructor's lesson rang true for Paula. Her professional experience had taught her that if she gave a client a positive affirmation to recite which wasn't in *vibrational alignment* with the client's *self-image*, then the positive affirmation would quickly be replaced with thoughts that were in vibrational harmony with their *poor self-image*. So, a positive affirmation such as *I'm Successful and Abundant*, would be replaced by thoughts in vibrational harmony with emotions, such as fear, scarcity, anger and resentment.

If her clients emitted low energy vibrations due to negative thoughts, they attracted people and experiences that had low, negative, and fearful energy. In turn, when her clients had high, fast and positive vibrations due to their positive self-image and positive thoughts, they attracted people and experiences into their lives that fostered inspiration and opportunity because *like attracts like.*

The instructor continued her lesson, but as she did her voice began to fade. Paula found it harder to understand her words, and then the vision of Ms. Angel was gone. She felt herself slowly slip from the classroom back into the kaleidoscope of colors. The pull of her Consciousness once again gave her the sensation of traveling at incredible speed, and in a flash, she was back in her living room with Mark.

Paula wore an expression of amazement on her face. As much as she had become accustomed to her multi-sensory spiritual journeys, it was still jarring to switch from a formless state of consciousness to her physical body so quickly.

Mark grabbed his pen and notebook and immediately began the debriefing process, which Paula and Mark had now mastered. "How was it? What did you see this time?"

"Oh, this was a wild session. I felt like an extrasensory Ping-Pong ball!" Paula was always filled with enthusiasm, but she was particularly exuberant this time. "First, I visited a college campus and learned about quantum physics. Then, I was catapulted to a construction site where I watched a saw blade teeth appear and disappear. And then, I observed a Self-actualization intensive about the secrets of vibrational transformation."

With his head down, Mark wrote furiously while he listened. "That sounds pretty intense. Tell me more."

It took some time, but Paula gradually recounted all the specific details of her vision.

Mark's pragmatic notes made grokking Paula's Vision Quest adventures invaluable. He possessed the unusual ability to intuitively translate Paula's metaphysical adventures into a well-organized summary. "OK, so here's what I have from today..."

As Mark read his notes, Paula closed her eyes to concentrate, but her mind became distracted. She thought back to when she had first met Mark, and grief was the dominant part of his personality. Now, after months had passed, she was beginning to experience another side of him that was lighter and more pleasant. *He's even a little charming*, she thought. She smiled to herself and quickly reverted her focus back to Mark's summary which he proudly recounted:

Secrets of Vibrational Transformation

1. **Everything in the Universe Is made of vibrating energy** including you, me, sound, light, and matter, which is why at a quantum level we are interconnected.

2. **Everything vibrates at a unique vibrational speed.** This means that everything in the Universe has a unique energy signature and vibrates at a certain frequency.

3. **Quantum Scientists** have proven that your thoughts have a direct effect on your physical environment, mood and body because **your vibrational frequencies create your reality.**

4. **The faster your body vibrates, the healthier your body will be.** Research has proven that to achieve your goals, your thoughts must be in **vibrational alignment** with the **vibrations of your Soul.**

5. The **Law of Attraction** states that if you emit low vibrations due to negative thoughts, illness, poor diet, etc. then you will draw to you people and experiences that match your low vibrational frequencies. In turn, if you emit high, fast and positive vibrations, then you will attract people and experiences into your life that foster inspiration, opportunity, and expansion because *like attracts like.*

6. The most important **Secret of Vibrational Transformation** is for you to consciously and consistently **raise your vibratory frequencies** with positive thoughts, nutrition, exercise, and

meditation. These consistent practices will produce the Life Force Energy that you need to create a Self-mastered life.

With that, Mark lowered his notebook and looked earnestly at Paula. "How is that? Am I on point?"

Paula, felt flushed with joy. "Mark, you never cease to amaze me. Honestly, your ability to organize each session in such a concise manner is amazing. I might go so far as to call it a Divine gift."

Mark nodded with humble appreciation. "Thanks Paula. I don't know why. I just have a knack for ingesting and organizing new information quickly."

"You really do. Having your help is such a tremendous blessing. Actually, without your help this process would not have been possible."

"Thanks Partner. As we learned during this session, we humans must learn to accelerate our vibrational frequencies to increase our *willpower if* we want to save humanity from extinction. I'm just trying to do my part!"

Paula looked into Mark's eyes. She felt a distinct fluttering sensation, the same as when she heard him call her "Partner" for the first time.

Lesson #6 Of
Transformational Awakening Is...

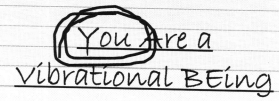 You Are a
Vibrational BEing

The Secrets of Vibrational
Transformation will help you raise
your vibratory frequencies, so you
can create and enjoy a Self-mastered
life.

Dig One Deep Well

Do You Seek Mastery or Mediocrity?

It was early morning the day after the spiritual partners drafted their lesson on Vibrational Transformation. Mark was in his home office reviewing one of his work cases. He liked to get a head-start on his work week in the morning to allow him more time to work with Paula on the Spiritual Awakening course.

Paula's number flashed on the display, as the phone rang.

"Hey, Paula." Mark answered, surprised to receive a call from Paula so early. "What's up?"

"God morning, Mark. Sorry, I know it's early. I was just about to head out the door, but I had an *aha* moment that I wanted to share with you."

"Sure. What came up?"

"I have a strong gut feeling that it might be good for each of us to... to take a break from our work and spend some time alone today... like a day off. I feel we would both benefit from a relaxing Self-care day to refresh and renew our energy."

"Are you sure you want to take a whole day? We could meet after dinner and just have a short session. You know. Just to keep the momentum going?" Mark knew the value of Paula's proposal but felt somewhat uneasy about it.

"We could do that. But I feel that having a whole day to reflect in solitude would go a long way toward rejuvenating our creative juices. This way, when we meet tomorrow, we'll feel refreshed and we can create with renewed enthusiasm."

Mark knew it was important to take one in seven days to just BE. He put his reservations aside and agreed. "That's fine. I could benefit from some alone time. We'll meet tomorrow then?"

"Definitely. I'll text you, and we'll hash out the details. Create a feel-good day, Mark."

**

Paula decided to start her Self-care day by taking the scenic route to the shore. She enjoyed driving on the long winding road through the woods by her home. The early morning sun had just begun to rise, and the tall pine trees surrounding the road dimmed its light. This created a dramatic contrast between the dimly lit forest and the bright eastern sky above her. Paula usually listened to music or her own pre-recorded affirmations while driving, but on this occasion, she chose to drive in silence and quietly contemplate the events that had transpired over the past few months.

Eventually, the dimly lit forest road gave way to a clearing where she was met with a beautiful view of the ocean. The road brought her right up to the coastline where the sun's rays reflected brilliantly. Paula parked her truck near a remote private stretch of beach ideal for her planned meditation. As she began walking, she surveyed the beach and headed to a stone jetty that extended far into the ocean. The jetty had a particularly large boulder that would provide a natural shield from the wind. She knew it was the perfect place for her. When she reached the jetty, she put down her backpack, spread her beach blanket and assumed a meditative pose.

She reflected on the past few months and what they meant to her. After a few minutes of deep contemplation, she closed her eyes and began to meditate using the God-sound chant, "Aaaaaah". As she eased deeper into her meditation, she reached a state of deep relaxation. Paula remained in the God-gap between her thoughts for quite some time until she was stirred by the salty fragrance of the ocean air. At that moment, she felt complete. She opened her eyes and was mesmerized by the beauty of her surroundings. The sea was a deep blue, which starkly contrasted the bright white waves which crashed onto the outer edge of the stone jetty.

She felt a deep sense of inner peace, and it was within that space that she began to process her feelings. With vibrancy, she declared, "I feel so fortunate! I grok that I'm neither my body nor my mind, but a vibrational BEing of light and love. I'm happy I discovered my reason for incarnating, and that I get to fulfill my spiritual purpose with my soul friend Mark. Thank you, God!"

She reflected on her relationship with Mark and realized that it was having a synergistic effect on the evolution of her soul. She could sense that co-creating the course with Mark had increased her vibrational Life Force Energy, which in turn accelerated the growth of her Godlike powers. The co-creation process helped them dive into a single spiritual path in which they found omnipotent wisdom.

The realization brought Paula back to when she was a young spiritual sampler, experimenting with many kinds of spiritual practices. She first encountered the concept of *digging one deep well* from the Kabbalah, but when she first read it, the meaning was lost on her.

However, she was honest enough to own that she was one of those seekers who had dug many shallow wells.

Over the years Paula worked with many other seekers. Through their interactions she realized that, like her, many of them didn't understand the difference between enlightenment and empowerment. She learned that these two terms needed to be distinguished so as not to confuse *knowingness* (studying, philosophizing, conceptualizing) with *doingness* (implementing, experiencing, actualizing). Her own trials and errors taught her the importance of this lesson: enlightenment alone only leads to intellectual faith, and that faith without action usually manifests into Self-delusion. For a soul on a journey to Self-mastery, there is nothing worse than Self-delusion.

As a young spiritual seeker, she frequently got *lost* playing emotionally seductive roles such as *powerless victim*. Her spiritual sampling created a wealth of mental confusion and emotional turmoil. Back then, her ego-mind believed that the *shallow wells* she dug would bring her to "the end." But after decades of emotionalizing her studies, Paula realized that her lack of commitment to one spiritual path was the primary source of her mental confusion. This prevented her from using tools such as the *Seven Spiritual Truths*[22], as a compass to guide her back to her authentic Self.

Eventually Paula came to accept that she needed to commit to one spiritual path to discover her spiritual reason for taking a human birth. She resigned to keep digging deep, until she experienced the cool clean water of her true Self. Through her experimentation, she found solace in the knowledge that her trials were just part of God's perfect plan for her.

She grokked that there is no one single 'right' path that is for everyone. Even when Paula's coaching clients had reservations, she told them "It doesn't matter which path you choose, whether it be Buddhist monk, minister, priest, yoga or meditation teacher, nun, meditation or Tai Chi. All rivers lead to the ocean of God's bliss." She frequently repeated, "When you find the spiritual method that works best for you, just keep *digging* until you train your ego to serve you, as opposed to you serving your ego."

Ram Dass, one of her most influential spiritual teachers, taught her that the spiritual path is a journey of inner exploration anyone can take, provided they have the *emotional courage* to examine the roles they play, and

---

[22] Seven Spiritual Truths, contain the essence of the sixteen lessons contained within Master Coach Hu's *Self-mastery… a Journey Home to Your Inner Self* textbook.

to understand that they are not those roles. As his student she learned that Westerners are enthralled with their minds to such a degree that it interferes with the use and development of their intuition.

Over-achievement, which creates a "bigger, better, faster" mentality, is perceived as a measure of success, and has conditioned Westerners to worship the "golden calf" of our materialistic culture. It saddened Paula that she lived in a society where people incorrectly think that they can't be "too rich or too thin," where power and materialism are valued above kindness and sensitivity, and where technology has evolved faster than the *Namasté Consciousness*[23]. She knew that this misguided attitude led society to believe that other levels of knowing are unproductive, to the point where intuition has almost become a dirty word.

Paula's guru, Swami Muktananda, taught her that the rational mind is a very limited processing system and that there are other meta-systems that are golden gates into the Infinite Mind[24]. He told her that these spiritual gateways can only be accessed by transcending the

---

[23] Namasté Consciousness: an awareness that underneath our minds, bodies, roles and identities, we are all spiritually inter-connected as One.
[24] Infinite Mind: the quantum field of infinite potential, infinite wisdom, and infinite possibilities.

logical, analytical mind with meditative practices, such as the *Five Disciplines of the Initiates*.

These memories flooded Paula's mind as she sat among the stones and fresh salty sea air. She felt calm and at peace with herself. Within that state, she organized her thoughts and wrote a single statement:

The astonishing diversity of individual karma means that everyone has their own unique spiritual path to follow. Seekers need to find a spiritual path that feels right to them, and then dig a deep well until they discover who they are 'not.' They aren't their body, or their intellectual mind, or their roles such as a parent, teacher, or coach.

She reflected on what she had written and was grateful for such a deep Self-realization.

Paula spent the rest of the day meditating, walking along the beach, napping, and journaling. After a full day in solitude revitalizing her soul and de-charging her body, she felt complete. She packed up and headed home, eager to organize her notes.

As she left the beach and sand behind, she wondered how Mark did with his day in solitude. At that moment, she was inspired with an idea that would positively alter their visualization method. Although she was very excited to share her new idea with Mark, she controlled her egoic impulse to call or text him immediately.

Instead, she decided to let it permeate more until they met the following morning. Even after making this decision, she still couldn't stop the feelings of excitement that flowed through her.

She missed Mark despite that she had seen him less than a day ago. She was awash with anticipation to see him and continue their creative process. As she glanced at the beach in her rear-view mirror, she was struck with another realization; her excited feelings to continue working with Mark were due to more than a desire to co-create a spiritual course. She thought back to Mark's compliment earlier in the week when he compared her to his fiancé, and she remembered blushing like a teenage girl. She realized that somewhere, at some point, she had stopped seeing Mark as merely a spiritual partner. She knew it was strange, but she started to see him as a rather good-looking man, with a kind and warm heart. She couldn't help but hope that maybe one day they could be something more than spiritual partners.

**

That same morning, Mark drove to an isolated stretch of woods where he liked to hike and meditate in nature. He considered the progress he had made since first meeting Paula and Coach Sarah. When he'd first begun his grieving work, he felt uncomfortable spending time alone. But since he'd learned to properly deal with his emotional trauma, he realized he enjoyed spending time in solitude in the woods, where he felt peaceful, calm and safe.

Mark entered the forest with his hiking apparel, a backpack, and his notebook. It was a gorgeous morning. Sunrays shone brightly throughout the evergreen forest, and a scent of pine was carried on a light breeze. He hiked at a fast pace for several miles while enjoying the sights, sounds and scents of the forest. He intentionally stayed present and prevented his mind from drifting to thoughts about his job or anything else. All he wanted to do was to slip into the God gap between his thoughts remembering that he was a *human BEing*, not a *human doing*. He intended to enjoy his day so he could refresh, recharge and renew his creative energies.

Eventually, he reached a cluster of tall trees next to a clearing with a wide view of the sky. He'd meditated under these trees several times before and he felt that it was the perfect place just to BE. The area had a rich fragrance of pine and provided easy access to shade or sunlight depending on the weather. On this day, the temperature was warm, so he chose a spot under his favorite evergreen that had plenty of shade. He leaned back, closed his eyes and began to meditate.

Mark took deep, slow breaths and gradually his heart rate slowed. He fell into a relaxed state of Consciousness.

When he was done meditating, he didn't immediately open his eyes; instead, he reflected on the events of the past few months. Since meeting Paula, he had made a dramatic paradigm shift, and he wished to simply digest all the new things he had yet to fully process.

***

As Mark reflected, a memory of one of his first sessions with Coach Sarah was triggered when she'd asked him, "Are you a pre-mature positive thinker?"

"I don't know what that is." He answered.

"Pre-mature positive thinking happens when you are *only* willing to see the positive aspects of your experiences and deny or minimize the negative aspects. It is a New Age belief system erected upon the chants of the positive attitude self-help advocates who preach affirmations such as, 'Think positive, think positive, only think positive thoughts.' Psychologists refer to pre-mature positive thinking as 'magical thinking,' because pre-mature positive thinkers believe, *If I just ignore it and think positive thoughts, this negative, painful thing will go away on its own.*"

At first, Mark's ego rejected the whole concept of premature positive thinking. He asked himself, *How can being positive be negative?* But, little by little, he realized that he had been using pre-mature positive thinking as a defense mechanism.

Coach Sarah had explained to him, "Once you've owned the certainty that your premature positive thinking is nothing more than an ego defense; the next step is to discover your inner truth. To do this, you need to dig deep and commit to a single spiritual practice. And I'll warn you now, Mark, many of your inner truths will have bad breath and will be unpleasant! And that's perfectly normal. The key is to stop denying the truths, even the stinky ones that lie deep in your heart. This is important because if you're looking to create change, you must first see things as they are because nothing will change until you allow it to be what it is."

"OK. I'm scared, but I'm also ready and willing to see what I have repressed. I want to know what these things are about so I can learn from them and move forward with my life. It sounds a little scary, but I'm committed to this!"

Through coaching sessions, Mark realized that his parents weren't perfect; but as a child, his ego mind needed to see them as perfect so their less-than-perfect parenting would appear "normal" to him. His child's mind had idealized[25] his parents as a defense mechanism. Through this process of parental idealization, he had denied and repressed the truth about

---

[25] Idealized: viewed as perfect; having no flaws.

his childhood hurts. Once Mark realized and understood the truth behind this, he and Coach Sarah established a "Mark-ology" rehabilitation plan, which included the *Five Disciplines of the Initiate* exercises to help him process his repressed feelings.

Mark learned that his repressed negative emotions recycled the same painful feelings over and over, which led to recurring painful experiences and the same old question he kept asking himself, *Why did this happen to me again?* Through his committed Self-work, Mark dug in and plowed through his psycho-spiritual exercises under the guidance of Coach Sarah.

Coach Sarah explained to Mark, "Holding on to your negative feelings is keeping you emotionally connected to your past hurts. If you secretly or unconsciously hate or fear your caretakers, you will remain attached to them emotionally. On an unconscious level, this gives you a perfect excuse to remain emotionally immature. As Carl Jung said, 'Enlightenment is not about imagining figures of light, but of making the darkness conscious.'"

By being emotionally honest with himself, Mark could see and express his true feelings. He released pounds of unfinished emotional business that he had been carrying around for years. He learned that as a child, he needed his parents' love, nurturing and emotional support to make him feel safe, sane, and secure; but as an adult, he needed to transition from needing his parents' love to needing his own inner God love, inner peace and emotional serenity.

He now understood that it was his sole responsibility to fulfill his own emotional dependency needs, because no one else could or would do it for him. It taught him that to heal, he needed to see the whole truth about everything that had happened to him without judgment, regret, or shame.

Mark also faced the truth of his past tragedy. This allowed him to see the deep resentments that had caused him to unconsciously place blame and to feel shamed and victimized. Owning these truths freed up huge amounts of his Life Force Energy, which he put to good use by empowering himself, and it helped him to understand why he incarnated.

**

After a full day of being alone in nature, recharging and refreshing his mind, Mark started to hike back to where he parked his car. On his way back, he thought of an idea that could improve the visualization method which he and Paula were using. Though he was excited to share his idea with Paula, he refrained from calling her because he knew that there is time enough for everything, and everything happens in God's good time.

As Mark hiked, his thoughts lingered on Paula. He knew his spiritual partnership with her was having a positive effect on him. He enjoyed co-creating the Spiritual Awakening course with her, and he knew that their interactions were providing a miraculous support system that magnified his Life Force Energy. With Paula and Coach Sarah's help, he had begun digging one deep well into his omnipotent wisdom. He felt very grateful to have both these people in his life.

He reached his car and packed up his belongings. He couldn't stop thinking about the positive impact Paula was having on his life. With her help, he had not only managed to put his life back together after a brutal tragedy; but he was also able to reconnect to what his parents tried to teach him while he was growing up. For the first time since before the accident, Mark felt complete, and he had Paula to thank for it.

Mark couldn't stop thinking about Paula. And he couldn't ignore his rapid heartbeat or the sensation of butterflies in his stomach.

Lesson #7 Of
Transformational Awakening Is...

<u>Dig One Deep Well</u>

Commit to Digging One Deep Well using one spiritual path until you discover the omnipotent wisdom that reveals your spiritual reason for incarnating on your Journey Home to Your Inner Self.

Self-Parenting Mastery

Only You Can Give You What You Didn't Get

The following day, Paula and Mark met early in the afternoon. It was a bright crisp summer day, the kind of day that invigorates the soul just to be alive. Paula prepared for Mark's arrival. As she often did, she set up a workspace in her living room and laid out their research materials. She began reviewing the notes she had taken the previous day at the beach. As she read through her notes, she became keenly aware of a fluttery feeling in the pit of her stomach. She tried her best to ignore it; but as hard as she tried, she could not subdue the sensation nor deny what she thought it meant.

After a short while, there was a knock at her door exactly on time, as usual. Paula eagerly jumped to the door to let Mark in and welcomed him with a big smile.

"Hey Paula."

They greeted each other in the doorway with a warm affectionate hug. As soon as they broke their embrace, Mark looked into Paula's eyes with a glow of lighthearted enthusiasm and said, "I have something exciting to share with you."

As Paula's eyes met Mark's gaze, she felt the fluttering sensation grow stronger. She started blushing and quickly tried to hide it by looking away.

Misinterpreting her actions, Mark asked, "Hey. Everything alright?"

Paula's face reddened. "Oh. Yeah, I'm fine. I just have my head in the clouds today. I have something important to share with you too. But you go first. What did you want to share?"

"Well," with a humorous undertone, Mark shared, "I spent my Self-care day in the woods hugging trees. After six or so hours, I felt recharged and started hiking back to my car. On the way back, I got an idea that might improve our Spiritual Awakening course..."

Paula's face beamed with pure joy as she laughed and interrupted, "The miraculous power of synchronicity!"

Mark raised an eyebrow. "Wait. What? What does that have to do with my idea?"

Paula pointed toward herself with a slight smile, "I *also* received an idea yesterday about how we could improve our course. And *that* is synchronistic!"

Mark looked at Paula with a blank expression and smiled sheepishly, "So, I've got to be honest. I've heard the term 'synchronicity' many times, but I don't actually know what it means."

"Synchronicity happens because all living things, like you and I, are interconnected on a quantum level. In our case, even though you were in the woods and I was at the beach, without either of us realizing it, the God Source synergistically sent both of us a course improvement idea. It's like we were listening to the same radio station at the same time while we were miles apart!"

Mark nodded in agreement. "That's pretty cool and sounds simple enough." He smiled slyly, "Is it okay if I come inside now and finish sharing my idea?"

Paula giggled. She had gotten so caught up in their conversation that she hadn't realized they were still standing in the doorway. "Of course! Sorry! I'm even more excited than I realized." And she let him in.

The two took their usual seats in the living room where Paula had a freshly brewed pot of tea waiting for them. After getting situated, Paula began to explain, "The concept of synchronicity really helped me to understand that nothing is an isolated event; it only appears to be. Everyone on earth is interconnected and only experiences disconnectedness when they neurotically fixate on their fear-based thoughts instead of the quantum energy that is shared among all of us.

My teacher, Deepak, taught me that we are non-material spiritual BEings having a human experience; so, we're not subject to the limitations of space, time, matter and causation. Rather, we exist within a field of Universal Consciousness, which is the core of our BEingness.

Our Universal Consciousness is *Omniscient* - all knowing, *Omnipresent* – everywhere present simultaneously, and *Omnipotent* - all powerful."

"Wow. That's profound. Can you say that again?!"

"Sure! Our Universal Consciousness is Omniscient, Omnipresent, and Omnipotent. All knowing, everywhere present, and all powerful."

"Wow." Mark tapped his finger against his mug as he processed Paula's statement, "I'm not sure why that feels so empowering to me."

"Maybe at some deep level, you know that in a synchronized state of grace the God Source can hear your thoughts and can fulfill your dharmic goals even before *you* are fully aware of them.

Even though we were physically separated yesterday, we were still connected spiritually. Our Universal Omnipotent powers transcended space and time. Even though we weren't in the same space, our thoughts were connected, and that is what *some people would call a miracle.*"

Mark was happy to learn about synchronicity, but he was bursting to share his idea with Paula. He carefully placed his mug on the table and stared into Paula's eyes, "So, I thought we would improve our course if we perform the Vision Quests together as equals." With a meek tone and a big smile, he continued, "I think we would get a big surge of creative energy if we *synergistically* co-created the space together. It's like you're always telling me, 'Where two or more are gathered in God's name...'

Another idea that surfaced for me yesterday is that since the first-half of our course is designed to enlighten our students about the Laws of the Universe, I feel that the second-half should empower them through Self-mastery exercises. Then they will be able to emotionalize their desired changes, which will help them achieve their desired changes... permanently."

Paula quietly contemplated Mark's suggestion. After a few moments, which felt like an eternity to Mark, she shared, "You know. I shouldn't be amazed when synergistic events unfold, but I am! I know this 'coincidence' was a co-created event. But even so, it's still so humbling to experience how the infinite organizing powers of the Universe connected our like-minded souls yesterday." Paula slowly sipped her tea, "What I'm saying is I had a very similar idea yesterday about our meditating together. And I agree that the second-half of our course must include empowering action exercises. This will help our students make the changes they need to achieve their objectives."

Mark leaned forward and sipped his tea. As he did, his eyes met Paula's, and he felt a warm, comforting sensation wash over him. He smiled and said, "It is truly amazing that just a few years ago I would have thought that this was just a weird coincidence."

Paula smiled back. Though it was very subtle, Mark could see a glimmer in Paula's eyes that he'd never noticed before. "Yup! No coincidences in a perfectly evolving Universe."

With enthusiasm Mark stood up and said, "Well enough talk! Let's experience our first Vision Quest together, Partner. Are you ready?"

Paula laughed, "I was born ready!"

The spiritual partners reorganized their workspace. They sat facing each other in a meditative pose with their knees almost touching. "So, how do we start this? Is it just like any normal meditation?" Mark asked.

"Well. Mostly." Paula smiled and continued, "Before we start, I'll let you know that this may feel a little weird to you; we'll be able to communicate telepathically. And you'll be able to feel and hear what all the characters in the vision are feeling and thinking. You'll even be able to feel what I'm feeling and hear what I'm thinking... as if we were all one soul with multiple minds."

With a gentle authoritative tone, she continued, "First, just relax. Be quiet, and try to clear your mind. I'll walk us through the process. Let's start by making a conscious intention to surrender to the God Source by opening our sacred hearts. Next, we're going to focus on our breathing. Our thoughts will naturally slow down with each deep breath we take until our heart rate slows. With each exhale, we're going to focus our attention on the mantra word 'Namasté.'"

They both knew that surrendering to their higher powers would open their subconscious minds to receive their next spiritual lesson. They were moving forward on the faith that they would receive what they needed to learn from their co-created Vision Quest.

They discovered that the longer they meditated, the faster the mystical revelations unveiled themselves. For Paula, the experience had become intimately familiar; but for Mark, this experience was entirely new. As his thoughts gradually slowed down, Mark was astonished by his sensation of weightless freedom.

**

Slowly, Mark saw a vision emerge from the darkness. He was observing a small group of climbers about halfway up a sheer cliff. His eyes were focused on a tall thin man who hung upside-down tangled in his repelling safety rope. The man's head was cut and bleeding steadily, and the rest of the members in the group were yelling, asking him if he was okay. Mark could also see a bearded, burly-looking man repelling down the steep cliff to save the man who was in danger.

Mark felt confused as to whether what he was seeing was real or just his imagination. He also wondered if Paula was seeing the same thing.

Surprisingly, Mark heard Paula respond to his thoughts, even though he never spoke a word to her, "I see it too Mark. The vision is real, it's not just your imagination. That's Howard, the man I saw fall during my vision on willingness".

They both watched as Tom repelled down, untangled Howard's ropes, and slowly lowered him to safety. As they watched the rescue unfold, their vision began to speed up as they observed the scene play out many times faster than in real time. The vision blurred, and the scene of Howard's rescue faded.

After a few moments their vision slowed down, and a new scene unfolded. They found themselves again observing Howard's tall thin frame, but he looked much older than he appeared just moments earlier in the previous vision. He now appeared to be about 20 years older, in his 70s. His hair was totally gray, and his skin was covered with wrinkles and age spots.

Paula and Mark listened to Howard's distinctive English accent, as he taught a small class in a living room. On a whiteboard, he had written:

Self-Parenting exercises will help you fulfill your emotional dependency needs that were not met by your caretakers.

**

Paula psychically commented, "It's great to see how far Howard has spiritually evolved since his near-death experience. I guess it helped him to learn some very important life lessons."

"Yeah. This is incredible. I feel honored to be able to witness this man's life like this."

***

Howard told the small group that his most important life lesson was learning how to *Self-parent*[26] his inner child. He courageously lowered his egoic walls and shared, "My childhood wounds affected my adult life in many dysfunctional ways. If I could only teach you one thing, it would be how to Self-parent your inner child. After practicing these Self-parenting exercises for several years, my 'Little Howard' feels almost real to me. I feel what he is feeling, especially when the person or thing triggering me is anchored to a childhood feeling, like when 'Little Howard' felt scared, lonely or hurt."

One of Howard's older male students blurted, "I'm sorry. I'm not trying to be disruptive, but this sounds ridiculous."

"I know what you mean, Larry, because that's exactly how I felt when I was first introduced to this empowering work. It wasn't until I met my outdoor adventure coach, Tom, that I was able to transcend my Self-parenting doubts."

---

[26] Self-parent: refers to self-nurturing exercises that will help you fulfill your emotional dependency needs that were not met when you were a child.

Howard could see that Larry was not satisfied with his answer. He carefully considered his student's criticism and continued, "Alright, Larry. Let me explain it another way. How old are you?"

"How old am I? Um. 58. Why?"

"You'll see. OK. I'd like you to imagine the stump of a 58-year-old tree that was sawed down. If you examined it closely you will see one ring for each year of the tree's life; so, for your life you would see 58 rings."

"And upon closer examination, you would see that the rings varied in thickness. The thickness of the rings indicates the degree of nourishment the tree absorbed through its roots for each year it was alive."

Larry stared at Howard blankly. "I'm not making the connection. What do the tree's rings have to do with Self-parenting exercises?"

"You're just like that tree, Larry. You are an accumulation of 58 years of experiences. During some of those years you received a lot of love and emotional support, while other years you didn't. For the tree, in some years it got all the water and minerals it needed. You can tell those years by its thick rings. While in other years, its nourishment needs weren't met. You can tell those years by the thin rings.

Like the tree, all your years of tough life experiences, or 'learns and burns', as I like to call them, still live within you. So, if you emotionalize your Self-parenting exercises you will fortify and nourish the years when you didn't get all of your emotional dependency needs met."

Joey, another of Howard's students, raised his hand and asked, "How exactly is saying loving things to myself supposed to change my childhood wounds?"

"Good question, Joey. Before I answer, I want you to know that your skepticism is perfectly normal. I couldn't move past my disbelief either until I realized that practicing these exercises just a few times would not create the changes I sought. They aren't magical, mystical, and they aren't mysterious either. They are well-grounded, psycho-spiritual exercises that work for anyone willing to do the required work."

Howard observed Joey uncross his arms and sit up straight to the edge of his chair. He knew Joey's doubt was beginning to wane because his body language had shifted, which motivated Howard to explain further. "Joey, the Self-parenting exercises work for the same reason physical exercise works. Imagine that a bathtub filled with 100 proof whiskey represented all your negative childhood experiences. Then imagine that for every Self-parenting exercise you practice, you diluted the whiskey with 16 ounces of water. If you only did a few Self-parenting exercises, they would make little to no difference. But if you consistently practiced Self-parenting exercises for 30 minutes a day for 100 days, slowly but surely the water would begin to dilute the whiskey.

With each Self-parenting exercise, you would dilute the emotional intensity of your painful childhood memories, and you would replace them with unconditionally loving memories. And if you fully committed to this healing process, then in a year your improvements would be clinically quantifiable.

The Self-parenting techniques take the abstract theoretical concept of Self-parenting and break it down piece by piece into a simple and specific set of emotionally self-nurturing exercises.

Self-parenting exercises will help you to fulfill your emotional dependency needs that weren't met by your caretakers. Fulfilling your own needs is a Self-parenting process that is designed to teach you four things."

Then on the whiteboard, he wrote:

1) How to be emotionally intimate with yourself and others

2) How to be unconditionally loving and accepting of yourself and others

3) How to nurture yourself and others

4) How to maturely protect your boundaries so that you will feel safe in the world

A tall beautiful dark-skinned woman raised her hand. When Howard acknowledged her, she asked, "What's the difference between inner child work and Self-parenting work?"

"Another great question! First, I'd like to take a moment to make sure that you fully grasp what this term 'inner child' means. It's your childlike memories and beliefs that are anchored to a time when you only had the power, knowledge, and physical strength of a small child. It takes time, but eventually your inner child will learn to trust the adult you as you consistently protect and nurture him or her with the adult powers that you didn't possess when you were a small powerless child.

So, to answer your question, inner child work is to Self-parenting as arithmetic is to algebra. Self-parenting takes inner child work and integrates it with clinically proven, spiritually based exercises that use a step-by-step, specific set of nurturing drills that have been clinically proven to create permanent behavioral change.

When I first learned to Self-parent 'Little Howard' it felt like I was trying to sweet-talk a newly adopted child to trust me as his new adoptive parent. My macho ego tried to devalue Self-parenting, but over time the exercises helped me to dis-create my emotionally dark mental habits. These permanent behavioral changes enabled me to cultivate many intimate relationships, which had a huge, positive effect on my well-being.

Slowly but surely, Self-parenting exercises taught me how to be my number one fan, advocate, encourager, comforter, and best friend. They also taught me how to do the same thing with the people I love, like my spouse, children, and friends."

He turned his back to the class and wrote on the board:

Self-parenting exercises are a fast, safe way for you to surface, release and heal your emotionally dark, repressed feelings.

He faced the class and continued, "You can *rewire* your internal programming with new healthy healing feelings. I can prove it! Close your eyes and imagine that you are sucking on a lemon. What you will notice is that you'll start to salivate. Why? Because your mind can't tell the difference between a real lemon and an imaginary one.

Therefore, when you practice your Self-parenting exercises repeatedly, your mind won't be able to tell the difference between your real childhood experiences and your empowering Self-parenting visualizations.

There are three especially striking, clinically quantifiable things about Self-parenting exercises." He then wrote on the board:

1) The speed with which you will feel better
2) The depth of your emotional healing
3) And how fast it develops your multi-sensory psychic powers

***

Mark was completely captivated by his out of body experience, but he didn't lose focus on the lesson he intended to learn. He mentally communicated to Paula, "I'm sure we are being guided to empower our students with Self-parenting action exercises that will help them achieve their spiritual purpose for incarnating."

Paula responded, "Yes, and it will also help them create the permanent behavioral changes that they need to achieve their personal and career goals."

***

Howard continued his lesson by teaching the class why *validating* is the most *esoteric*[27] skill of Self-parenting, "Validation means to give value to your healing feelings with well-grounded evidence as to why your feelings aren't right, wrong, good, or bad; they are just what you are experiencing in that moment. *Validation is the opposite of egoic resistance.* Therefore, when you validate yourself, your ego is out of a job, because it has nothing to deny, repress, or minimize about what you are experiencing.

---

[27]Esoteric: difficult to understand; mysterious; meta-physical.

Validating does not mean that you are condoning or excusing your behavior. It means that you are accepting what is *as is*. A Self-mastered person will use validation techniques every time their ego gets triggered, and they will keep validating until they feel better.

Mastering *personal boundaries* is another very important element of Self-parenting. Mature boundaries could be compared to a medieval drawbridge that you leave open to let love, abundance and intimacy in; but which you can quickly close when someone violates your boundaries. Boundary literacy is one of the most important elements of healthy relationships. If you don't learn how to maturely protect your boundaries and respect other people's boundaries, you will use childlike ego defenses such as withdrawing or retaliating to defend yourself.

Let's move on to another aspect of Self-parenting: Forgiveness." He then asked the class, "Why is Forgiveness a Self-protection mechanism?"

Silence.

Howard continued, "*Forgiveness* does not mean you condone what happened to you, only that you refuse to accept it as a toxic influence in your life. Forgiveness sets the prisoner free, and the prisoner is you. Not forgiving someone is like taking poison and hoping the other person will die. Or as some people would say, it's like cutting your nose off to spite your face. It drains you of your Life Force Energy, and it anchors your pain to you. Whereas, forgiveness frees up huge amounts of your Life Force Energy, which you can then use to create emotionally mature relationships that you so richly deserve."

Howard took a deep breath; and with a lot of passion he shared, "As a child, I needed a parent's love, nurturing, and emotional maturity to fulfill my emotional dependency needs, but now I am an adult. I still need to get my emotional dependency needs met, but now I fulfill my needs from within. As a Self-parented adult, I have gone from needing a parent's love to needing God's love; from wanting toys to wanting inner peace and emotional maturity."

Howard paused briefly before emphatically stating, "Understand class. Your *reward* for not forgiving someone is to remain enmeshed[28] with them, which is why it is your Self-parenting job to remember the lesson and forget the experience."

* * *

As Howard's final words rang, Paula and Mark's vision began to fade. Slowly, they left Howard and his class

---

[28] Enmeshed: Emotionally and psychologically over connected with another personal typically a parent.

behind and their formless state of consciousness was consumed in a kaleidoscope of colors. The pair felt their formless bodies pull, twist, and turn radically as though they were being pulled through a hole in space and time.

The experience was familiar for Paula, but for Mark the sensations from this first experience were a little difficult to bear. But as quickly as it began, the colors faded to black, and their formless bodies returned to a resting state. When they opened their eyes, they were still facing each other in the same meditative pose in which they had started.

Mark reflected on his first Vision Quest with a mixture of shock and awe. It was strange to have psychically felt what Howard and Paula were feeling and hear their thoughts as if they all shared one mind. The experience had been an eclectic mix of surreal and enlightening at the same time. He hardly had enough time to drink it all in when Paula broke the silence.

"The God Source's Omniscient powers taught us exactly what we need to do. Now we know how to instruct our students how to fulfill their emotional dependency needs!"

Paula was awash with joy. Her first Vision Quest with Mark was a complete success. She was pleasantly surprised by how easily Mark followed her instructions. She understood that the synergistic effect of doing their

Vision Quest as partners would accelerate the development of their Spiritual Awakening course.

She intuitively knew that she had shared numerous lifetimes with Mark, sometimes as friends, sometimes as mother and son, sometimes as siblings, and sometimes as husband and wife. She felt blessed to know that the synergy their spiritual partnership created would enable them to tap into the Universal well of Omnipotent wisdom.

With all these thoughts running through her mind, Paula looked at Mark. She saw the man that pulled her unconscious body from the ocean and saved her life when he'd lost the will to save his own. She saw the man that lived through an unspeakable tragedy and somehow emerged on the other side stronger and wiser than he had been before. She now saw something that she had never seen before. Beyond all the positive traits she had already observed, now she saw that he was a handsome, smart soul who was willing to do the required work to change his old paradigms. After contemplating this, she knew that it was time to stop denying that her feelings about Mark were just an infatuation.

Mark was silent for several minutes, so Paula asked, "Hey, you okay?"

"I'm more than okay. I'm feeling a deep sense of gratitude that I got to experience this Vision Quest adventure with you."

Without saying a word, they both stood up and gave each other a long tender hug knowing that they were both blessed to have shared a transformational experience that most people only read about in books.

As they embraced, Mark noticed the same feelings he'd had earlier. *What is this?* He wondered. At the same time, he couldn't deny the sense of admiration he felt for Paula. This woman had helped him in so many ways. *How can I ever repay her?* he wondered.

At some deep level, he knew he was willing to spend the rest of his life trying to answer that question. He profoundly appreciated how much Paula had changed his life for the better. He not only came back from the brink of despair, but he was also more psycho-spiritually grounded than ever before, and he had Paula to thank for it. He wanted to make sure that she knew how much she meant to him.

At that exact moment, Mark had a thought that simultaneously both excited and scared him because his intuitive heart already knew what his mind wasn't willing to own yet.

Lesson #8 Of
Transformational Awakening Is...

✱Self-Parenting Exercises

Are experiential exercises designed to fulfill your emotional dependency needs that weren't met when you were a child. Emotional dependency needs are the intimacy, nurturing, unconditional love and boundary protection that you need to feel safe, sane, and secure in the world.

CHAPTER 13

Spiritual Communications

Using the Language of Your Intuitive Heart

The following day should have been an ordinary day at work for Mark, but it was anything but normal. He arrived at the office the same time as usual. He processed a few new cases and continued with his usual routine, but he couldn't stop thinking about Paula. Several times throughout the day, he stared blankly at his monitor, consumed by conflicting emotions.

He looked at Paula differently now than when they had first started working together. Now he felt affection toward her; but at the same time, he felt guilty. Ann had been the love of his life. If things had gone differently, he would have married Ann, had children and spent the rest of his life with her. Nevertheless, he couldn't deny the positive effect Paula had on him. As much as he missed Ann, working with Paula made him feel good about himself. Interacting with her made him feel more holistically grounded than he had ever felt in his entire life. He longed to be with someone as wonderful as Paula, but his feelings for Paula made him feel as though he was being disloyal to the memory of his deceased fiancé. He wrestled with his thoughts, and eventually his mind concluded that it would be best to ignore his feelings for Paula. *I just can't*, he thought. He just wasn't ready.

***

Paula spent her morning organizing her notes, preparing for the next Vision Quest, and working on the next lesson plan. After several hours of focused work, she felt pleased with her progress and decided to do her favorite yoga workout on the beach and set aside some time for inner reflection.

When she arrived at the beach, she set up her mat and did a brief meditation to clear her mind and get grounded. As she started her yoga routine, she couldn't resist the flood of emotions that kept surfacing about Mark. He had become more than just a spiritual friend. When he released his victim identity and revealed his true Self, her feelings toward him shifted.

Paula longed to be in a consciously awakened relationship with a man she loved and respected, but she thought there were too many red flags for being in a relationship with Mark. Barely a year had passed since he had lost his fiancé; and even if he didn't seem like it, he was still mourning. Mark was essentially a widower. No matter how much she wanted to, Paula couldn't pursue her feelings of attraction for Mark with a clear conscience. She respected the emotional bond Mark had shared with Ann. She realized that making any advances toward him in his emotionally vulnerable state would not only be unwise, but it would be unethical and a violation of his boundaries. She cared too much about Mark to disrespect his grieving process, so she resigned to keeping their relationship strictly professional and repressing her true feelings for him.

* * *

When Mark arrived at Paula's that evening, they greeted each other with a warm hug and immediately started making necessary preparations for their next Vision Quest. They set a conscious intention to *surrender* to the God Source and open their hearts, so they could receive the next lesson of their Spiritual Awakening course. They faced each other in a meditative pose and focused their attention on the mantra word, "Namasté." They took deep slow breaths. The longer they meditated, the quieter their minds became and the faster they fell into an alpha state of Consciousness where their minds gradually harmonized as one.

As the spiritual partners continued to surrender to the God Source, a vision began to unfold. As it gradually became clearer, Paula immediately recognized the scene. They were observing a woman perched on the side of a jagged stone jetty in a ravine sandwiched between tall sheer cliffs. Beneath her, waves violently crashed into the stone walls of the gorge. As the waves receded, they revealed copious amounts of sea urchins wedged among the rocks between the woman and the open water. The woman seemingly had no way out of the situation other than diving into the tumultuous sea. She wore a terrified expression on her face as she observed the tidal patterns.

Delighted to see the continuation of her earlier vision, Paula psychically shared with Mark, "Oh my God, I know this scene! We've been brought to the moment when Donna was about to jump into the water!"

Even though it was only their second Vision Quest together, the experience of hearing each other's thoughts felt perfectly natural for them. They telepathically communicated with effortless ease as if they had done so for years.

"Looks like we'll get to find out what happened to her after all." Mark replied.

***

Donna studied the details of the ravine's floor and realized the task was even more perilous than she had initially thought. The sea urchins were adorned with ten-inch-long spines, and they rested in every crevice. She knew their spines were filled with poison and it was critical that she make her escape without so much as brushing against one. She observed the wave cycles for almost an hour, until she recognized a narrow window where the water was deep enough to swim to safety. Her timing needed to be perfect; if she waited too long to jump in, the next powerful wave would slam her onto the rocks and into the venomous urchins.

She slowly inched her way onto the jetty with fins in one hand and snorkel and mask in the other. She only had a few seconds to put on her equipment, jump in, and swim 30 feet to reach the safety of the open sea. She paused briefly to build her confidence and say a short prayer. She tried her best to repress the anxiety which was building inside, but she knew that there was nothing left to do other than take the plunge.

With no further delay, she took a deep breath and surrendered her fate to God, knowing it was now or never. She jumped in screaming at the top of her lungs, "HELP ME, LORD!" Instantly, Donna's adrenalin kicked in, and she swam with all her might, fighting the powerful incoming waves until she reached the safety of the deep ocean.

***

The spiritual partners felt Donna's emotional sigh of relief as she left the hazardous ravine behind her and silently thanked God for saving her life. Mark and Paula felt honored and humbled that they had been granted the opportunity to experience this life-altering adventure with Donna.

"Wow. I felt like I was in the water with her. The moment Donna jumped into the water, I instantly felt a chill pass through my whole body! Have all your previous visions been this kinesthetic?" Mark telepathically asked Paula.

"They have. It's why I've been so enthusiastic to continue pushing our work forward at the pace we've been keeping. It's truly an incredible experience." Paula responded.

***

Donna could see the ocean floor through the clear water on the Atlantic side of the Caribbean. Although she found the depth of the water visually uncomfortable at first, after a few moments her depth perception adjusted, and she could easily perceive the beauty beneath her. The exquisiteness of the underwater tapestry was so mesmerizing that she momentarily forgot about her situation and became absorbed in the beauty of nature's aquatic creations. After she regained her composure, she steadily worked her way back to where her adventure had begun hours earlier. She maintained a safe distance from the shore to avoid getting slammed by the waves into the jagged rocks which lined the coast.

Estimating that she had circumnavigated roughly 80 percent of the island, Donna slowed her pace. Her heart rate returned to normal, and she was able to be fully present and appreciate the extraordinary view that extended in all directions. She was astounded by the contours of the sea floor as it plunged hundreds of feet in some places while it dipped only thirty feet in others. The multicolored coral and schools of brightly colored fish bathed her eyes with an exuberant sense of wonder. But that all changed when she noticed three large sharks patrolling the ocean floor roughly 75 feet below. Her blood ran cold, and her heart started pounding. The theme from the movie *Jaws* boomed in her head as her breath quickened and her mind ran through every terrifying scenario she could think of. Without realizing it, her swimming accelerated to a frantic pace. She was wise enough to know that panicked activity attracted sharks, but she was unable to resist her instinctual urge to flee.

Donna didn't realize it at the time; but at that moment, her intuitive Self took control. Her breathing began to relax, which in turn slowed her panicked strokes. She heard a small voice within her repeatedly say, *I am one with nature. I am one with nature.*

As her mind calmed, Donna reassessed her situation and realized that the sharks were so far below that they didn't even notice her; or if they did, they weren't the least bit interested. At that point, she stopped fearing for her life and started appreciating the beauty and grace of these creatures which have existed since before dinosaurs.

Eventually, the sharks swam away and disappeared into the deep blue of the ocean. Donna popped her head up to check her bearings. She surveyed the shoreline and realized that the last bend she had passed was only a few hundred yards from the beach where she had left her friend several hours earlier. Eventually, the sea floor grew more and more barren until the vibrant coral reef gave way to white sand. She continued swimming until it was more practical for her to take off her fins and walk. As soon as she stood, she heard Deb yell, "Where have you been?! I was ready to call the coast guard! What happened to you?"

"I'm sorry I scared you." Donna said as she reached dry land. "I will tell you what happened. First, I need to rest. Is that alright with you?" She said with a slight defensive tone.

"Of course. I was just worried sick. I thought something bad had happened."

Donna laid flat on her back to stretch her tired lower back muscles and to recuperate from her long stressful swim. She closed her eyes and reflected on her adventure. She was thankful that she was able to receive spiritual communications, especially when her life was at risk. As a spiritually-based therapist with decades of experience, she knew that spiritual communications *weren't conceptual* and to receive them she needed to transcend her thinking mind. She thought back to all the clients she had coached and how she'd taught them to feel their feelings. It troubled her to consider that such a vital ability could be so easily overlooked because society incorrectly rewards people for suppressing their emotions. As a result, people have little incentive or motivation to learn how to tune into their intuitive communications.

Most of her clients were conditioned to process their feelings through their thinking minds as a defense mechanism to avoid feeling their uncomfortable feelings. Countless times, she had told her clients that they can't *think* their feelings; they either *feel* what they are feeling, or they repress what they are feeling with thoughts. With that thought, Donna fell asleep for some much-needed rest.

***

Mark shared with Paula, "Learning to interpret the language of my intuitive heart is one of the most valuable spiritual lessons that Coach Sarah is helping me to master."

"Yes, it's one of the most valuable life lessons for all of us incarnates to learn." Paula added.

***

Donna woke from her nap feeling refreshed and rejuvenated with an empowering realization. She realized that every time her life was threatened, her mind shut down and her intuitive spiritual communications turned on. Her intuitive Self kicked in when she slowed her breathing, calmed her mind and focused; and when she *surrendered*, her intuitive Self *guided* her to take the necessary survival measures.

Slowly, she sat up ready to share her ordeal with Deb.

Deb was upset, but she was wise enough to give Donna a few moments to compose herself before she asked, "You swam off, and I thought you would be back in 20 minutes. But as the minutes turned to hours I became more and more frightened. Why were you gone so long? You scared the hell out of me!"

Donna spoke softly, "Listening to my sacred heart saved me, Deb."

"What do you mean, 'saved you'?! What the hell happened?"

Donna recapped the highlights from her aquatic adventure, and how she had surrendered to her intuitive Self at each critical junction in order to survive. Retelling the details of her experience triggered a memory of a guru who taught her that Consciousness is in her sacred heart, not in her mind or brain. She had never really grasped what he meant, but her reflection created an epiphany. Up to this point, she had only *intellectualized*[29] what her guru had said; but because of this life-threatening experience, she was now able to *emotionalize* this valuable life lesson.

She looked at Deb with love in her eyes and said, "My fear of dying shut down the egoic part of my mind. This allowed me to experience brief moments of clarity where my intuition, not my thinking mind, took control and guided me to what I needed to do next. Deb, it's why I survived the most terrifying experience of my life.

When I was most frightened, I surrendered to God. As soon as I did, a warm calm feeling came over me, and I

---

[29]Intellectualized: Intellectual knowledge is easier to acquire than emotional knowledge because conceptual thought does not require you to change your behavior. Self-Mastery, A Journey Home to Your Inner Self; Renaissance Publishing 2008; page 19,

knew that it was coming from my sacred heart. When I felt *most* afraid, my sacred heart took control. I now realize that I'm always in communion with my inner God Self, even when I don't realize that I am.'

***

Upon hearing Donna's inspirational words, Paula was struck with a revelation of her own, which she telepathically communicated to Mark, "Hmm. Donna's realization reminds me of a quote from the Unity Church Founder, Charles Fillmore. He said, 'Intuition is the wisdom of the heart.' I now understand what he meant. Charles knew that the heart's intuition is a much more powerful processing system than the intellectual mind.

I believe that on a subliminal level, we all know that the heart is the center of Consciousness, and the physical heart is a visible expression of the invisible sacred heart."

Mark added his insight, "When I first started seeing Coach Sarah, she taught me that spiritual surrender is the intersection between acceptance and change. At first, I didn't fully grasp the concept; but now I realize that every time I consciously connect to my sacred heart, it helps me muster up the emotional courage to unconditionally accept God's Will for me."

"That's very profound Mark." Paula continued to share, "I memorized a poem many years ago that I think you'd appreciate. It helped me understand why my 'disturbing feelings' are reasons for celebration, not aggravation. It goes like this:

When I regard a so-called disturbing feeling as a mistake,
my spiritual practice becomes a path of needing to fix myself.
Thus, my spiritual practice becomes the long path.
If I indulge in my so-called disturbing feeling, "thinking"
it's something concrete when it's only relatively real;
then my disturbing feeling becomes
the cause that binds me to my karma.
But if I look directly into my so-called disturbing feeling,
and I don't deliberately reject it, or regard it as a fault, or
indulge in it concretely, or see it as a virtue; if I just feel it and
allow it to be what it is, an intuitive message from my Spirit;
then all my so-called disturbing feelings that arise
are wisdom the moment
I relax enough to feel them with the awareness that
what I'm feeling is perfect for
the evolution of my immortal soul."

***

Donna's story had triggered Deb, because as a young girl she had nearly drowned. To *deflect* her scared feelings, she shared something a psychology professor had taught her, "You need to honor your intuitive communications by facing them, embracing them, and then releasing them. I like to tell my clients that their objective is to feel and release what happened if they want to stop unconsciously reliving it. I say, 'It's better to feel your pain for 10 minutes to release it, than to keep reliving it repeatedly in your mind for the next 10 years.'

To be honest Donna, I know I still have some feel and release work to do from when I almost drowned. The intensity of my reaction to your story was way over the top, which proves I too haven't yet fully processed my feelings about almost drowning."

Donna said with a big smile, "I commend your emotional honesty. Yeah. And to be perfectly honest with you, in the past I only changed when the pain of holding onto my pain became greater than the fear of taking the required action needed in order to transcend it."

***

Without warning, Paula and Mark's vision began to fade, and they found themselves drifting out of their formless state of Consciousness into a kaleidoscope of colors. They opened their eyes, and Paula smiled when she saw Mark's look of astonishment. For her, the Vision Quest experience had become ritualistic, but she could see that it still amazed Mark.

Seeing Mark's reaction reignited reverence within her for being part of this Vision Quest evolutionary process. With awe, Paula shared, "Mark, many souls like us spend years collecting and consuming metaphysical books and audios and attending workshops until we finally reach a point where we are spiritually ready to sit quietly with an open heart and consciously listen to our own inner intuitive wisdom."

Paula's words filled Mark with warmth. She was so intelligent and spiritually grounded; and yet, she had an innocent, loving quality that was enchanting. He smiled back at her and shared, "I think I understand now, Paula. My rational mind cannot fully understand or appreciate the spiritual communications which I yearn to receive because my rational mind can't fully comprehend them."

"That's heavy, Mark. And it's why we must go beyond knowing to a place where we are spiritually one if we want to hear our spiritual communications. We must go beyond form to transcend our roles and identities and receive the spiritual communications that our sacred heart is sending us."

Paula and Mark exchanged notes and shared their thoughts and feelings about their joint vision. Paula was as astute as always in her observations, and Mark's contributions really impressed her, especially since it was only his second time to share a vision with her.

As they conversed about their vision and lessons learned, Paula felt a tranquil sensation take hold of her. Mark had changed so much since she'd first met him. The broken man who pulled her from the ocean was gone.

Over the past few months, she began to see him for who he truly is; a caring soul who had transcended some very challenging 'learns and burns.'

Mark was steadfast, strong-willed, and kind. Yet as much as he had learned, there was still an innocence in the way he processed life. He was relatively new to the metaphysical world, but he tackled the challenge with an enthusiasm that was enviable. Paula was impressed. She felt blessed to be on this spiritual adventure with him. Even if it was only as a friend and coworker, his companionship filled her heart with warm loving feelings.

Paula looked up from her notebook. Mark had a puzzled look on his face. She could tell he was thinking about something, so she smiled and asked, 'What are you processing?"

Mark met Paula's glance, and he said. "Well. I was thinking about what you said; about going beyond form and transcending our identities. And I realized that this whole time we've been floating down our Vision Quest's river without a rudder. It got me thinking, what if we could intentionally direct our Vision Quests?"

"What do you mean?"

"Well. I feel that it would be a huge benefit to master how to intentionally direct our visions to include Universal knowledge on things we specifically want to learn more about. For example, one of the most important transformational lessons Coach Sarah taught me was how to dis-create my negative beliefs. Do you think we could ask the God Source to teach us about dis-creation in our next Vision Quest?"

"I don't see why not! Regardless though, I don't see any harm in experimenting with your idea. Let's try it! Let's see if we have the ability to be the directors of our Vision Quest adventures!"

Lesson #9 Of
Transformational Awakening Is...

SPIRITUAL
COMMUNICATION

Is the language that allows your life
to be directed by your Intuitive Heart,
the source of infinite wisdom, love,
and compassion. It is what
synergistically connects you
with all living things via the
Namasté Consciousness.

CHAPTER 14

Dis-Creation is the Missing Link

You Need to Clean Your Mind of Negative Programming

Together, Paula and Mark organized their notes and prepared for their next Vision Quest session. As they did, Mark thought back to when Coach Sarah first taught him about dis-creation. She told him it would clean his mind of negative beliefs, and in turn, create space for new positive ones. He was surprised to learn that the creation cycle had been taught by metaphysicians for centuries. It originated with the ancient Greeks. *Dis-creation, however, is a new rediscovery.* It is the missing link in the conscious creation process. Aristotle taught his students that the mind is a clean tablet upon which experience writes, and it is believed that the term *Tabula Rasa*, which means "clean slate", came from this philosophy.

Mark remembered his first coaching session, when Coach Sarah said, "If you desire love, but your mind is filled with failed relationship beliefs, these contradictory thoughts will nullify your positive efforts and stop you from attracting the loving relationship you desire." Coach Sarah taught Mark that every experience of his life was inscribed on the slate of his psyche. And if he didn't periodically clean his mind, it would eventually become layered with opposing thoughts, such as "I'm loved and accepted" and "No one likes me." She had told him, "You cannot keep your mind focused on "I'm loved and accepted" and "No one likes me" at the same time because no two objects can occupy the same space at the same time."

Psychologists have proven that people produce over 50,000 thoughts a day and that 80 percent of those thoughts are negative. Mark reflected, I'm 33 years old. I've had over 600 million thoughts, and since 80 percent are negative, my mind is layered with nearly a half-billion negative thoughts. So, even if I do 100 positive affirmations a day, my mind would still be filled with 50,000 negative thoughts to the contrary. That would be like trying to bail out a sinking boat with a thimble!

The affirmation-only concept assumes that I've had a holistic life with nothing but functional role models. It assumes that my mind is a clean slate, free of past pain, loss, and dysfunctional experiences. That definitely is not the case!

According to this theory, people can pile on positive affirmations over a dysfunctional past and still create the reality they want; but as Mark discovered during his early sessions with Coach Sarah, the "pile it on" theory alone does not work. When Mark was younger, he repeatedly tried to use positive affirmations to create the reality he wanted, but to no avail. Through his sessions with Coach Sarah, he learned that the more he piled on without getting the results he desired, the dirtier the slate of his mind became. This was why he initially had trouble motivating himself to continue doing his self-help work. He was grateful that Coach Sarah was intuitive enough to be aware of his difficulties, so she helped him clean his mind of old negative beliefs. With Coach Sarah's help, Mark learned that his mind was so cluttered with contradictory information that it was preventing him from inputting the new programs that he desired to experience.

Mark learned that he couldn't create the permanent positive change he desired until he dis-created his old unwanted programming. To erase his negative beliefs, he first needed to see the whole truth of what happened to him in his past, without judgment, regret, or shame. Only after his mind had been cleaned of negative beliefs would he be able to create the reality he wanted by using affirmations.

Mark remembered a quote from the highly esteemed psychologist Carl Jung that he had read about in one of his Self-mastery assignments: "Until you make the unconscious conscious, it will direct your life, and you will call it fate." Mark chuckled to himself. At the time, he couldn't fully appreciate Jung's words. But he now fully understood that reciting affirmations without cleaning his mind was like putting on a white shirt after working in the mud and not understanding why the shirt was dirty.

***

Mark snapped himself out of reminiscing, and asked Paula, "You ready to begin?"

Mark sat down and assumed his meditation position while Paula prepared the room for their third Vision Quest adventure together. She lit a candle and some incense and added some ambiance by playing a soundtrack of Tibetan bells in the background. When she was satisfied with the atmosphere, Paula took her position across from Mark and together they began their spiritual grounding ritual. This time they added an intentional prayer and asked the God Source to manifest a vision about dis-creation. They focused their attention on the word "Namasté" and breathed slowly until they drifted into a deep state of bliss. Soon they were greeted with a vision that became clearer and clearer the more they surrendered to the precious *be-here-now* moment.

As their vision came into focus, the pair found themselves in an open, empty room with tall ceilings and tables cluttered with ancient-looking scrolls. A map hung on the wall with a grossly inaccurate representation of the Earth's continents. In the farthest corner of the room, there stood a detailed marble statue depicting a muscular man prepared to throw a disc.

With intrigue in their hearts, Mark and Paula began to investigate their fascinating surroundings. Mark focused his attention on the table in the center of the room and tried to determine the language on the open parchment scrolls. Though he wasn't an expert on linguistics, he surmised that the text was Greek. This theory was supported by the disc-thrower statue as well as the architectural columns and small arches in the room.

Paula's focus wandered to the far side of the room where she explored through an open doorway and down a flight of steps which opened to a large courtyard. There, Paula was provided with a remarkable view of the surrounding area. She was perched near the top of a high mountain which overlooked a large and seemingly ancient bustling city.

"Hey Mark, you have to come see this!"

Mark reached the courtyard and was astounded by the view.

"It's incredible, isn't it? The architecture and clothing look characteristic of ancient times. Where do you think the God Source has brought us?" She asked.

Mark surveyed the city below. "Well. I'm not an expert but look at the clothing. Everyone has a toga draped over their shoulders. And notice the architecture of the buildings. With the porticos and large marble columns," he chuckled to himself, "I'd say we're in ancient Greece."

"What's so funny?"

"It's just that I've always loved the stories about the Greek gods, the Trojan War, and the Spartan warrior society, and now I'm experiencing it as if I were transported back in time. It's incredible!"

"It definitely is."

The ensuing silence was broken by the sound of voices in the distance.

"You hear that?"

"I do. Let's check it out." Mark said with excitement.

The pair marveled at the beauty of their environment, as they followed the faint sound of the voices through the garden. They progressed deeper and admired the garden's many statues, manicured shrubs and shallow reflecting pools. Eventually they came to a clearing where a group of about a dozen men gathered. An older man faced the group and lectured. He looked to be in his early 60s. He had gray hair and was dressed in an untidy white toga. The audience sat on ornately decorated wooden benches, and they furiously scribbled notes on parchment scrolls while they listened to the lecture. The speaker's face wore signs of age, experience, and wisdom. He spoke slowly, putting proper emphasis on his words and choosing each statement carefully. It was evident to the spiritual partners that the speaker was an esteemed teacher, not just because of the way he carried himself, but because of the amount of attention he commanded from his audience.

Paula and Mark were amazed that, even though the man spoke in a foreign language, they understood his words as if he were speaking modern English.

They intently watched as a tall, young man raised his hand and asked, "Sir, I don't understand. Why is it so important for me to clean the slate of my mind?"

"It is important because your mind is a tablet upon which experience writes, you cannot write new positive ideas over conflicting negative beliefs. Two objects cannot occupy the same space at the same time."

***

At that moment Mark grokked why the God Source had taken them back to ancient Greece.

"Oh my God, Paula! I know exactly why we are here! Tabula Rasa. Ancient Greece. We've been taken back to Aristotle's school in Macedon. That must be him. We're watching one of his lectures about Tabula Rasa!"

"I know. It's so exciting! Let's see what else he has to teach us."

***

Aristotle explained that to create the reality his students wanted, they needed to create a detailed vision of their desire as an already accomplished fact. But first, they had to clean their minds of negative thoughts before any action plan they designed could create the positive change that they desired.

"But what if my life doesn't match my vision?" Another tall young man asked.

"My dear Alexander. The only place where that can happen is in your mind. You can visualize the object of your desires. You have a body that can act on your plan, but you won't manifest your desire to conquer the world if your mind is a dirty slate filled with fear." Aristotle answered.

***

Aristotle's words triggered an unexpected memory for Paula. She learned from her own experiences that before she could create a loving relationship, she needed to learn how to dis-create her old dysfunctional beliefs. She knew that once she cleared her repressed feelings and defensive reactive behavior about her former partner's less-than-perfect behavior from her mind, she could attract the functionally mature relationship that she longed for.

She remembered a powerful quote by St. Thomas, "If you bring forth what is within you, what you bring forth will save you. If you do not bring forth what is within you, what you do not bring forth will destroy you."

She knew that every day there are many kind, loving people who are unconsciously imprinting negative programs deep into their minds. These people are unknowingly creating the same pain and loss repeatedly because our subconscious minds do not judge, reason, or think. Instead, our minds replay our old fear-based programs, memories, feelings, and beliefs no matter how dysfunctional they may be. And this negative cycle continues until we learn how to clean the slate of our minds with dis-creation exercises.

**

Paula brought her focus back to their vision just in time to catch Aristotle explaining to his students that the Tabula Rasa process (dis-creation) is based on Three Laws of Healing:

Nothing changes until it becomes what it is

No two objects can occupy the same space at the same time

Your beliefs create your reality

***

Unexpectedly, Paula and Mark's vision began to fade. They found themselves drifting out of their formless state of consciousness into the kaleidoscope of colors.

Mark opened his eyes to find himself facing Paula. She met his gaze, and the two shared a brief reflective silence until Mark shared, "When I learned that 80 percent of my beliefs are below my conscious level of awareness and that I see right through them as if they were glass, it made me appreciate how important my dis-creation exercises are."

Paula nodded her head in agreement. She considered her feelings and what she had learned during their Vision Quest and humbly admitted, "I was shocked when I first surfaced my unconscious negative beliefs. As a student of positive thinking, I thought I was a positive person! But I didn't have a clue how much negative programming I had unconsciously downloaded into my mind."

Thousands of years ago, Aristotle taught that we couldn't dis-create what we couldn't hear ourselves sub-vocalizing[30]. Before we can effectively create desirable

---

[30] Sub-vocalize: to utter words or sounds silently, especially when talking to oneself.

changes in our behavior, we must methodically train our minds to be consciously aware of our negatively programmed beliefs

Mark remembered something Coach Sarah taught him which simplified this lesson. "All you have to do is re-create what feels good and dis-create what doesn't feel good. The choice is yours, to choose love or fear."

Experience taught Paula that when a client avoided doing their dis-creation exercises, it was usually because their ego-minds were afraid to feel and release their repressed, painful feelings.

Paula felt very proud of what she and Mark had accomplished. Their joint Vision Quest had been a tremendous breakthrough, but their newfound ability to consciously create a vision to learn a precise lesson was above and beyond exciting for them. Suddenly nothing was out of their reach. If there was knowledge they needed to learn for their Awakening Course, they only needed to focus their attention on their desire and the God Source would provide it for them. She bowed her head and asked Mark to join her in a short prayer.

"Dear Lord, since dis-creation is the missing link of the conscious creation process, I pray that we humans will learn how to use it to remove the unconscious roadblocks that are short-circuiting our divine ability so we can unite as one via the Namasté Consciousness to help save humankind."

By the time Paula and Mark finished their debriefing, it was well into the evening. Feeling delighted with the breakthrough they had made, they decided to conclude their session for the night. Their discussion remained focused on their work until Mark felt his stomach rumble.

"Well. It's late. I hate to say it, but I'm going to get some fast food on my way home."

Paula smiled widely at Mark. "Mr. Celli. You are a guest in my home. I could never, in good conscience, let you do that to your body after we just shared such an empowering evening together. I insist you stay for dinner! I'd love to cook us something healthy."

Mark raised an eyebrow and returned Paula's smile. "Well, if you insist, then I guess I have to. Out of respect. I'd hate to be rude." As he followed her to the kitchen, his mind analyzed the phrasing she'd used in her invitation. It was hard to put his finger on it, but he recognized somewhat of a flirtatious tone in her voice.

Mark put the thought out of his mind. "So, what's on the menu?"

"I was thinking something vegetarian. I don't want to brag, but I do make an especially tasty Ratatouille with Polenta."

"Sounds delicious. I'd love to try it." Mark had never heard of the dish, but he always enjoyed vegetarian food and was willing to try anything. Paula set about preparing the ingredients. She stepped away from the stove and searched through one of the kitchen cupboards. After a moment of careful deliberation, she produced a bottle of wine and two glasses, which she placed on the table next to Mark.

"Oh." Mark sighed with a worried tone in his voice.

"I figured a little something special to celebrate is in order. We did make a significant discovery tonight," Paula said as she poured herself a glass. She paused and made eye contact with Mark, not wanting to pressure him into drinking if he didn't want to. Mark grinned and extended his hand to ask for the bottle.

Paula handed Mark the bottle, and he read the label.

"Everything all right?" she asked, hoping she had not somehow offended him.

"It's fine. In all honesty, I haven't drunk anything since the night we first met. I guess I still associate some of the emotions I felt back then to alcohol."

"I'm sorry. I didn't know. I have V8 juice or water if you prefer?" Paula's face reddened. Suddenly she felt strangely nervous about entertaining her guest. Mark finished examining the bottle and looked back at Paula with a slight smile.

"It's fine. I've come a long way since then." He poured himself a glass and took a small sip. The two continued to sip their wine while Paula prepared the meal. When she finished, Mark was treated to a beautiful plate of well-seasoned vegetables and mushrooms, which he eagerly dove into.

Before they realized it, one glass had led to several while they enjoyed each other's company and holistic conversation. "I've got to say, Paula, thank you so much for this delicious meal. I haven't had home cooking since... since before the accident I suppose."

Paula noticed Mark's nonchalant tone while referring to his past. When she first met him, it was hard for him to speak about what happened without getting choked up. She didn't know if it was because of all the progress he'd made through his coaching sessions or if it was the wine that was doing the talking.

"Did Ann cook, or did you do the cooking?" Paula asked, taking advantage of Mark's newfound openness.

"Believe it or not, I cooked most of the time." Mark declared with a proud grin.

"Get out! I wouldn't have pegged you for a cook."

"Oh yeah. Well, with work I wouldn't always have the time. I have a few fancy dishes up my sleeve. Maybe next time I can cook dinner for you."

Paula shot a glance at Mark. She knew they had both been drinking, but she was still capable of detecting a line when she heard one. She smiled slightly and took another sip of her wine. She knew Mark felt a certain sense of pride in showing off for her. He'd displayed it every time he had a chance, especially when he wanted to show off some meta-knowledge he'd learned. She decided to put her concerns aside and play along.

"Careful Mister. You're getting my hopes up. You better hope you can make good on your offer. I hate being disappointed." Paula said in a faux stern and severe tone, as she furrowed her eyebrows and frowned slightly. She looked into Mark's eyes trying her best to hold the serious expression on her face. The two broke into laughter at the absurdity of Paula's uncharacteristic tone.

Mark took another sip of wine and gazed at Paula. Without any thought he asked, "Have you ever been married, Paula?"

Paula's expression shifted. Her eyes widened slightly and darted about the room before she refocused on Mark and answered, "No."

Mark noticed Paula's tentative behavior and felt compelled to push further. "I'm a little surprised to learn that someone with your compassionate and nurturing spirit never got married."

Paula took a moment to sip her wine. She stared off into the distance and occasionally looked back at Mark until she shared, "There was one guy that I dated for several years. I'd always thought that we'd get married. But one day, he just left. And that was it. Since then, I have been working on taking down my protective walls to allow me to be in an emotionally intimate relationship again. I'm a work-in-progress, and my method is to keep teaching others what I most need to learn and heal."

"I'm sorry," Mark said with a solemn tone. He wanted to find out more about what happened, but the wine made him talk without thinking, "For what it's worth, if this guy just left, then he may not have been mature enough to be in a relationship with you anyway. You deserve someone who is equally as capable of being in a spiritual relationship as you are."

Paula looked back at Mark. He looked straight back at her and smiled. She could tell by the look in his eyes that he had no ulterior motive or agenda. He only wanted to comfort her and offer his honest opinion to nurture her as she had nurtured him so many times before. Paula used her sleeve to wipe her teary eyes. She returned Mark's gaze and smiled, "Thank you, Partner."

Mark and Paula continued making small talk as they finished the wine and cleaned the kitchen together. All the while, Paula couldn't help but feel the now familiar flutter in her stomach. When they finished cleaning up, Paula saw Mark to the door.

As he stepped out, he turned to face her. "Thank you, Paula. This was a night to remember. The session, the home cooked meal, and just getting to chat and hang out. I had a lot of fun."

Paula looked into Mark's eyes and smirked. "Just remember Mr. Celli, you owe me a dinner."

Mark's gaze met Paula's, and for a moment neither of them spoke. Only the ambient sounds of chirping crickets echoed through the surrounding woods.

As Mark stared into Paula's eyes, he felt a familiar feeling. He instinctively knew what was supposed to happen next; this was the moment when he would usually lean in and kiss a beautiful soul like Paula goodnight. Yet he felt paralyzed. For as much as Mark's intuition told him what to do, his egoic mind said it was just too soon to try and escape the memory of his fiancé.

He leaned forward and gave Paula a friendly hug. He looked into Paula's eyes once again and said with a smile, "Goodnight, Paula." And he headed to his car.

"Goodnight." Paula echoed. She stood in place and waved as Mark pulled out of her driveway.

Within a matter of seconds after leaving, Mark realized that he had too much wine to be driving. He could have easily kept driving, but the memory of the traffic accident that killed his family surfaced to his consciousness. Mark would never risk being the cause of such pain for another human being, so he turned his car around and headed back to Paula's house.

As he stepped up to the door where Paula was still standing, the two of them looked at each other with knowing grins. Few words were needed. Paula intuitively knew what had just happened. She laughed, "One too many eh? I'll get you a blanket and pillow."

As Mark drifted off to sleep on Paula's sofa, he realized that they had just taken their relationship to a higher level. He felt deep gratitude toward Paula and enormous anticipation for how their relationship was evolving.

Mark awoke early the next morning. He wrote a quick thank you note and signed it with a big smiley face. He hurried out the door to get home and shower before going to work.

A few hours after Mark had left, Paula awoke. She instantly smiled when she read Mark's note, but then a feeling of deep sadness overwhelmed her. She knew that he was still in mourning, but she was no longer willing to deny that she longed to feel the comfort of his embrace.

Lesson #10 Of
Transformational Awakening Is...

Dis-Creation is
the Missing Link

Of the Conscious Creation process because
you must clean the slate of your mind
before your self-programming
affirmations can create the reality
you desire.

CHAPTER 15

The Magic of Emotionalizing

Makes Your Changes Permanent

While driving to work that morning, Mark was polarized with conflicting emotions. His mind kept dissecting his lack of action when he said goodnight to Paula. He knew that his thoughts were merely the product of his mind, but he couldn't stop wondering what might have happened if he had acted on his romantic instincts. Despite the myriad of thoughts, one was notably overpowering: that he couldn't do that to Ann. Regardless of what he might have done or felt, he was resolute in his decision to keep his relationship with

Paula strictly friendly and professional because he wasn't ready to move on with his love life just yet.

* * *

Later that afternoon, Paula sipped a tea as she awaited Mark's arrival. She had gotten an early start on her prep work for the day's session. She grabbed a pen and began to organize her thoughts. As she pondered what else they needed to learn for their course, she raised her notebook and wrote the word "Emotionalize[31]" at the top of the page. The word had repeatedly surfaced during her morning meditation. She felt strongly that they needed to learn more about the concept and how it could help their students create the permanent behavioral changes they desired. She firmly believed that creating permanent change would be one of the most important aspects of their course.

Paula continued making notes until there was a knock at her door. She eagerly jumped from her seat to greet Mark; and as she did, she felt the familiar sensation in her stomach. They welcomed each other with a hug, but Paula detected some uncharacteristic rigidity in Mark's energy. Her thoughts immediately returned to the

---

[31] Emotionalizing: helps to create permanent behavioral change because when you emotionalize your feelings with passion creates electromagnetic energy that changes your neuro pathways. Self-Mastery, A Journey Home to Your Inner Self; Renaissance Publishing 2008; page 19,

previous night when their hug lingered for a moment longer than usual. Paula was all too familiar with what *did not* happen that night. She knew she could be misreading the situation, but her intuitive heart said otherwise. The more she thought about it, the more she realized that she and Mark had the core ingredients to form a consciously awakened romantic relationship.

Ultimately, her analyzing had little value. Even though she was deeply attracted to Mark and viewed him as a man who had what it took to be her spiritual partner, she reminded herself that he still thought of himself as a widower. Any romantic actions would need to be initiated by him, lest she overstep his boundaries and damage their professional relationship, as well as their friendship.

After inviting Mark in, Paula handed him a cup of tea while they discussed their itinerary. Mark started reviewing Paula's notes, and she began telling him why she wanted to set an intention for the God Source to teach them about "emotionalizing". Mark enthusiastically agreed. It was exhilarating for him to know that by setting an intentional Vision Quest goal, they would receive what they needed from the God Source.

As excited as little children, they couldn't wait another minute to begin their next spiritual adventure. With their prep work completed, they began their ritual of playing Tibetan bell music, lighting a candle and incense, and sitting in their meditation positions facing each other. Together they slowed and synchronized their breathing and prayed to receive a Vision Quest about emotionalizing. They focused their attention on their mantra word until they drifted into a deep state of bliss. After 20 minutes they were greeted with a vision that became clearer the more they let go and surrendered.

***

They found themselves floating high above a five-acre sports complex a few hundred yards from a large river. Closer examination of the surroundings revealed a large expansion bridge with plenty of marine traffic passing below. From the volume of cars passing over the bridge and the numerous ships passing under, it was apparent that Mark and Paula were in a major metropolis.

The large athletic field bustled with activity. Though the players looked as tiny as ants to Mark and Paula, they could see a wide variety of athletes. As they descended, the school's insignia gradually came into focus until they could read it clearly: *Sacred Heart High School.* They watched a team running sprints as well as a few high jumpers and a lone shot putter practicing their skills. They also noticed a few dozen men in helmets and shoulder pads completing football drills on the artificial turf.

Mark telepathically directed his thoughts to Paula, "Hm... you know, after visiting ancient Greece, coming to a typical high school athletic field feels a little disappointing."

"Take a deep breath, Partner, because I'm sure the God Source brought us here for a purpose. We just have to be patient and see."

**

The partners' vision then focused on a grey-haired football coach with a large pot belly. They watched as his team of players took a knee and listened with great intensity as he delivered a motivational pep talk. He spoke in a firm and powerful voice, "If you expect to win the state championship, you need to COMMIT wholeheartedly. Being an all-star football player needs to be the most important thing in your life.

Secondly men, you must Study the game of football the way you would study the game of chess, because for us to win the state championship we must be smarter than our opponents.

Next, you must diligently Practice your football skills, because studying alone only creates knowledge, and you need a strong, fast, lean athletic body to play like an all-star.

Lastly, and most importantly, you must Emotionalize what you are learning about the game of football. When you learn to emotionalize your football knowledge, your behavior will change and the imprint will be permanent. Emotionalizing will change the way you play so you can be the state champs."

The coach paused a moment and stared into each player's eyes. After slowly scanning his team, he asked them in a stern loud tone, "WHO ARE YOU?"

The team immediately yelled back,

"STATE CHAMPS!"

"WHO ARE YOU?"

They stood up excitedly and yelled,

"STATE CHAMPS!"

"WHO ARE YOU?"

The team completely let loose jumping and screaming, "STATE CHAMPS! STATE CHAMPS! STATE CHAMPS!"

***

Without warning, the spiritual partners were abruptly ejected from their football vision. The shift happened so suddenly that they felt nauseated, as though they had been thrust upward with enough force to blast them into outer space. They continued rocketing upward until, just as suddenly, their stomachs dropped as they rapidly descended until everything went black.

After several minutes, a faint light came into view, like a flashlight in the distance of a pitch-black cave. The light slowly grew brighter and brighter until it became so blinding that they had to close their eyes. Slowly, the light faded, and the spiritual partners found themselves on the bank of a slow-moving river. It was a starry night without a cloud in the sky. Behind them stood a mansion with tall glass windows and an inviting light streaming from them.

As they approached the mansion, they heard light-hearted chatter and laughter emanating from within. They entered the house into a very large room where a few dozen people in Halloween costumes were gathered and energetically socializing.

Mark and Paula's attention was drawn to a dark-haired woman in a Native American costume making her way toward the center of the room. When she reached it, she greeted a tall, powerful-looking woman dressed as the Statue of Liberty. She whispered, "Anita, I think now is a good time to make your toast."

Anita tapped her glass with a spoon to call her guests to attention. When the room quieted, she spoke, "I want to thank everyone for making the first year of our Holistic Learning Center a huge success. It's because of all your hard work that we are here today. I want each of you to grok that regardless of the nature or degree of your participation; you have contributed to the conscious creation of this important center of psycho-spiritual education. I so deeply want each of you to absorb and take in to your soul that this Center would not be what it is today without you. She paused for several seconds, looking around the room at all the guests. Please raise your glass to our success as we each continue to teach what we most need to learn and heal, one soul at a time starting with our own."

The room resounded with thunderous applause, and the guests joyously sipped their drinks. Anita smiled and waited for the room to quiet. She invited one of the guests to come forward. A gray-haired, middle-aged man in a Plato costume made his way and stood beside her. Anita introduced him as her spiritual friend and mentor and said, "Please put your hands together to congratulate our Director of Training, Saul, who will say a few words about spiritual transformation."

When the applause ended, Saul thanked Anita and began speaking. "I want to thank you for the love and support you have shown me this year. I'm proud and blessed to be a member of our Sangha[32] training team. I hope that we all remember that 'team' is an acronym for 'Together Everyone Achieves More.'

---

[32] Sangha: a spiritual community

For the next few minutes, I'm going to ask you to indulge me as I speak one more time about the very important teaching technique of emotionalizing by using first-party communication[33]. I ask you to indulge me because most of you have studied, practiced, internalized and emotionalized the first-party communication techniques. And even though we have trained ourselves to be alert to our mind's tendency to say, 'I already know that', I'll bet you a glass of wine, your mind just said, 'I already know that.'" Everyone in the room laughed as they nodded in agreement.

"I'm asking you to indulge me as we delve into this technique one more time. It cannot be over taught. As I review this technique again, I am asking you to listen from a place of 'I don't know' or from a place of 'there is more to understand about this first-party communication technique, the knowing of which could make all the difference'. If you will agree to hear me one more time from this perspective, lift your glasses for a toast in agreement." Again, the room filled with laughter as everyone lifted their glasses.

As Saul launched into his discourse about first-person communication, he reminded the guests that it's a technique that he taught all his students who sought

---

[33] First-party communication: speaking from the perspective of I, me, my, mine.

spiritual transformation. He reinforced that this meant saying "I" or "me" instead of "you" and that if one used the word "you" in a communication it usually meant that the person was philosophizing, conceptualizing, and theorizing. He shared that all the meta-knowledge people have collected over the years through reading books about spiritual enlightenment, attending self-help seminars and listening to transformational audios, needs to be *emotionalized*, and one way of doing that is by using first-person communication when they discuss what they have learned, felt or experienced.

***

As Saul spoke, Mark considered his prior skepticism and telepathically directed his thoughts to Paula, "I must admit, when we arrived at that football field, I wasn't convinced our vision would tie into emotionalizing. I can't believe I had such little faith in the God Source."

"Don't beat yourself up. It's great that you noticed that, and now just observe and correct quickly to adjust your behavior." Paula reminded Mark with a loving tone.

***

Saul continued addressing the group, "Permanent behavioral change happens when you emotionalize the transformational knowledge you have been studying until it becomes a part of your Consciousness. Another benefit of first-person communication is that it mechanically trains you to hear what you are vocalizing and sub-vocalizing, which is tremendously beneficial when learning the Self-mastery skill of dis-creation. Eastern philosophers call this 'conscious listening' because it requires you to take the witness/observer[34] position. When you consciously use first-person communication, you are training yourself to *hear* instances when your words are sourced from negative programming, as opposed to times they're sourced from your inner God-Self."

His speech slowed, as he considered his next words carefully, "First-person communication helps you identify your Self as a Godlike BEing, instead of incorrectly identifying yourself as your roles or job titles. This, in turn, helps you stay awake to your higher Consciousness. In my opinion, the ability to remain consciously awake is the most important benefit of the first-person communication technique."

Saul paused a moment, and with a strong sense of knowingness, he delivered his final words. "When you communicate at this level of Conscious awareness you are One with the God that dwells within you as you. Think

---

[34] Witness/observer: Standing outside a situation or circumstance and watching as if viewing a movie.

about it, you have a car, but you are not your car. You live in a house, but you are not your house. You exhibit positive and negative behaviors, but you are not your behaviors. I hope this helps you understand why it's so important for you to understand that you are a spiritual BEing who has incarnated to experience these things, but you are not the things that you are experiencing."

The audience whistled and applauded loudly. Anita stepped forward to shake his hand and thank him. As Saul returned to his place in the crowd, Anita turned to the audience. "Thank you, Saul, for those words of wisdom. Now I'd like our resident scientist, Dr. Joe, to come forward. He's going to explain why emotionalizing is a scientific fact."

A man in his late 40s stepped out from the crowd. Dr. Joe was a well-groomed and handsome man, despite his silly tomato Halloween costume. He smiled and waved, showcasing his natural charisma and stage presence. Anita greeted him with a warm hug, and she quickly stepped off to the side.

Dr. Joe explained, "When we communicate in first-person with passion, that passion is more than just an emotion; it's electromagnetic energy... or simply electricity! The more electrical energy you run through your brain, the faster your neural pathways will change and the faster your belief systems will change.

Remember the video I shared with you a while ago? You could see the nerve cells of the subject's brain firing as he passionately recited positive affirmations. And you could see specific nerve cells activate and fuse together to form new neural pathways. And the more times a specific thought is repeated, the deeper and more solid the neural pathway becomes. It's like walking through snow. There's only a faint imprint when you walk through it a few times, and you may walk slightly different paths each time; but when you walk the path dozens and dozens of times, it creates a deep, lasting impression. Eventually, and without any thought, this will become the single path that you'll walk each time. Picture this when you think of your behaviors and how your subconscious mind works. The thoughts that are repeated the most are the thoughts that create the beliefs that will drive your actions.

It's important to note, that this same video showed that this process works in reverse as well. So, when you *stop* stimulating neural pathways anchored to negative thoughts, such as 'I'm not good enough' those neural pathways dissolve and are dis-created.

This, my soul friends, scientifically proves that when you emotionalize your thoughts, you change your brain on a cellular level! And this helps make your changes permanent."

***

Mark was astounded by Dr. Joe's explanation. He had never known such scientific evidence existed, and this helped him to make more sense of his earlier struggles. He directed his thoughts to Paula again, "I think one of the most important things Coach Sarah ever taught me was that I can't achieve spiritual transformation without being willing to accept what is. I remember you saying that 'people want things to change, but their egoic minds resist change.' Hearing it broken down so simply makes so much sense. It's all because our brains were wired in those ways! I could kick myself for not understanding this sooner."

"Mark, don't be so hard on yourself. Change triggers our egoic mind's need for safety and control, which can stop us from making positive changes. It's perfectly normal that you experienced resistance. We all go through it. If you are willing to remain steadfast eventually you will overcome your ego's roadblocks."

Paula's words rang true for Mark. Life had taught him that he couldn't remain the same and still grow. He learned that nothing *changed* in his life until he *accepted* what is "as is" about himself, life, and the circumstances he was experiencing, especially the painful ones. Mark learned that his mind created rational lies to escape the trauma of the painful experience that happened to him.

But his egoic denial blinded him from seeing what he needed in order to heal.

"Thinking about my life, as opposed to experiencing it, was my ego's attempt to try to feel good without doing the required transformational work."

"Mark, the truth is that transformation is only possible after we transcend our ego identification. It's only after we stop thinking we are our roles and behaviors that we can stop chronically placing blame and shame and playing the role of victim.

We're all creatures of habit, and change is always challenging; it doesn't matter if we choose to change intentionally, or if it's thrust upon us. We need to be aware that when we decide to Self-program what we want to experience, things often get worse first! This happens because what we begin to experience does not fit into our already existing habitual thoughts, feelings and actions, and this is disconcerting to our egos. Like Dr. Joe explained, change causes us to trudge through the deep snow alongside an already well-beaten path. And before things will change, we need to surface, heal and dis-create old negative beliefs that are blocking us from manifesting our desires.

God may have created us, but we made ourselves what we are today, one habitual belief at a time. We're the architect and builder of the reality we experience, and we created that reality thought by thought from the moment we were born."

***

Once again, the spiritual partners were abruptly ejected from their vision. The mansion blurred into streaks of assorted colors, and they rapidly descended until the array of colors faded to black. After a few minutes, a faint light appeared in the distance, and as it did, they were met with a bird's eye view of an expansive forest stretching as far as they could see. As they descended, they took in the breathtaking view of the surrounding area. The trees were on display in their most vibrant fall colors of orange, yellow and red.

As they broke through the forest canopy, they saw a deep ravine with a beautiful, fast-flowing stream at the bottom. Thirty feet to the right of the steam were two men; a muscular, bearded man in a flannel shirt collecting firewood, and an older-looking portly gentleman in a hooded sweatshirt setting up a tent. The older portly man appeared to be in his 50s, while his younger, fit companion looked roughly 20 years younger. The two men worked together to set up their campsite. With their work completed, they unfolded a pair of lawn chairs and sat comfortably around the blazing fire they had built.

The campers enjoyed a beer while they passionately discussed whose football team was best. Their discussion escalated to the point where it turned into a friendly argument. When their quarrel reached its peak, the two men shared a hearty laugh. They seemed like a pair of old friends who understood each other well enough to have a heated debate without losing their composure.

As their laughter subsided, the younger man solemnly shared, "Jim, I'm 28 years old. I've meditated, and I've learned how the laws of life work, but my life still isn't getting any better. What do you think I'm doing wrong?"

Jim looked deep into his friend's eyes. "Well Tommy, I can't say for sure, but it's probably because you are only intellectualizing what you have been studying. To manifest positive changes, you must emotionalize what you've learned. Embed it deep into your subconscious mind using Self-programming affirmations until they become a part of your Consciousness. Over the last 30 years, I've coached thousands of people, but very few of them have ever mastered the art of Self-programming."

"Why do you think that is?"

"There are plenty of reasons, many of which are quite complex. But generally, I'd say that a person's ego-intellect is addicted to excitement and resents boring, repetitive work... which is basically what Self-programming requires.

Self-programming taps into the power of your subconscious mind. Your subconscious mind is much stronger than your conscious mind, which is why it is such a powerful transformational technique. Did you know that your subconscious mind is so powerful that it orchestrates 10 trillion chemical reactions per second for your body to function properly?!

Learning how your conscious and subconscious minds work is a major component of mastering the Self-programing process. Your subconscious mind doesn't reason, balance, judge, or reject your thoughts. It simply accepts all the suggestions your conscious mind gives it, whether they are constructive or destructive.

Your subconscious mind is always programming, but *who* is doing the programming, and *what* is being programmed? Much of your subconscious programming happens without you even knowing. In fact, we're consistently being programmed by advertisers, social traditions, caretakers and even by our own fear-based 50,000 thoughts that we think every day. So, it's up to us. We can either allow ourselves to be unconsciously programmed or we can intentionally reject unwanted thoughts and beliefs using dis-creation techniques and then consciously program what we want into our subconscious mind using Self-programming techniques."

"So, let me see if I've understood you correctly. I remember learning that my subconscious mind is connected with the Universal God-mind, which is Omniscient, Omnipresent, and Omnipotent. And even though my conscious mind doesn't have all the powers that my subconscious mind does, it has a huge responsibility, which is to act as my computer programmer and deliberately Self-program what I want to experience. Is that correct, Tommy?"

Tommy gave his friend a light, goofy clap.

Jim smiled and bowed modestly in gest.

"I couldn't have said it better myself. Now, how about we get some food on this fire? I'm starving."

**

Without warning, the vision began to fade. Paula and Mark drifted from the campfire scene and out of their formless state of Consciousness. The scene blurred into a kaleidoscope of colors until everything went black.

When Mark opened his eyes, he felt a trail of tears running down his check. It didn't surprise him, because this had been an emotionally challenging Vision Quest for him.

"Wow. This was a very empowering adventure for me, Paula."

Paula returned his gaze and nodded in agreement. "Yeah. I got a lot out of it too. It taught me why it's so important for us to help each other remain consciously aware that our external conditions express anything that we emotionalize and Self-program. There's just so much to discuss and talk about!"

Mark nodded in agreement as he grabbed his laptop and turned it on. "I'm right there with you. Give me a few minutes so I can note what I grokked while it's still fresh in my mind." Mark began to type furiously. He read aloud as he typed:

"Eighty-five percent of the work required to create permanent behavioral change comes from having the emotional courage and willingness to take the required actions to surface what our egos have repressed, denied or intellectualized. Our ego-intellects created these "defenses" to help us feel safe when we were in situations that really weren't emotionally, sexually, financially or physically safe. So, we must dis-create our ego-created defenses that kept us feeling safe back then because now they can stop us from achieving our goals.

When we *Self-actualize*[35] what we have surfaced, we won't feel afraid anymore because we will grok that the karma we are burning off is just old FEAR... False Evidence Appearing Real. When we emotionalize our

---

[35] Self-actualize: - an *action* that you perform from a state of Conscious Awareness.

deep desires, we will be able to manifest what we wish to experience."

When he was done typing, he looked up. "And the more empowered souls there are in the world, the more we can affect the positive changes that are required to create the critical mass to transform humankind on a global level."

Paula smiled, impressed by his work ethic. "Do you mind if I look at your notes?"

"Not at all!" Mark said proudly, "Come have a look."

Paula made her way to Mark's side and leaned over his shoulder as she read. "Mark. This is remarkable. You just boiled down the essence of this entire Vision Quest adventure into a few paragraphs."

Mark chuckled, as he fished for more praise, "It's that good?"

"It's incredible! Hey, I've been doing this work a long time, and people don't usually grok this psycho-spiritual stuff as fast as you have. It really is extraordinary!"

"Maybe, it's because I had such a good teacher." Mark said in a humorous tone.

Paula turned her head to thank Mark at the exact same moment he turned his head to face her. Paula immediately felt the familiar feeling in the pit of her stomach as their eyes locked. Mark leaned toward Paula, and his romantic instincts took over.

Paula slowly raised her hand to his cheek offering a gentle caress. Their eyes closed just as their lips met. Their first kiss was soft and gentle, and each subsequent kiss resonated with an intense feeling of bliss. Mark gently placed his hands behind Paula's head, as he began to kiss her more passionately. He felt every curve of her beautiful body against his, as he drew her closer with a sensual embrace.

Their hearts synchronized with an intensity that Paula had never felt with anyone before. For a moment, they both felt as though they had found heaven on earth. But as quickly as the romantic encounter began, it slowed and stopped. Mark drew a deep breath as he placed his hands on her shoulders, and with gentle pressure, he slowly pulled back.

Paula's eyes opened to see that his expression had changed from one of desire to one of regret.

"I'm sorry... I can't."

As soon as Mark had said that, Paula's mind exploded. She was perplexed and struggled to understand what she was feeling.

"Oh God. Mark, I'm so sorry. It's just I..."

"Don't be sorry, Paula. We didn't do anything wrong. Really. Why don't we just... continue dissecting this lesson?"

"Okay, Mark," Paula said trying to hold back her tears.

Each tried to deflect their emotions and avoid what they were feeling by staring at their laptops.

Mark's mind was working overtime. He was trying to block his true feelings, but his heart knew what his mind wasn't willing to process: it was time to unconditionally accept what had happened in his past and start the next chapter of his romantic life with Paula.

Lesson #11 Of
~~Transformational Awakening Is...~~

The Magic Of
Emotionalizing

Creates the Permanent Behavioral
Changes that you seek if you invest
the time and energy to Self-program
what you emotionalize based on your
transformational Self-realizations.

CHAPTER 16

Transcending Your Incarnational Story

You Are Not The Story That You Are Experiencing

When the spiritual partners returned to work the following morning, they reviewed what they had learned from their last Vision Quest while sitting on the couch and sipping green tea. Neither of them spoke a word about their romantic encounter, but beneath their silence was an obvious layer of sexual tension. Mark worried that he'd made a mistake by pushing Paula away, while Paula's mind was troubled that she might have violated their professional boundaries. Despite their nervous concerns, there was a longing in their hearts that neither was ready to address just yet.

They put their concerns aside to focus on their work. They reflected on the need to teach their students the importance of Self-programing[36] their personal realizations that surface from emotionalizing their Self-mastery lessons. Mark and Paula learned from their own experiences that Self-realizations are quickly lost if they are not immediately Self-programmed. They needed to find a way to help their students clearly understand how pivotal Self-programming is in creating desired permanent behavioral changes.

Mark shared, "After last night's Vision Quest, I'm beginning to ask myself if I'm intentionally Self-programming what I want to experience, or unconsciously programming what I don't want to experience."

"That's powerful, Mark. And since our last visual adventure, I've started thinking of Self-programming as my daily medicine, like a daily vitamin. When our students emotionalize their spiritual lessons, they will feel sad and scared; sad because their old ego defenses that kept them in 'blissful ignorance' will no longer work, and scared because their new spiritually based boundaries haven't solidified yet. When our students

---

[36] Self-programming: five tools you can use to consciously change your behavior by reprogramming your thought patterns. Self-Mastery, A Journey Home to Your Inner Self, page 50-51,

emotionalize their transformational lessons, it will uproot their fear-based beliefs. When this happens, it will be perfectly natural for these transformational changes to make them feel emotionally vulnerable at first.

It's the old Self-actualization trainer's joke that 'the truth shall set you free, but not before it scares the hell out of you.' We must remind our students that their uncomfortable feelings are proof that they are headed in the right spiritual direction," Paula said with a confident giggle.

Engaging in their empowering work helped them to release some of their romantic tension, which allowed them to mastermind their next Vision Quest action plan. During their discussion, they agreed that all too often they became completely absorbed in their egoic thoughts and mistakenly identified themselves as the 'voice inside their heads'.

With emotional courage Paula looked at Mark and said, "As you know, I've been doing inner Self-mastery work for decades. But I must admit, there are still days when I unconsciously think that I am my roles, especially with my 'I'm not good enough' identity. But even if the role I'm playing is highly functional, it still isn't who I am."

"I know what you mean. I've noticed that when I'm spiritually grounded, I watch my thoughts come and go like ocean waves. I experience them, but I am not them any more than I'm my house, car, body or my relationships. This work has taught me that I'm not my feelings, and I'm not my thoughts. I experience them, but I am *not* them."

Paula quickly typed what Mark had said. When she finished, she looked up at him with a warm grin, "I must say, I really appreciate your ability to quickly create concise thesis statements. Once we are ready to put these lessons and exercises into a training manual, they are going to be very helpful."

"Thanks." Mark said smiling, "I'm not sure how I do it... they just come to me naturally."

"We need to teach our students how to *objectively* listen to the voice inside their head as a witness-observer. This will help them feel the subtle difference between who is doing the *talking*, their ego, from who is doing the *listening*, their Spirit."

Mark followed right along. "Right. And the Spiritual Distinction Meditative Exercise will help them with this."

"Exactly. And once our students can make these distinctions, it will free them from identifying with their incessant mind chatter. Their reward will be their ability to step back and view their thoughts objectively without being seduced by them. They will only *observe* their thoughts and grok that their nonstop mind-chatter is *not who they are!*"

After brainstorming for about an hour, the spiritual partners knew exactly what their next lesson needed to be: teaching their students how to transcend their incarnational stories[37] so they could create the permanent behavioral changes needed to spiritually transform.

Satisfied with their progress and excited to see what the God Source would reveal next, the spiritual partners prepared for their next Vision Quest. They maintained their ritual of playing spiritual music, lighting a candle and incense, and sitting in meditation positions facing each other. Together they asked the Universe to reveal the best way to teach their students to transcend their incarnational stories. They chanted the mantra "Namasté" while they breathed slowly and slipped into a deep state of bliss.

***

THREE FIRES CEREMONY
FIRST FIRE

---

[37] Incarnational stories: stories with which we become identified, such as mother, doctor, not good enough, coach, fat, fit, etc.

1st Speaker

After a half-hour in an alpha state of Consciousness, a vision began to emerge from the darkness and became clearer as they relaxed into their experience. The spiritual partners found themselves floating a hundred feet above a rural park. To the west was a sunset sky rich with indigo, violet, fuchsia and golden rays of light pouring through the clouds. Beneath them were acres of rolling hills covered in well-manicured lawns and dozens of large oak and maple trees. As they descended, they spotted a raging bonfire surrounded by a large group of people, of which about a dozen were adorned with black hoods, and each hooded *Spiritual Initiate*[38] was accompanied and guided by a sponsor. There were another two-dozen people dressed in casual wear, scattered around the blazing fire. The entire group listened attentively to a man bearing striking resemblance to Mark. He stood atop a wooden box and faced the crowd as he read from a large weathered book decorated with ornate gold trim.

The partners sensed a solemn, ceremonial energy resonating from the group. They drew closer until they came to a stop about 10 feet above the crowd. As they hovered over the crowd, Mark was astonished to see

---

[38] Spiritual Initiate: a student who is being inducted into a Spiritual community.

himself speaking to the crowd beneath them, "That's me with gray hair and wrinkles! I guess we were brought to see a vision of ourselves in the future?"

"It seems like it. This is weird."

"Sure is."

***

The Spiritual Initiates were as quiet as mice as they listened to the older-looking Mark read from the ceremonial book.

"Welcome my soul brothers and sisters to our Three Fires Ceremony. Since the founding of our school, we have been performing this sacred ceremony to initiate new members to our spiritual organization. We are not the first to do this type of ceremony. Such spiritual initiations have a proud, long-standing heritage. We are about to share secrets that have been passed down from one Spiritual Master to another for millennia. Please bow your heads and close your eyes, as I lead us in our ritual meditation."

The older Mark proceeded to lead a Spiritual Distinction Meditative Exercise. Once complete, he asked everyone to keep their eyes closed as he read from the ceremonial book. "The human school has a beautiful system of balance between the mind and heart. Your intellectual mind is the instrument of separateness, and your heart is the instrument of unity. What results is a profound polarized struggle, where your ego tries to preserve your separateness and your Spirit seeks to merge into the unity of all things.

Transformation means 'to go beyond form' to a level of conscious understanding that the real *you* exists beyond the physical form of your human body. You will spiritually transform, not through becoming divine, but through realizing that all your experiences have served the purpose of awakening you to your divine nature. There have been no unnecessary experiences, whether they have been pleasurable or painful, on your path to spiritual transformation. Therefore, you don't want to deny any element of your personal history, for each of your experiences has played a vital role in your spiritual awakening."

***

Mark looked on, transfixed by the scene below him. "I still can't believe this is real. Just being outside my body was one thing, but experiencing an older version of myself takes it to a whole new level! Do you have any idea why we are being shown this scene in such a strange way?"

"It's too early to tell, but I have my suspicions. It certainly is a strange experience though!"

***

The older Mark continued his speech, "Your incarnational experience requires you to embrace many paradoxes, such as: you are an infinite BEing in a finite body; you believe in a God that you can't see; you learn to love when there is so much fear; and you have been taught to accept an identity that is not the real you.

We have gathered here today to share with you the secrets that will enable you to transcend these paradoxes and identify yourself as a Godlike BEing of light and love with powers of deliberate, conscious creation."

Solemnly and slowly, he asked the group, "Do you believe that what you have just heard is a Universal Truth?"

The whole group answered with one empowered voice, "WE BELIEVE!"

2nd Speaker

The older Mark stepped down from the box, and a middle-aged African American woman stepped up to take his place. The class of Spiritual Initiates listened attentively as she spoke from the ceremonial book. "Change is what happens when the pain of holding on becomes greater than your fear of letting go. You use enormous amounts of Life Force Energy holding onto your pain and your past. This is why the word 'someday' can be a very dangerous word if you intend to change your behavior, because 'someday' can be a mental camouflage for 'never.'

My dear soul brothers and sisters, when things change, only two things can happen. One is obvious and the other is extremely subtle. The obvious thing is that you will manifest what you want to experience. The not-so-obvious thing is you will surface what you need to heal, forgive, dis-create, or learn before you can manifest what you want. Understand that if you go unconscious to the subtle second outcome, you will miss the God Source's diagnostic gift. But, if you have the wisdom and emotional courage to see, feel, and heal what you need to transcend, then your challenges become reason for celebration, not egoic aggravation."

The wise, old soul solemnly asked the group, "Do you believe that what you have just heard is a Universal Truth?"

The group of spiritually awakened souls answered with a single empowered voice, "WE BELIEVE!"

3rd Speaker

When the woman stepped down from the box, the spiritual partners were delighted to see an older version of Paula step up and face the crowd. "Look Mark. It's me! This must be our future."

"It could be. Or maybe it's one of many possible futures. Or it could be just a vision designed to teach us this lesson in the most effective way possible. We won't know for sure until the ceremony is over. I can't wait to hear what you have to say!"

***

The class of Spiritual Initiates listened attentively as the older Paula read from the ceremonial book. "We incarnated into a world where we exist on three levels of reality simultaneously. We have labeled these realities as the Experiential, Wisdom, and Transcendence Levels of Consciousness.

The first level of Consciousness is the Experiential Level. You incarnate to experience physical life, but the question is, are you experiencing your life consciously or unconsciously? If you are unconsciously experiencing your life, then you are an *actor* who is identifying yourself as the *roles* you are playing, such as mother, father, doctor, coach, victim, broken, addict, or saint.

The next level of Consciousness is the Wisdom Level. We call someone who has mastered this level of Consciousness a wizard, sage, guru, or saint. If you are at the early stages of this level, then you are a student of life who is using your human experiences to master the game of life. At this stage of your spiritual evolution, you are learning to be a deliberately conscious creator; to go beyond your form, mind and body identification via the never-ending process of trial and error. At this level, you are the *director* of your human experience because you see beyond the form that you are using to have an experience. You grok that you are not your body, thoughts, roles or your history.

The most evolved level is the Transcendence Level, which is where you witness your human life unfolding from a space of divine detachment. You know that no matter what your human incarnate is experiencing, be it pleasure or pain, it's all perfect. At this level, you realize there is nothing to do or fix. You are the *observer* of your human incarnate, with whom you are one, but who you are not. At this level, you are the *producer* of your physical life because you are producing the electromagnetic energy that allows you to play in the world as a deliberately conscious creator."

* * *

Those words triggered something within Mark. He telepathically directed his thoughts to Paula, "Didn't Ram Dass teach you that? As I recall, he taught you that the Experiential Level could be compared to a computer's hardware, the Wisdom Level is the software and the Transcendence Level is the electricity that runs the computer; and without it the hardware and software could not function."

"That's right. And it should be a part of our course. We need to teach our students that all three levels of Consciousness are happening simultaneously. One way we could do this is to ask them to imagine that they have a headache while they are talking to a friend with music playing in the background. Then, we'll point out that what feels more real to them is directly related to where they place their point of attention. Whether their point of attention is their headache, the music or communicating with their friend, their point of focus will become their reality. This will help them to experientially understand that whatever they place their attention on will be the reality they will experience."

"I didn't realize it at the time, but I actually learned this as a young child. I vividly remember having a severe sore throat, which completely went away when I watched a captivating movie at the theater. I now realize that my sore throat didn't 'go away'; my point of attention simply shifted from my sore throat to the movie, which changed what appeared real to me. Once the movie ended, the sore throat, sadly and painfully, returned." Mark chuckled lightly and added, "So now we're dissecting the lessons and debriefing before we even complete our Vision Quest!"

"I guess so. Isn't it exciting to see how far we've come?"

***

Paula and Mark returned their attention to their vision of the older image of Paula, as she solemnly asked the group, "Do you believe that what you have just heard is a Universal Truth?"

With a unified harmonious voice, the group responded, "WE BELIEVE!"

***

SECOND FIRE
1st Speaker

Mark and Paula watched as the sponsors took the right arms of the hooded Spiritual Initiates and slowly guided them through the rolling hills toward a second raging fire far in the distance.

Dusk turned to darkness before the mystical group arrived at the next fire. While they settled into their positions, a man with long straight brown hair and a full beard stepped onto a wooden platform overlooking the crowd. The class of Spiritual Initiates, sponsors and witnesses were quiet and attentive as they listened to him read from the ceremonial book.

"It is important to train your mind to be your 'servant' so you can consciously observe the world as it is, as opposed to what your mind wants it to be. When you first do this, you'll feel vulnerable, because your mind is accustomed to controlling what can't be controlled. Your ego-mind does this because it is trying to force your current experiences to fit into your historic paradigm box of fixed beliefs.

An untrained mind does this to feel comfortable when reality seems too painful to process. So, to cope with an uncomfortable or painful reality, your mind triggers ego defense mechanisms, such as denial, repression, disassociation, and transference as anesthesia to numb your pain. Until you can consciously transcend this *reactive* behavior, you will use your mind to buffer you from life instead of intentionally transcending it.

Spiritually awakened souls are aware of their mind's chatter, without thinking that they are their minds. They watch and observe the mental voices playing inside their heads, such as worry, distraction, and neurosis, knowing that they are not the voices. This is why training your mind with meditative exercises to notice this spiritual distinction is the launching ground of your spiritual liberation.

Eventually, my soul brothers and sisters, you will grok that the real cause of your 'so-called' problems is not life itself; it's the turmoil that your ego-mind creates about life.

Do you believe that what you have just heard is a Universal Truth?"

The group chanted as one strong voice, "WE BELIEVE!"

2nd Speaker

The bearded man stepped down, and a young Native American woman with long, straight, black hair stepped up to read from the ceremonial book as the participants and supporters listened attentively.

"You are a spiritual BEing who is having a human experience. You created a body to wear on the earth plane for the same reason an astronaut wears a protective suit to function in outer space. To attain spiritual liberation, you must be able to objectively watch your emotional disturbances instead of getting lost in them. The very fact that you realize that you are experiencing a mental disturbance means that you are not it.

The process of seeing something requires a subject-object relationship. The subject is called the witness because it is the one who sees what is happening. The object is what you are seeing, and in this example; the object being observed is your own inner disturbance."

***

"Wow. That explains why I must train my mind to be my servant, instead of my master." Mark exclaimed.

"And it explains how our thoughts dictate the way we experience the world." Paula added.

***

The Native American woman continued her speech, "You start by training your mind to observe. And what you are observing is your persona-mask, or personality, with all its strengths and weaknesses that are hiding the divine inner you.

Your egoic mind can become so absorbed in life's enjoyable feelings or frightening fears that it makes it nearly impossible for you to focus on what you want to manifest. It's these egoic dramas that drain you of your divine powers of conscious creation."

After a brief pause, she solemnly asked the group, "Do you believe that what you have just heard is a Universal Truth?"

"WE BELIEVE!" The group replied in unison.

3rd Speaker

The empowered young woman stepped down from the platform, and the older version of Paula stepped back up. Again, she read from the weathered ceremonial book and asked the group, "Are you ready to awaken to who you really are... Consciousness, the Atman, an Immortal Soul?

Ask yourself who hears the endless stream of thoughts that are always running through your mind. Who notices these endless distracting thoughts? It's the real you, the Self, the Soul, Spirit, God, Consciousness, the Atman or any other name which you feel comfortable using that represents the God Source energy of the Universe.

What distinguishes a person who is deliberately conscious from a person who is ego-identified? It's her ability to interact with other incarnates and the world as a witness/observer. She does this by not getting lost in, or identifying herself as, her duties, responsibilities, or roles, that her mind thinks she is."

***

Paula directed her thoughts to Mark, "I remember Ramana Maharishi saying that to attain inner freedom, I must ceaselessly ask myself this esoteric, soul-searching question, 'Who Am I?'

Ramana Maharishi would ask his followers, 'Are you your name, a collection of letters? Are you your relationships? Are you your age, height, weight, body or financial status? Then who are you?' He would tell them, 'You are a spiritual BEing having an incarnational experience.'"

***

The older version of Paula continued, "If you step back far enough and objectively listen to your endless thoughts, you will realize that they are online 24 hours a day, 7 days a week. The fact that your mind's obsessive thoughts are repeated so frequently makes them feel comfortable, but just because they feel comfortable, doesn't mean they are highly functional, which is why you need to meditate.

Your meditative practice is designed to bring about a temporary cessation of your endless stream of thoughts. This interruption of thoughts gives you a taste of what it feels like to be fully present and consciously aware of what is true and real in the present moment. Swami Muktananda, an awakened master, was once asked, 'What is real?' and he answered, 'That which doesn't change.'

It's important for you to grok that no amount of thinking can encapsulate the whole truth; at best, it can only *point* to it. Understanding this Truth - that thoughts are mere *pointers* - means that you grok that you are the Truth to which they point!

She solemnly asked the group, "Do you believe that what you have just heard is a Universal Truth?"

"WE BELIEVE!" harmoniously echoed through the night air.

THIRD FIRE

1st Speaker

The group disassembled and began making their way toward a third fire a hundred yards away. After a slow, contemplative walk, they settled around the fire, where a balding, gray-haired man dressed like a hippie stepped onto a wooden box and faced the crowd.

The class of Spiritual Initiates listened attentively, as he read from the ceremonial book. "Are you deliberately conscious enough to understand who you are NOT - your human roles, identities, bodies or minds? You will transform only when you realize that you aren't your thoughts and beliefs that are associated with your incarnational roles.

Your ego is so pre-occupied with trying to control your world, that the 'real you' gets lost in your historic stories. It's like the experience of watching a good movie that draws you in deeper and deeper until you forget that you are watching a movie. In the same way, you think the story playing inside your head is who you are, instead of the spiritual BEing who is listening to that story."

***

Mark projected his thoughts to Paula, "This vision is really helping me to see that the only permanent solution to my problems is to train my mind with meditation, so I can objectively watch the world as if it were a TV show, instead of getting lost in my egoic stories."

***

The balding man continued, "By God's grace, the founders of our spiritual organization developed five exercises to train your ego-mind to act as your servant. By ceaselessly practicing these Five Disciplines of the Initiates, you will begin to grasp that you are not your roles, duties, identities, responsibilities, thoughts or feelings. What you are is pure Consciousness, or what some religions refer to as the Atman, Soul, or Spirit.

When you practice the Five Disciplines of the Initiates until they become a lifelong habit, your vibrational oscillations will accelerate, and the faster they vibrate, the more powerful your conscious creation powers will become.

My soul brothers and sisters, just as the sun shines even when it is hidden behind a wall of clouds; your inner Consciousness, the source of your BEingness, is Omnipresent, whether you are consciously aware of it or not.

Do you believe that what you have just heard is a Universal Truth?"

"WE BELIEVE!"
2nd Speaker

He stepped down from the box, and the older version of Mark stepped up once again and read from the book as the class eagerly waited to hear his words. "One of the biggest challenges of life is to not mistake the image of reality for reality itself. Every time you identify with the essence of who you really are, your God-identified state of BEingness, you escape the prison of the intellect, and you enter the world of infinite, unbound freedom, serenity and abundance.

Did you ever wonder why you forget who you are? You forget because you have been socially conditioned to believe in the superstition of materialism, and to trust the illusions created by your body and senses. Our soul brother, Deepak, taught us that you are inseparable from, and are one with, the field of infinite intelligence that created the entire cosmos. Knowing this frees you from the hallucinations of a separate, ego-dominated self, and it helps you identify as Consciousness, which is the source of your power and freedom."

Do you believe that what you have just heard is a Universal Truth?"

With one empowered voice the group chanted, "WE BELIEVE!"

3rd Speaker

As the older version of Mark stepped down, the older version of Paula stepped back up to recite from the ceremonial book, "What is the key to lasting happiness? The key is to grok the distinction between your primary God-identified reality, which is immortal and infinite, from your numerous secondary realities, which are temporal.

It is imperative for you to understand that a silent mind is more important than a positive mind. Your silent mind is your God-mind, which is non-judgmental, non-analytical, and non-interpretive. We strongly suggest that you form the habit of meditating every day, so you can slip into the God Gap between your thoughts. This will help you grok that you are a human BEing, not a human do-ing. When you meditate, I want you to pay attention to your subtle intuitive messages. Intuitive spiritual communications are so subtle that most souls are only aware of them when they are meditating or praying. While in God's meditative silence, you will be able to comprehend the spiritual communications that are being sent to you via your sacred heart.

There is one last thing that we want to share with you, our new Spiritual Initiates. *Mastery* in any field of endeavor implies that the thinking mind is either no longer involved, or at the very least, is taking second place. When this happens a Universal power and intelligence greater than your ego-intellect takes over, and there is no decision-making process anymore. Spontaneous *right action* happens, and your ego-mind *isn't doing it*.

Mastery of life is the direct opposite of egoic control. Mastery of life happens when you are aligned with your inner Consciousness. This means that your divine

Consciousness acts, speaks, and does the work through you with effortless ease. This is why it is vital to surrender to your higher powers, knowing that the 'Father within you doeth the work'."

Do you believe that what you have just heard is a Universal Truth?"

"WE BELIEVE!" The group replied with thunderous zeal.

***

Without warning, Paula and Mark's vision began to fade. They found themselves drifting from their formless state of Consciousness into the kaleidoscope of colors until the scene faded entirely.

Mark opened his eyes and met Paula's astonished gaze with his own. He shared, "That was incredible! Seeing ourselves in our own Vision Quest. It was weird and Self-empowering at the same time."

"I know. It was a strange metaphysical experience! It gave me a unique perspective to witness what was happening on the earth plane, while simultaneously experiencing it. It made me reevaluate my own egoic stories from a witness/observer position, which was eye opening," Paula replied.

"The weirdest part for me, was that it doesn't matter if my egoic stories are true, false, painful, or not relevant to who I am now; whatever story is playing inside my head will keep creating the reality that I am experiencing until I dis-create it."

Paula and Mark leveraged their excitement to immediately capture what they had learned during their Vision Quest. They realized at a much deeper level why practicing their dis-creation exercises will clean the egoic stories that no longer serve them from the slate of their minds. They noted that after dis-creation work, the next essential thing is to Self-program the changes which are needed to transcend incarnational stories.

Paula closed her eyes to contemplate. After a moment, she opened them and shared, "It's a bit paradoxical that after I own my incarnational life lessons, the next step is to *intentionally forget* what I've experienced. This process will allow me, and our students, to live our lives as deliberately conscious creators who purposely design our incarnational stories based on what we want to experience, rather than what we were programmed to believe during our childhoods."

"Wow." Mark shared with awe and admiration for his partner's deep intuitive wisdom. "That was heavy Paula."

Their latest Vision Quest had reinforced that studying, practicing, and emotionalizing the Self-mastery life lessons which the God Source had taught them will help them to transcend their egoic stories, so their history doesn't have to be their future.

These Self-realizations inspired Paula and Mark to summarize all their lessons from their Vision Quest adventures. Mark opened his notes and began to read, while Paula typed as fast as she could to keep pace with his dictation.

- Lesson 1- Spiritual Partnerships- Consciously Awakened Spiritual Relationships are a miraculous support system which can help humankind evolve from a five-sensory species to a multisensory species, so together we can create the critical mass needed to help SAVE the... HuMans!
- Lesson 2 Paradox- To Spiritually Awaken, you must embrace the paradoxical dualisms of the earth plane.
- Lesson 3 Willingness- Having the Willingness to do whatever it takes to awaken spiritually is essential; because 90% of life is just showing up.
- Lesson 4 Spiritual Distinction- The ability to consciously feel the difference between the core distinctions of physical life by practicing the Spiritual Distinction Meditative Exercise is a vital ingredient of Self-mastery.
- Lesson 5 The Five Disciplines of the Initiate- Practicing the Five Disciplines of the Initiate will produce the divine fuel required to live a Self-empowered life.

- <u>Lesson 6 You Are a Vibrational BEing-</u> Since you are a vibrational BEing, you need to raise the vibrational frequency of your body and thoughts until they become matched with the vibrational frequency of your dreams, goals and desires.
- <u>Lesson 7 Dig...One Deep Well-</u> On your journey home to your Inner Self, you need to dig one deep well until you discover your spiritual reason for incarnating.
- <u>Lesson 8 Self-Parenting Exercises-</u> Self-parenting exercises will fulfill your emotional dependency needs that weren't met when you were a child.
- <u>Lesson 9 Spiritual Communications-</u> Spiritual Communications are the language of your intuitive heart, which will synergistically connect you with other deliberately conscious souls via the Namasté Consciousness.
- <u>Lesson 10 Dis-Creation is the Missing Link-</u> Dis-creation exercises are the missing link of the conscious creation process. You need to do these revolutionary exercises to clean the slate of your mind before you can create the realities you desire.
- <u>Lesson 11 The Magic of Emotionalizing-</u> Emotionalizing your Self-realizations will help you to create the permanent behavioral changes that you seek if you are willing to Self-program these Self-realizations deep into your subconscious mind.

— <u>Lesson 12 Transcending Your Incarnational Story-</u>
You are not your thoughts. You are not your feelings. You are not your body. You are not your real world, true stories. You are a BEing of Light and Love who incarnated into a human body to experience a curriculum made of life lessons and karmic burns.

"I don't know about you Mark but listening to you read these Self-mastery lessons made me feel like our research for our Spiritual Awakening course is now complete. How about you?"

"Yeah, it feels complete to me too."

"Then it's time for us to organize what we've learned into a training course, so we can go out into the world and share it knowing that what we give away, we get to keep."

Paula's face beamed with love, as she asked Mark in a whimsical tone, "Do you believe that the God Source has given us all the Universal Truths that we need to create our Spiritual Awakening course?"

They both answered with a harmonious, confident and humorous tone, "WE BELIEVE!"

Lesson #12 Of
Transformational Awakening Is...

Transcending Your Incarnational Story

You are not your thoughts. You are not your feelings. You are not your body. You are not your real world, true stories. You are a BEing of Light and Love who incarnated into a human body to experience a curriculum made of life lessons and karmic burns.

DONE!

Sometimes Dreams Do Come True

Conscious Relationships are the Closest Thing to Heaven You Can Experience on Earth

Paula and Mark began reviewing what they'd learned from their last transformative Vision Quest. Though they were both tired from their metaphysical journey, the spiritual partners were still exuberant from their experience. One lesson at a time, they examined all the empowering life lessons that the God Source had taught them. Paula's coaching experience, combined with Mark's ability to quickly organize notes into concise thesis statements, allowed them to make rapid progress. As the hours ticked away, they gradually converted their research into professional lesson plans and coaching exercises. Their work was still rough, but they had built the foundation for their Spiritual Awakening course.

Eventually, their fatigue drained them of their creative juices, and they put their endeavor on hold until the following morning. Mark wished Paula a good night and returned home for some well-deserved rest. After so many trips down the same winding road, he could practically drive it blindfolded. With this ease of unconscious operation, his mind became lost in an endless loop of thoughts. Something was lurking at the edge of his mind, and with each passing moment it grew in intensity. He was proud of everything he and Paula had accomplished that night, but his thoughts kept returning to the kiss he had shared with her. Eventually, his mind's preoccupation with the kiss superseded his feelings of accomplishment, until it became impossible for him to think about anything else.

Mark couldn't deny how much Paula had helped him change. He was no longer driven purely by ego or the desire to adhere to societal norms, because he knew that he was not the thoughts inside his head, nor his roles or actions. He still had a great deal of inner work to do, but he was in a place better than ever before, and he had Paula to thank for it. For the first time since he had lost Ann, Mark felt an emotional connection to someone else.

As he pulled into his driveway, he couldn't stop his mind from analyzing the distinctions between Ann and Paula. He entered his home, dropped his bag on the living room couch, and prepared a simple dinner as his mind continued to whirl. As much as he loved Ann, he'd never grown with her in the way that he had with Paula. This realization was hardly surprising because he and Ann were just teenagers when they'd met; but it did cause Mark to wonder, *What if I was never meant to stay with Ann? What if Paula is the one for me?* He pondered these questions as he finished his meal.

Mark retired to his bed and closed his eyes, anxious to get some rest from the conflicting turbulence of thoughts in his head. After 20 minutes of tossing and turning, Mark finally accepted that his mind was far too stimulated with thoughts of Paula and Ann to be able to sleep. He decided to put this energy to good use by organizing his course notes, but when he went to the living room to get his laptop, he found it wasn't there. A surge of panic washed over him as he rummaged through his bag somehow expecting his laptop to magically appear.

After turning his living room upside down, Mark slipped on a pair of flip-flops and returned to his car to see if he'd mistakenly left it there. When his search yielded no results, he realized he must have left it at

Paula's. He checked the time, it was late, but he decided to head back to Paula's to get his laptop anyway. Though he felt compelled to make the drive, Mark questioned if retrieving his laptop was his only motive.

* * *

In the meantime, after Mark had left Paula's she organized their research material and tidied up for the following day's work. As she did, she became acutely aware of a feeling of melancholy within her. The sensation puzzled her. After such an empowering evening, she should have felt happy. Instead, her morose feelings gradually became more pronounced.

She tried to keep her mind busy by focusing her attention on preparing dinner. She poured herself a glass of wine. As she cooked, her anxious feelings gave way to a sense of emotional release. By the time she sat down to eat, she realized that her emotional state was being triggered by her unresolved feelings for Mark.

Paula's years of being single provided her with the time and space to complete a significant amount of psycho-spiritual work. Through this work, she became an empowered, self-reliant woman. Although she'd had several short-term relationships in the past, she never felt a deep emotional connection with any of her partners in the way that she did with Mark. *Why was this time different?*

She reflected on when she first learned about conscious relationships - a unique type of partnership in which two souls commit to co-create a relationship where their primary goal is to support each other's psycho-spiritual growth. Back then she found the notion of conscious relationships to be holistically romantic and something she longed to experience. She was young and naive and didn't appreciate the intricacies of such a union. What had intrigued her most about conscious relationships was that they create a synergy that allows each partner to spiritually evolve faster together than they could on their own. This happens because each partner focuses on the subtle needs and desires of the other and is sensitive about the other's feelings, history and karmic challenges.

Paula finished her meal and began tidying up. As she washed the dishes, she reflected further on her relationship with Mark and the way their interactions improved the quality of her life. Before they'd met, she was strong yet still unsure of herself in some areas of her life. Even with all the time she'd spent learning Self-mastery coaching techniques, she struggled to understand her true calling. This left her adrift in the sea of life for years until her "chance" meeting with Mark. At first, all she wanted to do was help him heal; to save the man who saved her. But the more inner work they did together, the more she realized that it wasn't just about healing him. Paula cared deeply for Mark, and genuinely wanted to help him transcend his tragedy, but she also grokked that helping him was synergistically helping her as well. In many ways, Mark was the missing link in her life. Though she'd been independent and felt complete before, having someone else to inspire her creativity and share her experiences helped her to take her *theoretical knowledge* to new levels of *emotional understanding*

After Paula finished cleaning, she returned to her living room to ponder further. During the time they'd come to know each other, Mark had been emotionally honest with her and she with him. They'd reached a place in which they were more spiritually conscious together than they were alone. Together they were each willing to do whatever was required to push themselves forward on their journey home to their inner Self. *Isn't that the way a Conscious Relationship is supposed to be?* She thought.

Though she cared deeply for Mark, her mind told her that she was trapped by circumstances completely out of her control. As much as she wanted to reach out and be with Mark, she believed that he wasn't ready to move on yet. Even though she considered herself to be Self-mastered, at that moment, she felt powerless, like a small child. She contemplated the irony of her situation as tears rolled down her face. She was interrupted by a knock at her door.

As Mark waited outside, he felt a familiar, yet uncomfortable, sensation in the pit of his stomach. It was a feeling he knew very well, like a nagging pain from an old injury. *Why is this coming up now?* His attempt to process his feelings was cut short when Paula answered the door with a surprised look on her face.

"Hey! I didn't expect to see you again tonight. What's up?"

Mark noticed a faint glossiness in her eyes. It was subtle, but it looked like she might have been crying. He also thought that he might be over analyzing the situation.

"Hi. Sorry, I know it's late. I couldn't sleep, so I tried to get a little work done before bed... you know how it goes. But I think I left my laptop here. I figured, 'What the heck, it's not too late, why not just swing by and grab it?'" Mark chuckled anxiously. He felt embarrassed after hearing his own words. His rambling was a reactive behavioral pattern, which he knew he'd formed before his self-help work.

"Oh. I know exactly where your laptop is!" Paula replied with her usual chipper tone.

Mark entered the home and closed the door behind him, as Paula went to fetch his laptop. He couldn't help but notice that she was wearing a revealing camisole and pair of silky, skimpy shorts. Certainly, suitable sleepwear, but it was far more revealing than anything he'd ever seen her in before, which caused an involuntary physical reaction.

Paula returned with his laptop, raising it triumphantly. "Right where I left it... on top of a stack of notes! After you left, I organized everything to prepare for tomorrow's work."

Though her demeanor was as cool and calm as always, Mark's sense that she'd been crying grew stronger. He wanted to open the conversation, but he remembered how late it was, and he didn't want to further impose on her boundaries. "Well. It's late. I should go." He said with hesitancy in his voice.

The two exchanged a friendly hug, and just as Mark reached for the doorknob, Paula blurted, "Mark. Are we just not going to talk about it?"

Mark turned to face Paula, and he noticed that her stance stiffened and her eyes began to gloss over again. He felt his stomach tighten, "What's on your mind?" He asked, wanting to give her the opportunity to share her feelings.

"Mark, I know it would be so easy for us to write off what happened as just a one-time thing, but I don't think it's that simple. I feel there's something more between us... and I think you feel the same way. Don't you?" Paula asked, earnestly.

"I don't deny that. I feel something too, but I'm not exactly sure what that is. There's a lot of things I'm wrestling with right now. I know that I care about you very much, but I don't want to rush into something out of a desire to feel loved again. That would be immature and careless on my part... and you deserve better than that."

Paula interrupted Mark with a surprising strength in her voice, "Mark, when it comes to you and me... us... nothing has been ordinary, especially how we met! The God Source didn't bring us together by accident. Our relationship isn't just the byproduct of some random series of events. The way we've evolved together gives a taste of what we stand to gain as individuals if we agree to intentionally create a conscious relationship.

You've changed so much from a heart-broken, grieving soul who saved me from drowning into a well-grounded man standing now before me. It's hard to believe you're the same person. And it's more than that; you bring out the best in me. Before I met you, I wasn't sure how I could manifest my dharmic reason for living. But now I'm clear, and I know what my spiritual purpose is." Paula's voice cracked as tears flowed down her face. "And I know if we're both *willing* to put our fears aside and give ourselves a chance, we have the opportunity to create something very special."

Mark was stunned. Paula had always been exuberant, but for as long as he'd known her, she'd never been as powerful and sure of herself as she was at this moment. He desperately wanted to say something, but the words wouldn't come. Dozens of thoughts whirled all at once, as his mind struggled to craft an appropriate response. All the while, Paula waited anxiously with tears steadily streaming down her cheeks. Mark ignored the myriad of thoughts in his head and slowly stepped toward Paula. He took her in his arms and gave her a tender kiss. As the two embraced, their hearts synchronized, and their pulses accelerated. Their rambling thoughts quickly fell away, and the only thing remaining was their romantic desire for each other.

Mark pulled Paula in closer and kissed her again, but this time with all the passion that existed within him. He never expected to have such an experience again. He was awed by the deep love that he felt for Paula. He had suppressed his love for her for so long, but at this moment it was undeniable, and it overwhelmed him with desire. When he felt her lips connect with his, nothing else in the world mattered. He wrapped his arms tightly around her, feeling completely enraptured.

He wanted to say something, but it felt as though his brain's connection to the rest of his body had been rendered inert. Still, he tried and said, "I've worked through heartache to achieve this conscious relationship with you. Since we met, we've taken a journey of a thousand steps together... one step at a time. But what matters most is the imprints you've left on my heart and soul."

At that moment, Paula could not hold back her passion any longer. She leaned forward and wrapped her arms around Mark, welcoming his every advance. They kissed deeply, as his hands gradually slid down her body from her shoulders to her lower back and beyond, igniting their physical passion and bringing their romantic desires to a feverish pitch.

I'm about to make love with the most amazing woman I've ever known, Mark thought to himself, as Paula seductively removed his shirt. Unwilling to wait another second, he scooped her up in his arms and swiftly made his way to the bedroom to consummate their love for one another. He gently placed her in the middle of the bed and slipped on top of her.

"I love you so much, Paula."

She placed her hands on his cheeks, smiling radiantly. "Oh, Mark. I never knew I could feel like this. You've changed everything for me."

Mark kissed her gently, whispering between kisses, "I never want to stop kissing you."

"Mmm," was her only reply.

"I want to make love to you," he said, as he gave her a sensual kiss on the neck.

"Yes," she whispered breathlessly.

Longing for skin-to-skin contact, he slipped the camisole from Paula's shoulders. As it fell away, he placed a kiss on the nape of her neck and gradually worked his way down her shoulders with a sensual tease. He pulled her in close and whispered, "You're the best thing that has ever happened to me. I want you to be mine and only mine."

Mark's words gave Paula comfort in knowing that, finally, he wanted her as much as she wanted him. And with that feeling of release and complete surrender between them, Paula slowly removed the remainder of their clothing and gave herself to him. They made love passionately late into the night with deep appreciation and reverence for their relationship; it truly felt like heaven on earth.

Physically exhausted and totally at peace, they fell asleep in each other's arms. As the night wore on, Mark slipped into a powerful, lucid dream. He found himself in an unfamiliar dark room, but his angst was quickly brushed aside when he felt encased by a comforting warmth. He turned and saw a figure bathed in white light descending toward him. Though her face was obscured, he intuitively knew who it was. The woman bathed in light slowly reached out and took his hands in hers. The instant they made contact, Mark's mood shifted. In front of him stood his first love, Ann, dressed in white angelic robes, smiling brightly, and looking as lovely as ever. Seeing her filled him with a bittersweet sadness. Tears rolled down his cheeks, unsure of what to say or do.

"Ann, I'm..." he started, but the words wouldn't come. He stared at her, unable to find the words to properly articulate his thoughts. His tear-filled eyes became too clouded to see her clearly. As he wiped away his tears, Ann leaned forward and gave him a tender hug.

"Mark, when I left my body, it made life very hard for you. I want you to know that I've been with you the entire time. Through every road you traveled and every person you've met, I've been sending you the guidance that you needed to heal and find your true purpose for incarnating."

Mark's tears flowed. "Ann... I don't even know what to say. There's a woman. Her name is Paula, and...."

"It's OK. You have nothing to feel uncomfortable about. I've been with you this entire time. I love you, and I don't want you to be alone. I want you to be happy and I want you to be with Paula. I want you to know that I'm in a place that is filled with nothing but the love of the God Source. I love you, Mark. I'll always love you."

Ann leaned forward and graced Mark with a tender, loving kiss. As soon as their lips separated, Ann began to ascend toward the light from which she came. Mark reached out and took her hand one last time. She continued to ascend, and as her form began merging with the bright light, she looked at Mark and smiled warmly, "Remember, my Love, everything that happened to you happened for a divine reason!"

When Mark woke, he knew his dream was a spiritual communication from the God Source. He turned to share with Paula what he had dreamt, but the bed was empty. He wondered where she could be so early in the morning, until he smelled the aroma of food. He followed the mouth-watering fragrances to the kitchen, where he found Paula preparing breakfast and humming a joy-filled melody.

Paula glimpsed Mark standing in the kitchen doorway, and she smiled the same alluring smile that she'd given him the night before. "God morning! I'm making omelets, toast, and freshly squeezed orange juice. I hope you like the sound of that!"

Mark wasn't surprised by Paula's nonchalant happy-go-lucky attitude. The few women he'd been with in the past usually showed signs of insecurity the morning after. But Paula was different and unlike any other woman he'd ever known. He knew he was a lucky man to have a woman like her in his life.

As Paula continued to cook, Mark walked toward her. She turned and was surprised to see him so close. "Oh. Hey you. Careful not to distract me... our eggs might burn." She said, flirtatiously.

Ignoring her warning, Mark pulled her in closer. He looked deeply into her eyes and smiled. He knew that he was right where he wanted to be, with exactly who he wanted to be with. With the sound of frying eggs in the background, he cupped her face with his hands and gave her a tender kiss.

"Being loved by you is the most satisfying thing I've ever experienced." He kissed away her tears of joy and continued, "I feel like I've won the lottery having you in my life."

Paula snuggled into the nape of his neck and murmured a sweet, "Thank you."

Paula glanced at Mark. Her eyes shone as bright as stars. She smiled and kissed him with passion.

Mark took a long deep and comforting breath knowing that their love was the cornerstone for their Spiritual Awakening course. He knew in his heart that their course had the potential to help humankind heal - one person at a time - and that together they could contribute to a global transformation to address the challenges facing humanity.

Their dharmic work would have to wait though, because at that moment they were fully present in the warmth of each other's arms and the smell of burning eggs.

Do The Work You Love

"If one advances confidently in the direction of his dreams and endeavors to live the life which he has imagined, he will meet with a success unexpected in common hours."

Henry David Thoreau

Twenty Years Later...

It was an early Friday evening when Mark and Paula were getting dressed to attend a graduation ceremony to certify their students as Spiritual Life Coaches. Paula carefully appraised her appearance in the full-length mirror to see if any last-minute adjustments were needed. Tonight, would be the 20th time that she and her husband would present diplomas to their graduates, and she wanted to look her best.

"How are you doing, Babe... almost ready?" Mark asked from across the room.

"Just about, Love."

Paula lingered at the mirror for a moment longer. Tears of joy rolled down her cheeks as she gazed at herself and reflected on the years of dedication that led to this moment. With her eyes still tearing she told her husband, "You know, most people overestimate what they can accomplish in a year, and underestimate what they can accomplish in a decade."

Mark stopped adjusting his tie and looked at his wife, "So, is that what's making you so emotional tonight?"

Paula turned her head and smiled, "Sort of. I was just looking back at everything it took to reach this moment, and it got me thinking... if someone had told me 20 years ago that our work would lead us to share these Universal Truths with thousands of souls, I probably would have laughed or thought they were pre-maturely positive."

"Yeah, I know what you mean. It's hard to believe." Mark commented as he fastened his cuff links. "Our transformational school expanded faster than I ever could have imagined. I've loved every minute of it. When I think of where we started, it feels surreal."

Mark took a final moment to adjust his tux, which he only wore once a year to honor his students. He wanted to look as sharp as possible. Feeling satisfied with his appearance, he turned and marveled at his wife's inner and outer beauty and said with a slight chuckle, "Time flies when I'm doing the work I love with my best friend and soul mate." With longing desire in his eyes, he added with a sigh, "Speaking of doing the things that we love doing together ..."

"Mr. Celli, are you making a pass at me?"

"Absolutely! I was just thinking... after the ceremony why don't we open a bottle of wine and try a new technique from the Kama Sutra?"

Since their marriage, Paula and Mark had been experimenting using the ancient teachings of Kama Sutra. To their surprise, they learned that Kama Sutra is not exclusively about sex. It contains a wealth of information about the nature of love, family life and other aspects of human sexuality. It taught them about desire – what triggers it, what sustains it, and how and when it is appropriate to use it. Practicing its techniques helped them keep their relationship fresh and exciting.

"Well," Paula replied teasingly, "if you're a good boy tonight, I think that could be arranged."

"I promise, I'll be on my best behavior. And remember, we have the whole house to ourselves tonight." Mark exclaimed in a playful tone. "That reminds me, did you get a chance to talk to Lenore today?"

"I did. She's so excited to go rock climbing with her big brother this weekend. She barely slept last night."

"Did you remind them to come straight to the campus tonight?"

"I did. Rudy said he wanted to get there early to help with the prep work."

Mark turned and slowly strolled across the room, beaming as he approached his wife. "I must say, you did an excellent job rearing our children."

"You helped a little too." Paula giggled.

"A little?" Mark asked playing along.

"Nope." Paula broke into a fit of laugher, "It was all me."

When their laughter subsided, Mark kissed Paula.

"I must say Mr. Celli, you look very handsome tonight."

Mark grinned proudly, "Thanks Babe. And you look positively stunning."

Paula embraced him. "Ready to go?"

"I am."

They locked up and made their way to the campus where the graduation ceremony was scheduled to take place.

Despite arriving an hour early, the parking lot was already half full of eager graduates and their proud families and friends making their way to the ceremonial grounds. The campus was beautifully landscaped with cobblestone paths, water ponds and cherry blossom trees. A plethora of blooming wild flowers provided a breathtaking backdrop for the distinctive occasion.

They began making their way through the campus to connect with their staff and volunteers. They passed the Self-mastery academy for students from kindergarten through to grade 12, the sweat lodge, labyrinth, and several statues of souls who had achieved a state of Self-mastery. They approached the school's three main buildings, which had been consciously built in a triangular formation to represent the spiritual trilogy of life. As they passed the Life Seminar building where their large weekend-intensives took place, Paula felt deeply blessed to have partnered with various spiritual organizations to co-host these transformational events. She was amazed at how these fundraising intensives rewarded them with soulful friendships and connected them with spiritual leaders throughout the world.

As they continued walking, they passed dozens of former alumni and current students along the way. They were filled with a warm sense of satisfaction in seeing so many turn out for the occasion. Twenty years ago, their first graduation class certified eight students, while tonight's graduation class would bestow Spiritual Life Coaching Certification to over a hundred students. With such a large number of graduating students they had to divide the Three Fires Ceremony into four groups.

Arriving at the meeting point, they could feel the excitement in the air. As they finalized last-minute ceremony details with the enthusiastic volunteers, Rudy and Lenore arrived. Rudy was a 20-year-old replica of Mark, while Lenore, 15 years old, had Mark's blue eyes and Paula's beautiful thick hair and smaller frame. Mark and Paula were proud of their spiritually grounded children. They were independent free thinkers, respectful in how they treated others, and just as importantly, how they treated themselves.

The family mingled and chatted until it was time to assume their positions for the ceremony. Paula and Mark gave their children a hug and took their places as they waited for the first group of initiates to arrive.

**

The Three Fires Ceremony went smoothly. As the campus cleared out, Paula and Mark proudly hugged Rudy and Lenore and bid them farewell as the children started on their weekend rock-climbing adventure.

As the last few volunteers left, Paula and Mark finally headed home. As soon as they entered the door, Mark rushed up the stairs to the bedroom. Paula followed closely. Mark couldn't rip his tux off fast enough. As he fumbled with his tuxedo, Paula walked slowly toward him and placed her arms around his waist. Mark paused and embraced his wife's caress as she gave him a soft, gentle kiss. She then leaned back and with an alluring tone said, "Mr. Celli, you have been such a good boy. I think you deserve a reward."

Paula whispered into Mark's ear, an ancient Hebrew passage wherein the wife asks her husband four questions, which he must answer before she will agree to make love with him,

"What makes you happy?"

"You do!"

"What's the most important thing in your life?"

"You are!"

"Where would you rather be?"

"Nowhere!"

"When will you leave me?"

"Never!"

"Then proceed, My Love!"

After making love, Mark laid on his back and stared at the ceiling in deep contemplation. He turned to face his wife. Even though she was sleeping, she wore a serene smile on her face. Mark grinned and returned his gaze to the ceiling feeling fulfilled and blessed.

He thought back to the day he married Paula. The memory was etched into his mind, and he could recall vivid details as though it took place yesterday. He could see their soul friends gathered in the chapel filled with fresh cut flowers. He saw the adorable flower girl leading the way for his bride as she slowly walked down the aisle. Paula had looked beautiful in her vintage wedding dress. The soft silky material hugged her fit body in all the right places, and the low neckline accentuated her feminine attributes. He remembered reciting their wedding vows, which they composed together. It amazed him that after so many years, they were still so deeply embedded within him:

We asked you here today to bear witness as we read our Life Partner wedding vows to each other.

We stand here as equal Life Partners;
and we promise that as long as we live,
we will support each other's
spiritual, emotional, and psychological growth
because there is nothing more important to us
than the holistic evolution of our immortal souls.
We know that together we will
evolve faster than either of us could on our own.
We promise to rise above old-world relationship models
and elevate onward to an emotionally mature, highly
functional technique called *Responsibility Communication.*
We own that we will not always have perfect behavior,
so we commit to correcting our imperfect
behavior as quickly as possible.

We commit to being emotionally honest with each other,
which is why we have co-created an environment
where it is emotionally safe to share our
most intimate thoughts and feelings.
We unconditionally accept that marriage isn't
a magical guarantee of happiness,
but an empowering tool that we can use
to keep aligning ourselves with our
spiritual purpose for living.
We pledge to adhere to our Life Partner Vows
because we know that a
consciously awakened spiritual partnership
is the closest thing to heaven which
we can experience on Earth.

Mark then thought back to the first time he saw Paula, that unforgettable day when he'd pulled her out of the ocean. He paused to give thanks that they found each other at that precise moment. Mark felt an inner knowing that he was exactly where he was meant to be and doing exactly what he was meant to be doing, for himself and for humankind to help create the critical mass needed to help **SAVE the... HuMans**™!

CHAPTER 19

Ancient Scrolls
of
Transformational
Awakening

LESSON #1
Spiritual Partnerships
Consciously awakened, Spiritual Partnerships are a
miraculous support system that can help
humankind evolve from a five-sensory species to a
multisensory species, so together we can create the
critical mass needed to help SAVE the... HuMans!

LESSON #2
Paradox
To spiritually awaken, you must embrace the
dualisms of the earth plane, especially the Healing
Paradox because inside of every karmic curse lies an
equal and opposite dharmic blessing.

LESSON #3
Willingness
The will to take whatever actions are necessary to
spiritually awaken, because 90%
of life is just showing up.

LESSON #1
Spiritual Partnerships
Consciously awakened, Spiritual Partnerships are a
miraculous support system that can help humankind evolve
from a five-sensory species to a multisensory species,
so together we can create the critical mass needed
to help SAVE the... HuMans!

LESSON #2
Paradox
To spiritually awaken, you must embrace the dualisms
of the earth plane, especially the Healing Paradox because
inside of every karmic curse lies an equal and
opposite dharmic blessing.

LESSON #3
Willingness
The will to take whatever actions are necessary to spiritually
awaken, because 90% of life is just showing up.

LESSON # 4
Spiritual Distinction
The ability to consciously feel the difference between your
Spirit and the core components of physical life --
body, mind and vision --
is a vital skill of inner Self-Mastery.

LESSON #5

The Five Disciplines of the Initiate

Prayer, Feeling Your Healing Feelings, Visualizations, Spiritual
Distinction Meditation and Dis-Creation will produce the
Divine fuel that will empower your life.

LESSON # 6

You Are a Vibrational Being

The Secrets of Vibrational Transformation
will help you raise your vibratory frequencies so you
can create and enjoy a Self-mastered life.

LESSON # 7

Dig... One Deep Well

Commit to Digging One Deep Well using one spiritual path
until you discover the omnipotent wisdom that reveals
your spiritual reason for incarnating on your
Journey Home to Your Inner Self.

LESSON #8

Self-Parenting Exercises

Are experiential exercises designed to fulfill your emotional
dependency needs that weren't met when you were a child.
Emotional dependency needs are the intimacy, nurturing,
unconditional love and boundary protection that you need to
feel safe, sane, and secure in the world.

LESSON # 9
Spiritual Communications
Is the language that allows your life to be directed by
your Intuitive Heart, the source of infinite
wisdom, love, and compassion.
It is what synergistically connects you with
all living things via the Namasté Consciousness.

LESSON # 10
Dis-Creation is the Missing Link
Of the Conscious Creation process because you must clean
the slate of your mind before your Self-programming
affirmations can create the reality you desire.

LESSON # 11
The Power of Emotionalizing
Creates the Permanent Behavioral Changes that you seek
if you invest the time and energy to Self-program what you
emotionalize based on your transformational Self-realizations.

LESSON # 12
Transcending Your Incarnational Story
You are not your thoughts. You are not your feelings.
You are not your body. You are not your real world, true stories.
You are a BEing of Light and Love who incarnated into
a human body to experience a curriculum made
of life lessons and karmic burns.

<u>Are You Willing?</u>

To Do Your *Inner* Work and Be Part of the Global Transformation?

By Christine Grauer, MSc, CSLC

This book is about more than a transformational love story - *it's about a Transformational Movement.* Just as Mark and Paula were drawn together by a force greater than themselves for a higher purpose, you were drawn to this book for a transformational reason. This book is just as much about *you* as it is about Mark and Paula. In a perfectly evolving Universe, it's no accident that this book ended up in your hands!

The spiritual partners were driven by a higher sense of purpose to create the awakening course. This would not have been possible had Mark not experienced *the dark night of the soul* and completed his personal work with

Coach Sarah. Through his coaching sessions, Mark awakened to his Divine nature; and through his awakening, he was able to co-create the Awakening Course with Paula. Mark and Paula created the course to help humanity awaken to their true nature and interconnectedness and to ultimately transform lives and the world at a critical point in time.

In *Cosmos* (1980), Carl Sagan predicted that the human species has a slim chance of surviving the next hundred years. But you don't need to read his book to know that the world is in a catastrophic state. Turn on the news, pick up a newspaper, take a good look at the cityscape and smog, or observe the drastic weather changes and environmental disasters around you.

The Current State of Humanity

The vast majority of us believe we are separate from one another, and this is evident through the inhumane ways in which we treat not only each other, but also animals and the environment. Humans are at the top of the food chain with no predators, yet we turn on ourselves for materialistic gain. Technology has advanced faster than humanity, and most technological conveniences, such as social networks, which claim to bring people together, actually foster a sense of separateness and contribute to the de-humanization of society.

Only after the last tree has been cut down, only after the last river has been poisoned, only after the last fish has been caught, only then will you find that *money cannot be eaten!*
-Cree Indian Prophesy

There is a worldwide imbalance of priorities. Major league sports players are paid millions of dollars, while teachers responsible for educating and basically raising children earn a mere fraction of that! Excessive focus on performance and profits has created a materialistic society where mass consumerism, fame and greed have prevailed over compassion, kindness and equality.

The unyielding ecological disasters and catastrophic state of world affairs is a reminder that the heavily burdened earth is experiencing its own *dark night of the soul*. But the condition of the earth is merely a reflection of the inner human condition, which is just as heavily burdened. No amount of positive affirmations will create the needed change. We can try to ignore and turn a blind eye to the devastating news that confronts us throughout the day, but that will not change the fact that the world is in a state of despair. Let's call a spade a spade.

Just as Mark's tragedy became a blessing in that it awakened him to his Divine nature, the political landscape in the US and around the world has helped many people awaken to the *need for change*. We are no longer able to ignore the unjust treatment of fellow citizens and the state that the country is in. And just as Mark could not begin his healing process until he recognized that he had issues that needed to be healed, the first step toward global transformation is recognizing that changes are needed for humankind to survive the next hundred years. The good news is that more and more people are owning what needs to happen, and this acknowledgement is the spark needed to ignite change.

Humanity has two paths: one toward self-destruction and the other toward a global awakening of Light and Love! Both possibilities exist simultaneously. The question is - will enough people take the required action soon enough to help *SAVE... the HuMans™*?

Saving Humanity Starts with You and Me!

Before a passenger plane takes off, the flight attendants instruct passengers on emergency procedures, one of which is that each capable passenger must *first* put on their oxygen mask *before* helping another put on their mask. *Why?* Because we must first help ourselves before we can successfully help someone else. Likewise, before we can help transform the world, we must each first transform ourselves.

By doing our inner work, we free ourselves from our limiting beliefs, which are creating our less-than-desirable reality and contributing to a disconnected society. As we do this, we awaken to our true nature, and as Mark and Paula experienced, we begin to expand our understanding of the world around us and feel interconnected with all. Healthy and empowering thoughts and behaviors prevail in our lives, and we begin to operate as a multisensory human with regard for the whole of humanity.

Just as all cells are interconnected in our bodies, all humans are interconnected in a single body called humanity. And just as changes in one cell affect the functioning of other cells in our bodies, awakening to our Oneness will contribute to the awakening of the whole of humanity. By the Law of Attraction, we will draw like-minded people into our lives, and we will help to transform those around us, just as ticking clocks in a room synchronize. Transformational awakening will happen when all humans act in unison as a single, harmonious organism called humanity. Stealing, polluting, injuring and violating will be known as strange occurrences of the past... a time when the human organism had a cancer and was killing pieces of itself.

We but mirror the world.
All the tendencies present in the outer world are to be found
in the world of our body. If we could change ourselves,
the tendencies in the world would also change.
As a man changes his own nature, so does the attitude
of the world change towards him.
-Mahatma Gandhi

It may seem hard to fathom that working on ourselves will help to transform the world, but there is no single, more important thing each of us can do to help save the world and humanity! If Mark had not done his inner work first, he would have remained stuck in a state of mental despair. *In such a desperate state, could he have transformed himself and created a course on awakening to help empower others?*

Know that you are not alone in your desire to create change. Millions of people feel their souls crying out for change and are awakening today. As each of us begins our journey to inner change, the rate of change among the many grows exponentially. Mark and Paula referred to the importance of critical mass in saving humanity, and it is this scientific phenomenon that will fuel the planet's global awakening.

The Miraculous Power of Critical Mass

Also known as the "tipping point", critical mass is a scientific process of evolution where a rate of change happens in such a way that it becomes self-sustaining and creates a self-propelling momentum to create further change; it's the quantity needed to sustain a chain reaction. Critical mass is observed in a variety of contexts, such as physics, politics, technology, and group dynamics. In social dynamics, it is estimated that critical mass occurs when about 10% of a given population adopts the same, new behavior pattern.

Lyall Watson described this phenomenon in *Lifetide* (1980), when he reported on Japanese primatologists who observed a species of wild monkeys. One young monkey began washing dirt off sweet potatoes by the shoreline. Over a period of about six years, all young monkeys and their parents adopted the behavior, while the older adult monkeys without offspring did not change their behavior. But then, as if a large conspiracy took place and *within a single day*, the *entire colony* (including the stubborn old adults), adopted the behavior. And get this... miraculously the same species on different, distant islands adopted the *same behavior!*

To save the planet and humanity a point of critical mass must be attained. We must reach a place as a global society where enough of us are conscious that we are Spiritual BEings having a human experience, and where we understand our interconnectedness and Oneness. Only then can we become consciously aware of the earth's ecological time bomb and realize that we have Godlike powers to help reverse the process.

Now What?

Despite what society may have conditioned us to believe, and from the perspective of quantum mechanics, there is only the *Now*. You may be accustomed to "holding out" for some event, thing or day in the future before you take action, like waiting for New Year's Day to lose weight or quit smoking. But when that project finishes, or when the next month or season starts, or when the kids get older, or when you get more money, or when you have more time, *another excuse* will come along and keep you in the dark and the world heading toward destruction. It's time to take action. Now! And this doesn't mean reading another book, theorizing about what you *could* do and sending positive thoughts to the Universe. It means digging in and taking steps to begin your journey within – your journey to Oneness.

There are dozens of spiritually grounded methods available which will help you discover your true nature and create internal shifts to help transform yourself, and ultimately the planet. In the chapter, *Dig One Deep Well*, Mark reflected on how important it was for him to find a single spiritual method and dig in; likewise, you must find a single method that resonates with you, and commit to it! One such method available is that which Mark did with Coach Sarah - the *HuMethod*™ - and it was through the exercises in this program that Mark was able to overcome his tragic past and transform his life by awakening to his true spiritual nature.

Through your spiritual work, not only will you awaken your inner spiritual powers to personally benefit and create the life you truly desire, but you will also contribute to the creation of a society centered on love, peace and harmony. Ultimately, you will contribute to the critical mass needed to create a shift in global Consciousness in order to help *SAVE... the HuMans*™!

Are You Optimistic about Humanity's Future?

Millions have already acted and transformed themselves, and this has had a positive impact on so many other souls. "Mindfulness" and "meditation" are now publicized on the cover of mainstream magazines. Just 25 years ago, those words were almost taboo, and anyone with the courage to admit that they meditated was usually considered a "hippie" or somewhat of a "freak". But those taking positive, personal action have noticed a change for the better in their lives, and word is spreading to the point where meditating is almost considered the "in thing" today. Likewise, few spiritual life coaches existed 25 years ago, and today, more and more people are seeing positive, palpable changes in their lives under the guidance of a professionally trained spiritual life coach. Word is spreading to the extent where having some form of a life coach is almost more common today than not. Celebrities, including Oprah Winfrey, Leonardo DiCaprio, Serena Williams, Chuck Liddell, and even the band *Metallica* have all benefited from having a life coach.

There is reason for celebration and hope! Not only are millions spiritually awakening, but humanity has made considerable improvements over the past hundreds of years. Thanks to medical and technological advances, the average human now lives longer (Roser, 2017); the number of undernourished individuals has decreased steadily over the past 20 years (Ritchie, 2017); and countless efforts are being made to promote global peace and to aid fellow humans in conditions of poverty and lack. Isn't it amazing how communities come together in times of crisis, especially during environmental disasters? All differences and judgments seem to effortlessly fall away, while people step up and provide support to those affected by these disasters... and *the lion and the lamb lay down together.*

After the tragedy of losing those closest to him, Mark's mind blamed others and used his tragedy as an excuse to justify his destitute, depressed and distressed life. Like

Mark, you also may have endured a tragic life experience. You can use your tragic story as an excuse to remain stuck in your uncomfortableness and sadness, and you can try to repress, deny or minimize the painful reality. Or, you can choose to do as Mark did and use your tragedy as an opportunity to learn, grow and fuel your path to spiritual liberation and happiness. Life tragedy, or *the dark night of the soul*, is often the spark needed to ignite spiritual awakening and the journey toward positive change. It is only through struggle, effort and action that the cocoon is able to emerge transformed and take flight as a butterfly.

> Problems cannot be solved by the same level
> of thinking that created them.
> -Albert Einstein

Are You Willing to Be Personally Accountable?

The Awakening begets the question – are you willing to commit to doing your own psycho-spiritual work, to shed your old, self-destructive beliefs and strengthen your God-given powers? Furthermore, this book is asking if you are willing to be held *personally accountable* for doing your own transformational work to help create the critical mass for global transformation, where each of us groks our interconnectedness with the whole.

Paula's and Coach Sarah's guidance supported Mark on his journey to higher levels of Consciousness; likewise, so will associating with others of a similar focus support your journey. Connect with people who are committed to transforming themselves and the world, and your journey to awakening will follow a paved path. Thanks to technological advances, this could be as easy and cost-effective as turning on a computer and joining a transformational movement. You could subscribe to a channel or blog, such as *TED, Gaia* or the *Oprah Winfrey Network*, which are committed to spreading hope and good news and educating people on the power to change attitudes, lives, and ultimately the world. You could join Holistic Learning Center's *Inner-Net of One Abundance Exchange* to receive free, monthly Self-mastery materials. Or you could join a local *Meetup* group or host a local self-help book club.

As important as connecting with like-minded people, consider disassociating from and eliminating toxic influences in your life. This could mean reducing your time spent consuming news media, which spreads fear and feeds feelings of controversy and retaliation. This could mean replacing toxic habits or substances with healthier ones. Or this could mean taking inventory and identifying the "energy-sucking" people in your life and either setting clear boundaries to protect yourself or eliminating all associations with these people.

As a graduate from Holistic Learning Center's Certified Spiritual Life Coaching program, I have personally experienced the power of the *HuMethod*™ healing modality and it has transformed me as well as my coaching clients. Thousands of coaching clients have transformed their lives through the *HuMethod*™ healing modality. This coaching program was developed over two decades and 10,000 pages of research developed from the research on over 150 spiritual masters, saints, sages, gurus and famous self-help authors. Through 15 years of clinical testing, this method was proven to create the *greatest degree of behavioral improvement, with the greatest number of clients, in the shortest period of time.*

For anyone willing to be emotionally honest with themselves and do their personal work like Mark did, I would recommend a *HuMethod* certified coach to fuel your transformational journey. *But if this doesn't resonate with you, then choose another means.* All rivers lead to the ocean of God Consciousness. Find the river that will help you transform yourself and help create the critical mass needed to save humankind. There is no wrong way! Just do something to transform *yourself,* so you can help transform the world and help *SAVE... the HuMans*™!

There are no more awards for predicting *apocalyptic rain*, only for doing the *required work* needed to build a *transformational ark!*
Master Coach Hu

The point is, do something! Take action toward your personal growth and transformation. And know that as soon as you take even the smallest step toward your personal growth, by the Law of Attraction, you will draw people, circumstances and events into your life which match your higher energy level and further fuel your journey to Self-empowerment.

Again, I ask... Are You Willing to Do Your Inner Work and Be Part of the Global Transformation?

With much Love, Gratitude,
Optimism and Hope.

Namasté,
Christine Grauer, MSc, CSLC

We Would Love to Hear from You

Email all comments, feedback
and testimonials to
Hu@HolisticLearningCenter.com
Or call HLC @ 888-HLC-0878

Holistic Learning Centers

About the Author

Master Coach Hu Dalconzo is an author, spiritual teacher and the founding father of the first spiritual life coaching healing modality, The *Hu*Method.™ His work stands shoulder to shoulder with other paradigm-shifting human potential movement greats such as Oprah Winfrey, Eckhart Tolle, Pema Chödrön, Wayne Dyer, Deepak Chopra, Louise Hay, Marianne Williamson, and Ram Dass. In 1993, Coach Hu founded Holistic Learning Centers, North America's oldest spiritual life coaching certification school.

Combining psycho-spiritual exercises and ancient spiritual practices, The *Hu*Method™ was developed from more than 10,000 pages of research. This transformational healing modality is clinically proven to create lasting behavioral change. The "Hu" in *Hu*Method™ refers to the subconscious, divine, and quantum powers that exist within all _hu_man beings.

*Hu*Method™ certified coaches are taught how to tap into these universal powers to coach their clients on how to create permanent change.

Hu is the son of blue collar, Italian immigrants who settled in Manhattan in the 1920s. In 1974, Coach Hu was the first in his family to graduate from college (cum laude) with a degree in education. After 10 years of coaching and teaching emotionally handicapped children in New York's inner-city schools, Coach Hu realized that helping students develop self-esteem was the key factor in their journey to growth, happiness, and independence.

The Awakening is infused with the wisdom gained from Hu's hard-knock New York City beginnings. His life-giving work with at-risk youth, and his own cathartic spiritual transformation, led to the establishment of his renowned coaching school, and this groundbreaking book. Author of 14 coaching textbooks based on more than 20,000 client session hours logged since 1993, *The Awakening: A Transformational Love Story* is Hu's first novel.

With his wife and soulmate of more than 40 years, Hu Dalconzo currently resides in New Jersey in a beautiful lakeside home just three short blocks from the shoreline. Their marriage was blessed with three *mastery* children reared using The *Hu*Method™ transformational coaching techniques.

Want to Discuss These Life Altering Ideas
With Your Potential Coaching Clients,
Friends and Family?

Start A
Book Study Group

 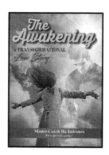 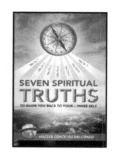

HLC will send you a Book Study Guide
that will make it easy for you to stimulate
intelligent conversation with the psycho-spiritual
topics contained in these three books.

As a Bonus, we will send you a 'Thank You' gift of the
Ancient Scrolls of Transformational Awakening
for helping us SAVE the... HuMans.

Call 888-452 0878
or email your request to:
Admin@HolisticLearningcenter.com
Subject: *[Book Title]* Study Guide

SAVE the... *HuM*ans™

Are You Willing to Be Part of the *Transformational* Solution?

"There are no more awards
for predicting *apocalyptic rain,*
only for doing the *required work* needed
to build a *transformational ark!"*
-Master Coach Hu

Are you willing to help us educate
our Human family about why we must
SAVE the... HuMans?™

We are asking you to commit to spreading the word
that a CRITICAL MASS of Light and Love is the
first step to *SAVE* the... HuMans™.

"You must not lose faith in humanity.
Humanity is like an ocean;
if a few drops of the ocean are dirty,
the ocean does not become dirty."
–Mahatma Gandhi

HLC is proud of the role we've played since 1993,
by educating people about our global challenges
via our educational campaign titled,
SAVE the... HuMans™!

Now, after two decades
HLC's *SAVE* the... HuMans™
educational campaign has evolved into the...
Inner Net of One
Abundance Exchange Campaign

This *progressive realization* of HLC's educational intention
is the next step in teaching our HuMan (god-man) family
about *Inner Transformation,* so together we can continue
to co-create the *Critical Mass* needed to help
SAVE the... HuMans™!

To Learn More About Our Campaign
and How You Can Contribute
Call 888-452-0878
Or Visit
www.HolisticLearningCenter.com/Monthly-FREE-Products

Inner Net of ONE
Monthly Abundance Exchange

Just a few decades ago it was unimaginable that millions of souls worldwide could be in contact with each other simultaneously. Today with the Internet and social networking, we can join our hearts and minds and educate the world as to why we need a *Critical Mass* of souls to help *SAVE the... HuMans™*.

We are all part of an *"inner net"* of the *Namasté Consciousness* where we are all **ONE** in *Spirit*. Using the synergy created when we combine the Internet and our Inner Net, we can quickly spread the word with passion and a sense of urgency on why we need to act now!

Are You Willing To Be Part Of The Solution?

1. **VISIT** - HLC's website on the 1st and 2nd day of each month to DOWNLOAD your <u>FREE Transformational</u> Products, which you can share with your clients, family and soul friends.

2. **STUDY and PRACTICE** - your transformational mastery products to manifest your own inner Self-transformation by transcending your ego-identification so you can be an effective Teacher of Global Transformation.

3. **TAKE ACTION** - use your divine powers to become a Global Transformational Teacher by starting a **Book Study Group** using either the Awakening, HuMan Handbook or the Seven Spiritual Truth books, and unite with us to *co-create* the *Global Critical Mass* that is needed to create a... *heaven on earth!*

For More Information
About the Inner Net of One Visit
www.HolisticLearningCenter.com/Global-Transformations

For More Information
About Starting A Book Study Group
CALL- 888-452-0878

The HuMan Handbook

> "It doesn't matter where you are on your Self-mastery journey because this book's transformational truisms are easily understood by everyone."
> -Deborah Giddings, CSLC

What does it mean to be a Hu-Man?

Coach Hu, utilized his two decades of professional field experience to piece together life altering truisms that contain all the essential lessons of how to live a Self-mastered life.

This inspirational "handbook" simplifies esoteric concepts into an easy-to-read format, so that they can be treasured by the novice as well as the seasoned self-help sage.

Coach Hu's talent lies in the fact that he delivers these abstract concepts to you in step-by-step easy to understand language. After decades of studying mastery principles, Coach Hu has captured the essence of famous self-help authors' overlapping truths and principles and presents them to you in small, manageable pieces, which makes them easy for you to understand and implement.

This empowering little book will teach you how to achieve spiritual transformation by using the Laws of the Universe to create the permanent behavioral changes that are needed so that you can manifest the reality you desire!

For Your Copy Call 888-452-0878
Or Visit
HolisticLearningCenter.com/The-Human-Handbook

Contents

1. What is Spiritual Transformation?
2. Presence & Beliefs
3. Self-acceptance & Approval
4. Relationships
5. Self-parenting, Boundaries & Forgiveness
6. Parenting
7. Laws of Manifestation & Creation
8. Ego, Paradox and more
9. Law of Detachment
10. Spiritual Distinction Transformation

Seven Spiritual Truths

> "I Want to Warn You That These
> Empowering Spiritual Truths
> Will Scare Souls
> Who Aren't Ready to Spiritually Awaken."
>
> -Master Coach Hu

A Compass To Guide You Back To Your *Inner*-Self

These Universal Truths were discovered after Coach Hu and his staff conducted three de-cades of research that

compiled over 10,000 pages of the teachings of hundreds of self-actualization leaders, Gurus, and famous self-help authors such as Dyer, Tolle, Williamson, Chopra, Hay, Singer and Ram Dass.

The research made it perfectly clear that there were sixteen over lapping lessons that all these Gurus, Self-actualization leaders, and hundreds of self-help authors were teaching.

Coach Hu took these Sixteen Universal Lessons and organized them into a transformational book called Self-mastery... A Journey Home To Your Inner Self. He discovered the Seven Spiritual Truths deep within the central core of these Sixteen Universal Lessons, and...

<u>We Now Pass These Empowering Universal Truths To You!</u>

Our hope is that you will use these Seven Spiritual Truths like a Compass, to guide you back to your Inner Self anytime you feel lost or disconnected.

For Your Copy Call 888-452-0878
or Visit
HolisticLearningCenter.com/Seven-Spiritual-Truths

<u>Contents</u>

82651659R00230